WHAT THE BIBLE SAYS TO THE
BUSINESS
LEADER

The Business Leader's Personal Handbook

WHAT THE BIBLE SAYS TO THE
BUSINESS
LEADER

The Business Leader's Personal Handbook

LMW

Chattanooga, TN

Dear Friend,

Surprisingly, God Himself tells us how to start and operate a business. God's Holy Word actually spells out how to be successful in business as well as in life. In fact, early in the creation process, God ordained labor to be one of humanity's major activities. When He created the first man (Adam), He immediately charged him to get busy and work, to subdue and manage the earth, to tend and look after it (Ge.1:28; 2:15). This means that having work to do, the privilege of a job, is of critical importance.

Think for a moment: What would the world be like without structured businesses? There would be no jobs to provide work or income, no companies to construct houses, make cars, or build stores, no products or services available to sustain human life. Indeed, without businesses, we would likely still be living in a primitive society. Humanity never would have progressed as it has through the centuries without businesses nor would we have achieved the quality of life we enjoy today. Knowing this should make business one of the most honored institutions on earth.

It is you, the business owners and professionals whom God has called and gifted to lead, who enable humanity to function as it has through the ages. Whether yours is a single-person operation or part of a huge conglomeration, you play an important role in providing the products, services, and flow of money that are essential worldwide. Likewise, you are key to the progress, development, and strength of communities and nations. You have an integral role in helping people meet their most basic needs:

- Their *physical* needs—by creating jobs through which people can provide food, clothing, shelter, and other necessities for themselves and their families

- Their *practical* needs—by supplying beneficial products or services that make life more productive, enjoyable, and comfortable

- Their *emotional* needs—by providing purpose, fulfillment, and satisfaction through meaningful work

- Their *spiritual* needs—by giving them at least one day a week for worship and rest, which enables them to support churches and other ministries that are helping the needy and taking God's Word to the world

Your call to business leadership, whether as an owner, executive, or manager, requires much of you. It requires wisdom, fearlessness, and fortitude—the fortitude to make difficult decisions and take extraordinary risks. Indeed, there may be days when you feel you cannot go on, that your situation is hopeless, that you are unprepared, or that your responsibilities are too great. In addition to everything else, you may feel all alone.

But, thankfully, you are *never* alone as you go through the long, difficult days. God is always there, always available for you. If you seek Him, He will give you wisdom and direction, and you will feel His power working in you. He will enable you to overcome your fears with an infusion of sound thinking (Jas.1:5). His presence will strengthen you and give you the courage to move forward (Is.41:10). In fact, He invites you to bring your heavy burdens to Him. Just ask Him for help and He promises to empower you to persevere through the darkest, most hopeless conditions. He will give you rest even when your troubles are so overwhelming that you cannot sleep (Mt.11:28-30).

God has promised you all of this and more, everything you need as you lead your business or area of responsibility. This is what *What the Bible Says to the Business Leader* is all about. This is what God says to you as a business owner, executive, or manager. The major verses and subjects in the Bible that *speak directly to the business leader* are here in this book. They are organized and arranged according to the crucial areas of the business leader's life. And, note, just like the Bible, most of the discussions address "you" as "you," using the second person singular. This makes the discussions far more personal—as though the instruction, challenge, or promise is for you.

What the Bible Says to the Business Leader is your own Personal Handbook—a resource or tool that you will want to keep at hand on your desk, computer, or another device. It is not a book to be read straight through or read once and then placed on the shelf. It is a *resource book* to be turned to again and again. Inside, you will find the help and encouragement you need from God's Word, all stated clearly and concisely. The thorough subject index will direct you to the pages where you will find God's wisdom for specific areas or challenges. We offer this book to you with the prayer that God will richly bless you through it, helping you daily to accomplish His purpose for your life and business.

With warmest regards, we are,
LEADERSHIP MINISTRIES WORLDWIDE

CONTENTS

CHAPTER 1

What You Can Do to Succeed Personally and Professionally

Contents

Chapter 1

What You Can Do to Succeed Personally and Professionally

1. *Strive daily to glorify God through your business or area of responsibility.*

> "So, whether you eat or drink, or whatever you do, do all to the glory of God" (1 Co.10:31, ESV).
>
> "Ascribe to the Lord, O families of the peoples, ascribe to the Lord glory and strength!" (1 Chr.16:28, ESV).

"Will it glorify God?" You should always ask yourself this question before making decisions. As Scripture so plainly teaches, everything we do should bring glory to God. Your commitment to glorify God should extend to the way you operate your business, or to the way you conduct yourself in your position of leadership in a business.

In every deal, every contract, every personnel decision, every policy, every response to customers or employees or suppliers—from the largest matters to the smallest—our first concern should be ensuring that our actions or decisions bring glory to God. God is glorified through your business when you...

- conduct business the way He would
- conduct business in a way that pleases Him
- obey His commands in everything you and your business do
- conduct *yourself*—your attitude, words, interactions—in a way that pleases Him
- value other individuals, treating each one fairly and respectfully
- use your business or position to advance the cause of morality and righteousness on earth

- acknowledge Him as the true owner of your business or management position and view yourself as a steward over it
- seek His help and depend fully on Him for everything you need
- give Him the honor and credit for everything you accomplish, every success you attain, for it is God who has given you life and the abilities you have

As you strive to glorify God first in your business, remember that there is no justification for unethical behavior, even for a worthy cause. That is, you should never do anything that does *not* glorify God in order to achieve something that *does*. Paying unfair wages to employees so that you can increase your giving to the church *does not* glorify God. Nor does reducing the quality of a product or service or violating regulations so you can support a ministry glorify God. God is glorified only when every facet of your business pleases Him. This should be your constant goal and driving motivation as you go about running or managing your business day by day.

2. *Obey God's Word in all things.*

> **"Only be strong and very courageous, being careful to do according to all the law that Moses my servant commanded you. Do not turn from it to the right hand or to the left, that you may have good success wherever you go. This Book of the Law [His Holy Word] shall not depart from your mouth, but you shall meditate on it day and night, so that you may be careful to do according to all that is written in it. For then you will make your way prosperous, and then you will have good success" (Jos.1:7-8, ESV).**

> **"Therefore keep the words of this covenant and do them, that you may prosper in all that you do" (Dt.29:9, ESV).**

God's promise is clear: the results of obeying His Word are prosperity and success. Therefore, the most important thing you can do to ensure your success is to make God's Word the basis or the manual for your life and your business or job. You will be successful, first, because the Lord will bless you for being obedient to Him. God's favor will be on you. He will lay His hand on you and your company, exercising His unlimited power in your behalf. In other words, you will have the full force of God's favor behind you, on your company's or job's journey to success.

You will also be successful for a second reason, one that is entirely practical: God's principles *work*. His principles for life and business are powerfully effective. When you follow God's commandments, you will see positive results. For example...

- when you treat your employees as God instructs, you will develop and retain individuals who are diligent, productive, loyal, and dedicated
- when you follow God's principles for managing your finances, such as limiting debt and building reserves, you will survive recessions and economic downturns
- when your customers, vendors, and suppliers experience your integrity in action, they will want to do even more business with you

God commanded Joshua to obey everything that Moses had written, all of God's Holy Word at that time. He has also commanded you to obey all the instructions of His Word, both in your life and in your work. Note exactly what God tells you to do with His Holy Word:

- Obey *all* of God's law—keep *all* of His commandments (v.7; also see Jn.4:21, Jas.1:25)
- Do not turn away from God's Word (v.7)
- Never stop sharing God's law or Word (v.8)
- Meditate on God's Word day and night (v.8)

Without question, obeying God is not always easy. We all know this. This is why the Lord calls you to be strong and courageous. He knows that adhering to His Word will force you to make difficult choices and take bold stands. In all probability, some people will despise and mock you and make false accusations against you *because* of your Christian stand. Some may even refuse to do business with you. Others may pressure you to compromise your convictions. Consultants and experts might give you advice that is contrary to God's principles. If you are in a retail business, you will have to decide whether or not you will sell certain products, products that are profitable but also detrimental to those who purchase them (for example, alcohol, tobacco products, or pornography). At times, you will have to act according to faith rather than according to details, data, and trends.

Knowing this, when the pressure is mounting not to follow God's Word in some area of life or business, you should cling to God's promise. You should believe that He will keep His Word. Indeed, if you will obey His commandments and operate by the principles of His Word, you will flourish and be successful. This is God's promise to you. He will bless and honor your commitment to Him. But note: this promise is given only to those who obey God faithfully and who truly trust in His Word in all areas of life and business.

3. *Be ambitious to serve others.*

> "They came to Capernaum. When he was in the house, he asked them, 'What were you arguing about on the road?' But they kept quiet because on the way they had argued about who was the greatest. Sitting down, Jesus called the Twelve and said, 'If anyone wants to be first, he must be the very last, and the servant of all' " (Mk.9:33-35, NIV '84).

> "Jesus called them together and said, 'You know that those who are regarded as rulers of the Gentiles lord it over them, and their high officials exercise authority over them. Not so with you. Instead, whoever wants to become great

**among you must be your servant, and whoever
wants to be first must be slave of all. For even
the Son of Man did not come to be served, but to
serve, and to give his life as a ransom for many'"
(Mk.10:42-45, NIV '84).**

Nearly all leaders are motivated, at least to some degree,
by ambition—a driving desire to succeed or excel, advance
or be promoted, achieve or accomplish something, gain respect or admiration, recognition, or earn more money or
other tangible benefits.

In these passages, Jesus directly addresses the subject
of ambition. He taught that good ambition is a virtue. It is
not wrong to desire to be great or to make a significant
contribution. Jesus never rebuked the disciples' ambition;
instead, He channeled it, which is exactly what He wants
to do for you. Jesus wants to steer your energy and motive
and efforts in the right direction.

a. **First, look at** the world's view of ambition. The world
    thinks in terms of power, fame, wealth, position, and in-
    fluence. Within the business world, people want a posi-
    tion that assures them of a high income, bonuses, pen-
    sion, recognition, privileges, and achievement. Some
    even seek powerful, prestigious positions for the pur-
    pose of exercising authority over others. They do not
    always think in terms of service or in terms of how they
    can help the company, their employees, their custom-
    ers or clients, their community, and society as a whole.
    Far too often, their thoughts are on themselves, on the
    honor, reward, influence, and benefits they receive.

    Sadly, most people in general are caught up to some
    degree in worldly ambition, seeking more and more
    of what the world has to offer. Few are totally void of
    worldly ambition. In fact, the majority of people tend to
    judge the success of others by their . . .

    * wealth
    * homes or vehicles
    * jobs or titles
    * influence or authority

- social standing

- fame or popularity

- clothing or other worldly possessions

b. **Second, look at** the Lord's view of ambition, which stands in direct contrast to the world's view. Godly ambition does not seek greatness for the purpose of exercising authority over people. It does not covet and strive for a high-ranking position simply to hold authority or to secure more money or benefits for oneself. Godly ambition is not self-centered or selfish, not worldly-minded.

Note Jesus' exact words: ". . . whoever wants to become great among you. . . ." It is acceptable to be ambitious, to seek after success and achievement, to seek to be great at whatever you do. But note a crucial point: you become great by doing what Christ says, that is, you do not seek greatness for your own sake but rather for the sake of serving others. Godly ambition seeks to serve rather than be served. It looks for people to help and for ways to help them.

What Christ means is this: you are to be a servant of others. True greatness is not found in holding a high position or in having authority over others, but in helping others. You become truly great when your driving ambition is to be *a servant of all*. Make this your goal and purpose, to use your position and influence as a business leader to help as many people as you can. From a broad, business perspective, your mission should be to help others by:

- providing a beneficial service or product for people

- providing legitimate jobs for people

- providing opportunities for people to find purpose and significance in doing honorable work

- creating opportunities and a culture in which people can thrive, advance, and better themselves

- helping to change society—inner cities, the deprived, jobless, downtrodden, third world nations—through setting up businesses, training people to use their resources, teaching a strong work ethic, and stirring up a passion within people to be productive and to better themselves

- guiding your business according to God's Word—principles and values of righteousness—simply doing what is right

- helping meet humanity's greatest need, the *spiritual* need, the need for the gospel and God's Word

The way to greatness is through humble service. If you wish to be great, then this needs to be your driving ambition. You need to actively seek to serve others.

As a business leader, you occupy a position of authority and influence over others. But no matter what your position is or how much authority you have, you are still called to serve. You are to actively work for the sake and benefit of others by producing the best product or providing the best service possible for your customers or clients, always treating your fellow workers and all others as you should. Your ambition should never be to lead just for the sake of holding a position of authority or for receiving more money, benefits, or honor from other people. Instead, your ambition should be to help as many people as you can. This is *true greatness!*

4. *Be a person of integrity—good character—above reproach.*

> "The integrity of the upright guides them, but the crookedness of the treacherous destroys them. Riches do not profit in the day of wrath, but righteousness delivers from death. The righteousness of the blameless keeps his way straight, but the wicked falls by his own wickedness" (Pr.11:3-5, ESV).

One way to contribute to success in your business is to be a person of integrity. It is not an easy task, especially in today's business climate. If you are—or wish to be—such a person, you will need to make decisions and operate your business or department just as God's Word instructs. You will need to do the right thing even when it is difficult or painful. You will need to refuse to do wrong and run from the temptation even if it hurts your business, costs you a promotion, or jeopardizes your job.

Doing the right thing when it concerns money is the theme of the above Scripture. This includes honesty in all business dealings (v.1). Integrity is a powerful quality, and if you possess it, you will be better prepared in all your decision-making (v.3a). If you have integrity, you will not be guided by...

- what your emotions or feelings tell you
- what your personal desires or ambitions are
- what others pressure you to do
- what yields the highest profit
- what gains the favor of a superior
- what makes a sale
- what wins you a contract
- what saves you the most money
- what is in your best interests
- what saves you the most money
- what is in your best interests
- what looks best on reports or financials

As a Christian businessperson, your integrity will lead you to do what is right in every situation. It will guide you according to God's truth. His clear instructions will guide you day by day and bring peace to your soul.

The *treacherous* in verse 3 are those who are crooked or dishonest in the way they conduct business (v.3b). Though they lack integrity, they may still prosper for a while. But the day will come when their crookedness finally catches up to them. They will be found out, and when they are, they could face the loss of their businesses, positions, criminal prosecution, or even worse.

When you are tempted to compromise your integrity, always remember this fact: one day you will answer to God for your life, including how you conducted your business and performed your job. Admittedly, countless individuals have accumulated great wealth through crookedness. But when they stand before God in the *day of wrath*—the day of judgment—their money will be entirely worthless (v.4). Nothing will stand between them and God's wrath. However, your doing what is right will deliver you from His condemnation.

Furthermore, God gives you a wonderful promise: if you allow integrity to guide you, you will travel a smoother road through life (v.5). This does not mean you will be free of problems, trials, or temptation, but that your integrity will *keep your way straight*—clear of the hazards brought about by dishonesty and crooked dealings. You will avoid the guilt that comes from defrauding others; the fear of being caught and punished; and the shame and lack of respect by family, friends, and all work-related associates. Add to that the months or years of covering your tracks and looking over your shoulder, and the devastating havoc that such dishonesty has on your business or career.

Instead of all the fear, trouble, and loss, you will experience true peace of heart and mind, a deep sense of purpose and fulfillment, and the priceless blessings of God. You will still suffer adversity, as we all do, but you will avoid the excruciating consequences that come to those who lack integrity.

In addition to the personal sense of peace, your career or business will reap the benefits of being *blameless* or unblemished by dishonest dealings. You will have a sterling reputation. Even more important, you will be a powerful witness for the Lord Jesus Christ. Those who lack integrity are a detriment to the gospel. Deceitful, dishonest business leaders who tout their church membership or claim to be

Christians have done great damage to the cause of Christ. But instead of bringing shame to His name—as the dishonest do—your integrity will bring glory to God, especially when others see you doing the right thing at great expense to yourself or your business.

5. *Work hard—laboring willingly and diligently.*

> "[Christian employees] whatever you do, work at it with all your heart, as working for the Lord, not for men, since you know that you will receive an inheritance from the Lord as a reward. It is the Lord Christ you are serving. Anyone who does wrong will be repaid for his wrong, and there is no favoritism" (Col.3:23-25, NIV '84).

As a Christian employed by a company, whether an owner, manager, or employee, you are to work "with all your heart" (v.23). This means that your labor should be for more than just a paycheck. Your service and work should arise from a desire to please and be obedient to the Lord. You are not working solely for a business or some executive or manager here on earth, but also for the Lord (v.24). You are working for the most important reason possible: The Lord Jesus Christ has instructed you to work and to work diligently. Jesus Christ is *your* Lord; therefore, as a Christian worker, you should do what your Lord says. There are, however, two other very important reasons you should work diligently.

a. **Workers who are diligent** will be rewarded by Christ (v.24). On earth, you may be taken advantage of, or even mistreated. But the Lord knows and sees all, and He is going to abundantly reward you if you are diligent in following His instructions to work hard. In fact, God's promised inheritance is simply astounding, expanding far beyond all that you could ever ask or think. This glorious reward includes a new, incorruptible body, one that is perfect and eternal. When that day comes, you will live forever in the new heaven and earth, where you will serve the Lord Jesus in positions of great leadership and authority.

> "Therefore, my dear brothers, stand firm. Let nothing move you. Always give yourselves fully to the work of the Lord, because you know that your labor in the Lord is not in vain" (1 Cor.15:58, NIV '84).

b. **Workers who are half-hearted,** lazy, or idle will be judged by Christ (v.25). Think of the people you know who perform their jobs poorly by being...

- lazy
- careless
- selfish
- prejudiced
- unfair
- unprincipled

- untruthful
- irresponsible
- untrustworthy
- unproductive
- inconsiderate
- indifferent

As a Christian worker, you should never be half-hearted, lazy, or idle on the job, for some day, you are going to face God. You will be called to give an account, not for your sins, because they have all been forgiven, but for your works. You will be judged for the works you have done while on earth. And God does not show favoritism. Regardless of your status here on earth, a day is coming when you and every other Christian are going to stand before God, at the judgment seat of Christ. Therefore, be prepared: work hard—laboring willingly and diligently, with your whole heart.

> "His master replied, 'Well done, good and faithful servant! You have been faithful with a few things; I will put you in charge of many things. Come and share your master's happiness!' " (Mt.25:23, NIV '84).

> "For we must all appear before the judgment seat of Christ, that each one may receive what is due him for the things [works] done while in the body, whether good or bad" (2 Co.5:10, NIV '84).

6. *Strive to walk humbly before all, especially before the Lord.*

"Humble yourselves before the Lord, and he will exalt you" (Jas. 4:10, ESV).

"He has told you, O man, what is good; and what does the LORD require of you but to do justice, and to love kindness, and to walk humbly with your God?" (Mic.6:5, ESV).

As you become increasingly successful in your business or career, always remember that certain dangers are inherent to prosperity and position. One of the deadliest dangers is that of pride. But in discussing pride, we must always remember this fact: there is both a good, healthy pride and a bad, unhealthy pride. Good, healthy pride is acceptable because it is a deep sense of self-respect and of confidence in one's abilities to do things—to act, work, labor, achieve, and succeed. Very little is ever accomplished by a person with little self-respect and no confidence.

On the other hand, bad, unhealthy pride is unacceptable because it thinks too highly of self and exalts self over others. It is a deep sense of feeling better, of more value and worth than other people. It is being conceited, egotistical, and condescending—all of which is hurtful and damaging because it debases others and takes advantage of them. It can even lead to domineering and oppressive behavior. In truth, unhealthy pride is the root of *every sin*. Why is this true? Because when we exalt ourselves and our desires over others, we are exalting ourselves over God Himself and His creation. When we consider ourselves to be masters of our own lives, then we feel free to act and to do anything we want—good or bad—no matter what God says. Exalting ourselves over God is a dangerous position in which to place ourselves.

Pride can also lead you to feel self-sufficient, totally forgetting that you need the Lord. You will need to diligently guard against having a self-sufficient spirit, one that overlooks calling on the Lord. God should never see a spirit in you that ignores His Word, that faces the temptations and challenges of life on its own, not even thinking about God and the strength He can provide. God wants to see you humbly coming into His presence, calling and depending upon Him for strength and wisdom every day of your life. With this in mind, you ought to consciously humble yourself before the Lord every day (Jas.4:10).

You are called to *walk humbly with the* LORD (Mic.6:8). What does this mean? How can you walk humbly with God? The Hebrew word for *humbly* suggests modesty. As one of God's followers, you are to walk modestly or meekly with Him, not proudly or arrogantly; you are not to exalt yourself over others, treating them as though they are of less worth than you. Instead, you are...

- to have a humble estimate of your own abilities and importance
- to be free from vanity, egotism, boastfulness, and pretension
- to trust the LORD and acknowledge Him as the source of your life as you walk through each day
- to constantly seek His mercy and forgiveness

If you are walking humbly with God, you will not be proud or self-reliant, depending only on your own strength. Rather, you will continually seek strength from God, calling on Him to help you, guide you, and deliver you from temptation. Walking *humbly* with God means you will not seek honor for your own name but for God's *Name*. All of this is because you know that it is God who has gifted and enabled you to achieve and succeed. Therefore, you want the honor and glory to be His. This is what it means to *walk humbly* with God.

7. *Do not think too highly of yourself, nor too lowly.*

> **"For by the grace given me I say to every one of you: Do not think of yourself more highly than you ought, but rather think of yourself with sober judgment, in accordance with the measure of faith God has given you" (Ro.12:3, NIV '84).**

As a business owner, executive, leader, or manager, you most likely occupy a position of respect in your company and in your community. Consequently, you might be tempted to think too highly of yourself. Too many people become arrogant when they are successful. As a believer, you need to resist every vain thought that arises, refusing to become *puffed up* with your own...

- importance
- position
- stature
- ability
- performance
- wealth
- possessions
- opinions
- education
- goodness
- title

You should never esteem yourself too highly or think of yourself as *better*—of more value in life—than others. God stands against such *puffed up* attitudes.

On the other hand, this verse is by no means suggesting that you ought to think of yourself more *lowly* than you should. Rather, you are to evaluate yourself with *sober* (sound, reasonable) *judgment.* You are to be wise and think of yourself accurately, making a sensible and realistic evaluation of yourself and your abilities. Thinking that you are more important than someone else is foolish, irrational, and vain behavior. Every person is equally important to God; every individual is meaningful and significant to God's kingdom, no matter the person's profession, wealth, or position.

Only when you know yourself—openly, honestly, and accurately—can you make the contribution you should to your family, company, society, church, and the world. If you think too highly of yourself, you will be proud, unapproachable, and often despised by others. As a result, no matter how successful you may become in the eyes of the world, you will end up failing in life. On the other hand, if you think too little of yourself, you will never reach your full potential. You will never do as much as you are capable of, nor will you make the contributions that you could have made. Only when you view yourself honestly and accurately will you be blessed by God and serve to your full capacity, thereby fulfilling your task on earth. Therefore, do as God instructs: think of yourself with sober, reasonable judgment. Be honest and accurate in your self-evaluation.

8. *Develop outstanding people skills: Learn to be gracious in all your interactions.*

> "But now you must rid yourselves of all such things as these: anger, rage, malice, slander, and filthy language [abusive speech, NASB] from your lips. Do not lie to each other, since you have taken off your old self with its practices. . . . Therefore, as God's chosen people, holy and dearly loved, clothe yourselves with compassion, kindness, humility, gentleness and patience. Bear with each other and forgive whatever grievances you may have against one another. Forgive as the Lord forgave you. And over all these virtues put on love, which binds them all together in perfect unity" (Col.3:8-9, 12-14, NIV '84).

So much of your success in life—both personally and in business—depends upon your people skills. In general, good people skills are described as the ability to listen, to communicate, and to relate to others on a personal or professional level. If your people skills are strong, you will be respected and well-received by others, which will help you significantly as you seek to move forward in life. But if your people skills are weak, you will be ineffective, and your business or career will usually suffer.

By being gracious in the way you relate to others, you will earn people's deep respect and admiration, even their friendship (Pr.11:16-17). Your employees will remain with you and do their finest for you. They will favorably receive your instruction, direction, and when necessary, correction. Your clients and customers will be loyal, giving you their repeat business and excellent referrals. Your suppliers will offer you exceptional pricing and unsurpassed service in order to retain your business.

God's Word has much to say about the way we treat and deal with others. The above passage consolidates much of the Bible's teaching on the subject into one passage (Col.3:8-14). Notice the specific behaviors or qualities we are commanded to avoid as well as those we are commanded to practice. Then grasp how they apply to the following people skills that experts agree are essential to effective leadership and business success:

- controlling temper and emotions—*anger, rage, malice*
- communicating appropriately and effectively—*slander, abusive speech, kindness, gentleness*
- tone and body language—*kindness, gentleness, humility, patience*
- honesty—*lying*
- showing empathy and understanding—*compassion*
- relating to others on their level—*humility*
- conflict avoidance and resolution—*malice, kindness, gentleness, humility, patience, forgiveness*
- *patience*
- tolerance—*forbearance*

We develop these critical skills when we commit to love others as we love ourselves (v.14; Mt.22:36-40). Love for others is the catalyst that empowers us to conquer our flawed human qualities and cultivate them into strengths and blessings. Love binds together all of the virtues mentioned in Colossians 3. If we develop loving hearts, we become much more effective in the way we deal with and relate to others. This, in turn, helps us become more successful in our businesses or careers as well as in our daily relationships with family and friends. Developing loving hearts truly affects every aspect of our lives.

9. *Build healthy relationships with helpful individuals, companies, and associations.*

> "Two are better than one, because they have a good return for their work: If one falls down, his friend can help him up. But pity the man who

> **falls and has no one to help him up! Also, if two lie down together, they will keep warm. But how can one keep warm alone? Though one may be overpowered, two can defend themselves. A cord of three strands is not quickly broken" (Ec.4:9-12, NIV '84).**

This passage states one of the most important principles for success in any and every area of life: You will be more successful with the help of other people than you will be alone. What a strong testimony to the power of relationships! In these four verses, you can quickly see at least four benefits of developing healthy relationships:

- You can accomplish more with the help of another than you can by yourself (v.9; 2 Chr.2:3-16).
- You will have help in difficult times, when you are struggling (v.10; 2 Ti.4:9-13, 21).
- You will have support when facing some need (v.11; Ph.2:25).
- You will have someone to assist you in overcoming obstacles and opposition (v.12a; 2 Sa.10:11).

Note exactly what Scripture is saying: two are better than one, three are better than two (v.12b). A critical point is being made, one that you should take to heart and incorporate into both your professional and personal lives: the more good, supportive relationships you have, the more successful you will be; the stronger your relationships, the stronger you will be (v.12b). With this in mind, guard against being so driven by your work and so busy that you neglect nurturing relationships with helpful individuals, companies, and associations. One of the worst mistakes you can make is to neglect building and maintaining beneficial relationships.

In every aspect of your business, solid relationships will contribute to your success. Obviously, as your company grows, you will need to add employees, because you cannot do all the work by yourself. Depending on the size of your company, you may even have executives and various levels of managers. But no matter the size of your company, you should never lose sight of this fact: strong relationships with everyone with whom you work will enhance everything in your work environment, including the success of your business or company. You can either regard your fellow workers as commodities, or you can value and care for them as fellow human beings. You can view them as being subordinates to you, or you can view them as associates or equally-important team members (1 Co.12:14-31). You can treat them as if they work *for* you or as if they work *with* you (1 Co.3:9). When the people in your company or business sense that you genuinely care about them, they will care about you. Failing to nurture relationships *within* your company will nurture division, dissatisfaction, envy, apathy, and a lack of dedication or loyalty.

Likewise, you need to develop *external* business relationships. Your business or company obviously cannot succeed unless you have positive relationships with customers and clients, those upon whom your business depends. The same is true with suppliers, vendors, or any others who provide goods or services to your business. Indeed, the more attention you give to developing strong relationships with those connected to your business, the more successful you and your company will be.

External business relationships also include those with other business leaders. Networking and interacting with others in the same profession or vocation serves as an invaluable source for fresh ideas, best practices, information, advice, and encouragement. It also offers you much-needed fellowship. For these reasons and more, being a part of various business groups or associations and cultivating close relationships with other business leaders will have tremendous benefits, helping you both personally and professionally.

When you or your company is financially able, you should draw on the valuable relationships you have built with other individuals and organizations and reach out to help the less fortunate in your community and around the world. While there may be worthy causes or projects for which you or your business can take sole responsibility at times, you can accomplish more overall by working with existing organizations and ministries. Your efforts to help the disadvantaged and needy within your community will be more effective when you join the efforts of local civic groups, agencies, and ministries. As you seek to fulfill Christ's Great Commission (Mt.28:18-20), you should work in partnership with ministries that are already effectively spreading the gospel and equipping God's people with His Word.

On a personal level, you would be wise to build a team of advisors and mentors who share your values and commitment to Christ. Such close confidants should be carefully-selected men or women who have proven themselves trustworthy. This type of relationship usually builds over time, progressing naturally as you become better acquainted, sharing burdens, encouraging, and praying for one another.

10. *Overcome a cynical attitude by focusing on the positive.*

> **"Finally, brothers, whatever is true, whatever is noble, whatever is right, whatever is pure, whatever is lovely, whatever is admirable—if anything is excellent or praiseworthy—think about such things. Whatever you have learned or received or heard from me, or seen in me— put it into practice. And the God of peace will be with you" (Ph.4:8-9, NIV '84).**

What you think is what you become. Or, put another way, your thoughts actually shape your behavior. This fact is an inescapable truth. Excellent commentator William Barclay says,

> ... *it is a law of life that, if* [you] *think of something often enough and long enough,* [you] *will come to the stage when* [you] *cannot stop thinking about it.* [Your] *thoughts will be quite literally in a groove out of which* [you] *cannot jerk them.*[1]

---

1 William Barclay. *The Letters to the Philippians, Colossians, and Thessalonians.* Published as a volume in the "Daily Study Bible Series." (Philadelphia, PA: Westminster John Knox Press, 1953), p.97.

Think about it: if you focus your thoughts only on the world and its things, you will live only for the world and its things: money, property, possessions, power, social standing, pleasure, and a host of other pursuits. The result of focusing primarily on worldly pursuits is tragic because it leads to…

- unhealthy anxiety and stress
- cynicism and distrust
- selfishness and greed
- emptiness and restlessness

A worldly mind never knows peace—not true and lasting peace, not the peace of God. God will never allow the worldly person to have that kind of peace because it is the restlessness or dissatisfaction of the human soul that He uses to reach people for salvation.

Similarly, if you focus only on the challenges and problems facing your business, you will become discouraged, fearful, depressed, and hopeless. And you will create and feed this same spirit of negativity in your associates and employees.

In your business as well as your personal life, God wants you to focus your thoughts on Him and on the good things of life. This is the primary reason God created the human race, to fellowship with Him (Is.43:10; 1Jn.1:3) and to do good works (Ge.2:15; Ep.2:10). For this reason, you should diligently strive to control your mind and to focus on things that encourage and build up the people with whom you deal every day. What you think is so important that God tells you what to focus upon:

a. **Focus on whatever is true:** the facts, what is accurate, correct, and certain. Whether dealing with employees, customers, investors, or other business leaders, or with problems that arise in your daily business affairs, do not fix your mind on lies, deception, or imaginations. Do not focus on what you wish would happen or had been done. Focus on the truth—the facts and the realities of the situation you face. When your thoughts are centered on things that are true and realistic, God will help you solve your problems, and His peace will continually fill your heart and life.

b. **Focus on whatever is noble:** honorable, worthy, up-right, and honest. Never consider the possibility of being dishonest in word or deed in your business—lying, deceiving, cheating, or stealing. If your thoughts and behavior are always honorable, you never need to worry about being caught in a lie, theft, or any other wrong. You can live in peace instead of being anxious or under stress, fearful of being discovered.

c. **Focus on whatever is right:** just and righteous behavior. As a business leader, you are to make the greatest contribution you can to your community and society. You are to treat your employees fairly, produce the best product possible, give the best service possible, and so on. When you keep your thoughts and behavior on doing what is right—just and righteous—your employees, customers, clients, suppliers, and everyone else will usually be pleased. And God will relieve any unhealthy anxiety you might feel due to outside forces, giving you a spirit of lasting peace.

d. **Focus on whatever is pure:** morally clean, spotless, chaste—whatever is free from moral pollution, filth, and impurity. As you walk about in the workplace and society, you are to protect your mind, keep your every thought morally pure. This can be difficult at times because some people seek to attract sexual attention by dressing, behaving, or speaking suggestively. You cannot help the first look, but you can the second. The first look is natural and unpreventable. But the second look is deliberate, and it is contrary to the teachings of God's Word. Looking and lusting after a person other than your spouse is adultery in the sight of God (Mt.5:28). We are to keep ourselves morally pure both for our spouses and children and for God. Then, and only then, will God give you a heart of lasting and permanent peace, a heart free of guilt and shame.

e. **Focus on whatever is lovely:** kind, gracious, appealing, pleasing—things that stir people to care and to be kind to one another. Whether dealing with customers or clients, suppliers or co-workers, superiors or employees, family or friends, your mind should never be filled with thoughts of...

- unkindness or meanness

- grumbling or murmuring

- criticism or reaction

Indeed, when dealing with the most serious problems, you, the business owner, manager, or executive, are to control yourself. You should not allow yourself to react in a destructive way. Even when handling serious problems such as releasing employees or breaking the relationship with a supplier, it is possible to act in a kind and constructive way. As a business leader within your community and nation, your thoughts (and life) are to be focused upon things that are kind and gracious (lovely)—that encourage and build people up, not tear them down.

f. **Focus on whatever is admirable:** reputable, commendable, worthy. You should fill your mind only with worthy, excellent thoughts, never with nonsense, foolishness, or junk. You should not listen to ugly or scandalous reports, no matter how intriguing or tantalizing they may seem. Nor should you fill your mind with filth—useless, misleading, destructive, and vulgar material—that bombards you daily through suggestive conversations and every type of media. As a business leader, your mind should be focused only upon worthy, admirable things, things that are reputable and of good report.

In summary, you should fill your mind with excellent (virtuous) and praiseworthy thoughts (v.9). As the Scripture above says: heed the Word of God, the things you have learned and received and heard, and follow noble examples. In fact, as a business leader, you should be a noble example yourself. You should be practicing and showing what a difference positive thinking and behavior can make within a work environment. God's Holy Word is clear: positive, holy thinking and behavior is the way to secure God's peace and to overcome a cynical, worldly attitude.

CHAPTER 2

What You Can Do to Help Achieve Your Vision or Dream

Contents

CHAPTER 2

WHAT YOU CAN DO TO HELP
ACHIEVE YOUR VISION OR DREAM

1. *Lay out your vision and plans.*

> "I will climb up to my watchtower and stand
> at my guardpost. There I will wait to see what
> the LORD says and how he will answer my com-
> plaint. Then the LORD said to me, 'Write my an-
> swer plainly on tablets, so that a runner can
> carry the correct message to others. This vision
> is for a future time. It describes the end, and it
> will be fulfilled. If it seems slow in coming, wait
> patiently, for it will surely take place. It will not
> be delayed'" (Hab.2:1-3, NLT).

Habakkuk, an ancient prophet, is a strong example
to follow as you carry out your vision or plans for your
business or career. As Habakkuk looked to the future, he
sought answers and direction from God. So should you. If
you seek the Lord's help, He will guide you.

a. **Be sure your vision** or plan is from God. Before moving forward, ask God to lead you, then wait on Him (v.1).
   Keep praying until He gives you clear direction. Do not
   move until you are convinced that your vision or plan
   is from God. Remember the crucial counsel of Scripture when making decisions: pray fervently, and let the
   peace of God guide you in determining what He wants
   you to do (Ph.4:6-7; Col.3:15; see ch. 3, pp.55-60).

   When God's answer comes, it will always come with
   deep conviction. The Lord will guide you if you wait on
   Him and are willing to obey His direction. His answers
   to your prayers may not come quickly and may not be
   what you expect, but God will answer and answer de-
   cisively. He will lead and give you peace as to what you
   should do.

b. **Communicate your vision** or plan clearly and enthusiastically (v.2). Whether you are starting a new business, adding a new service or product, expanding into a new market, launching a sales campaign, or embarking on any other project or objective, it is vital that you communicate your vision or plan clearly. It is just as important that you inspire your team to support and carry it out.

In any major undertaking or project, you need a detailed business plan to direct preparations, to help obtain any needed financing or permits, to navigate through the project, and to ensure success in accomplishing the overall goal. Thus, it is always wise to write out the plan, making it as thorough as possible. In addition to the comprehensive plan, you should prepare a simple and exciting presentation to help you convey your vision to your team. Getting their input and involving them in the planning will create even more enthusiasm among them. It will engage and unite them and encourage them to take ownership of the plan. This kind of involvement will inspire them to work tirelessly, make sacrifices, and do whatever is necessary to accomplish the desired result. Reminding your people of the vision regularly will keep them focused on the goal. But it will also encourage them to press on when setbacks and challenges arise.

c. **Persevere until your vision** or plan is accomplished, believing fully that God will bring it to pass in His time (v.3). Most visions are not accomplished quickly, and the larger they are, the longer they will take to achieve. When you know that God has led you in formulating your vision or plan, you can have confidence that He will, in His time—the perfect time—help you see it accomplished. Until then, you need to keep moving forward. You need to keep pressing on when obstacles come up. You need to keep working when you are at the point of exhaustion. And you need to remain hopeful when hope is hard to find.

As you work toward your goal, you may have to re-vise your plan, adapting it to changing times or unfore-seen circumstances. You may have to cut costs or cut certain elements of the plan. You may have to adjust schedules or timetables. In any case, you will definitely have to be . . .

- bold, yet prudent
- innovative, yet careful
- encouraged and encouraging, though cause for dis-couragement may abound
- determined, though all around you may be doubtful

When you face unimaginable trials, deep disappoint-ments, or crushing setbacks, you need to hold fast to the vision God has given you. You need to believe in what God has led you to do and know that, in His perfect time, God will help bring it to pass.

> **"And we know that God causes everything to work together for the good of those who love God and are called according to his purpose for them" (Ro.8:28, NLT).**

2. *Trust God as you set and carry out your goals: Re-member that your plans are subject to His will.*

> **"The preparations [plans] of the heart *belong* to man, But the answer of the tongue *is* from the LORD" (Pr.16:1, NKJV).**
>
> **"A man's heart plans his way, But the LORD di-rects his steps" (Pr.16:9, NKJV).**

A frustrating reality in business—as well as life in gen-eral—is the fact that things do not always work out as planned. Looking back at unmet goals, unfulfilled objec-tives, and disappointing results can be overwhelming and discouraging. And, in many cases, the disappointing out-comes are due to human failure, including:

- a failure to plan adequately
- a failure to follow through with plans
- a miscalculation or mistake in planning
- a failure to assign the right people to certain tasks
- a failure to foresee or overcome obstacles
- a failure by some to put forth their best effort
- a failure to oversee or properly manage a job

Human failure, however, is not always the cause of our lack of success or change of fortune. You and everyone involved in a project may do your absolute best and still fail to achieve expected results. In such cases, some other factor—perhaps a Divine factor—may be involved.

The truth of the two proverbs above is commonly summarized as, "Man proposes, but God disposes." In other words, you can make excellent plans and set reachable goals for your life or business and move forward to fulfill those plans or attain those goals, but God may have different plans entirely.

As a wise business owner or manager, you will plan your calendar and schedule according to your short- and long-term goals. You will chart detailed plans of action that are well-thought-out and then seek to follow those plans precisely, making necessary adjustments along the way. Ultimately, however, God determines your course. When your plans do not work out as you had hoped, it may be that God has a different plan for you. Out of His great love for you and those whom you lead, He may overrule your plans to accomplish a greater purpose.

When you have done your best but still fall short of your goal, you may feel as if you have failed. During these times, you need to remember this fact: God works through all the lives and affairs of this world to accomplish His will and purpose for the good of those who truly love Him (Ro.8:28). Trust God! Continue to follow Him! He will take care of you!

Keeping in step with *God's* plan is crucial for every Christian, but especially the Christian leader. Why? Because of the impact and influence you have on other people. Every day, you should ask God to direct you as you yield to His guidance. Notice that the Lord directs your *steps* one step at a time. This means He works in and cares about the *details* of your life. He has not only a calling for you and your business but also a plan to take you there. At times that plan—His plan—may look very different from yours. And God's plan will always be far better for you than any plan you could have ever developed.

It is crucial that you grasp this truth: God does not reveal in advance the entirety of His plan for your life. Nor does He reveal His complete plan for your business or area of responsibility—He only reveals *the next step*. In fact, Scripture issues a strong warning against boasting of long-range plans:

> **"Come now, you who say, 'Today or tomorrow we will travel to such and such a city and spend a year there and do business and make a profit.' You don't even know what tomorrow will bring—what your life will be! For you are like smoke that appears for a little while, then vanishes. Instead, you should say, 'If the Lord wills, we will live and do this or that.' But as it is, you boast in your arrogance. All such boasting is evil'" (Jas.4:13-16, HCSB).**

Making plans and setting goals for your business or some aspect of it is a vital part of leading a company and doing so successfully. But, as you do so, remain aware that God may overrule your plans. Every plan you make and goal you set is subject to God's will.

Now, does the fact that God guides or directs our paths mean that our free will is worthless, that God will do what He wants to do regardless of what we want? No, absolutely not! God guides and directs according to what is in our hearts. If we choose to rebel against God and His plan for our lives, God will not violate our free will. He will allow us to doom ourselves. But He will take our evil ways and use them to accomplish His purposes for the world and for the good of those who truly love Him.

Remember, God knows everything about you—your desires, your thoughts, and even your motives. So, if you desire to please God and seek His plan for your life and business, He will enable you to accomplish this.

God reveals His will to you through His Holy Word, and He will reveal His *specific* will for each day, each step of your life and work, if you will study His Word and seek Him through prayer. God will then direct your steps, one at a time. This is the very reason God has given you His Holy Word and His Spirit who lives within you as a believer. As you study His Word and ask the LORD for His direction, the Holy Spirit will lead you every day, guiding you in decision after decision and helping you carry out operation after operation.

Wise leadership is *seeking* God's will and plan in every decision and then *stepping forward* in faith and obedience to God's direction. God is perfectly good, and you can have confidence that He has a good plan for your life, both personally and professionally.

Note these Scriptures that speak further to God's plan and direction for you:

> **"And we know that in all things God works for the good of those who love him, who have been called according to his purpose" (Ro.8:28, NIV '84).**

> **"'For I know the plans I have for you,' declares the LORD, 'plans to prosper you and not to harm you, plans to give you hope and a future' " (Je.29:11, NIV '84).**

3. *Be sure you have sufficient resources to accomplish your goals.*

> **"Suppose one of you wants to build a tower. Will he not first sit down and estimate the cost to see if he has enough money to complete it? For if he lays the foundation and is not able to finish it, everyone who sees it will ridicule him,**

**saying, 'This fellow began to build and was not
able to finish' " (Lk.14:28-30, NIV '84).**

A modern-day example of this passage stands alongside
the main thoroughfare of a major American city. Eighteen
stories tall, a large office tower sits unfinished sixteen years
(at the time of this writing) after the organization responsible for it began construction. The partially-completed
building is considered an eyesore by the community, and
the organization is mocked, just as Jesus said.

Before you begin any kind of project, whether construction, expansion, an acquisition, adding new products or
services, hiring additional employees, or any other plan requiring a major financial commitment, you need to be sure
you have estimated the costs as thoroughly and accurately
as possible. You would be wise to add an additional percentage to that figure—perhaps ten to twenty percent—
for unexpected expenses. Then, before start anything, you
need to be sure you have sufficient resources to finish the
task.

As an example, this is precisely what David did prior to
the building the temple in Israel. He made extensive preparations for its construction, securing the needed workers
and stockpiling an enormous amount of materials before
construction ever began. Scripture records that he built
up specific quantities, indicating that he had painstaking-
ly estimated what would be needed to build a habitation
worthy of God's glory. Israel's wise king was confident he
had accumulated more than necessary to complete the job,
both in human and material resources (1 Chr.22:3-4, 14-
16; 29:2-5).

Naturally, there are always variables involved with any
major undertaking, just as there is always an element of
risk. You have faith that your plan will work, that the business will be sufficient to meet expenses, and that the outcome you are hoping for will be achieved. Still, you need
to be as certain as you can be about as much as you can.
Therefore, you need to be sure...

- that your plan is sound and realistic
- that your cost projections are accurate and complete
- that your financing is secure

Remember, projects rarely go *exactly as planned* or *right on schedule.* Be sure you have the resources both to finish the project and to sustain you until the expected results of the plan have time to come to fruition. And before launching any project, it is wise to prearrange access to additional funding in case it is needed. Until the business is established or projected increases in business and income materialize, be sure you have sufficient funds to finish what you have started!

4. *Be fully committed to the success of your business.*

"In the month of Nisan, in the twentieth year of King Artaxerxes, when wine was before him, I took up the wine and gave it to the king. Now I had not been sad in his presence. And the king said to me, 'Why is your face sad, seeing you are not sick? This is nothing but sadness of the heart.' Then I was very much afraid. I said to the king, 'Let the king live forever! Why should not my face be sad, when the city, the place of my fathers' graves, lies in ruins, and its gates have been destroyed by fire?' Then the king said to me, 'What are you requesting?' So I prayed to the God of heaven. And I said to the king, 'If it pleases the king, and if your servant has found favor in your sight, that you send me to Judah, to the city of my fathers' graves, that I may rebuild it.' And the king said to me (the queen sitting beside him), 'How long will you be gone, and when will you return?' So it pleased the king to send me when I had given him a time." (Ne.2:1-6, ESV)

"I also devoted myself to working on the wall and refused to acquire any land. And I required all my servants to spend time working on the wall" (Ne.5:16, NLT).

> "Sanballat and Geshem sent me a message:
> 'Come, let's meet together in the villages of the
> Ono Valley.' But they were planning to harm
> me. So I sent messengers to them, saying, 'I
> am doing a great work and cannot come down.
> Why should the work cease while I leave it and
> go down to you?' Four times they sent me the
> same proposal, and I gave them the same reply"
> (Ne.6:2-4, HCSB).

If you are going to achieve success in building a business, you have to be fully devoted to it, just as Nehemiah was to his task. You have to be totally committed. There is no other way to achieve success—not in starting or establishing a business.

a. **Being totally committed means** having to take risks and freeing yourself from other demanding responsibilities (Ne.2:1-11). Every venture has an element of risk. While many individuals have practical ideas or visions for businesses that are full of potential, they are often not willing to take the necessary risks to turn those visions into reality. Sometimes starting a business requires stepping out boldly, risking capital, or mortgaging home and property, or getting completely free of other obligations. One of the key differences between those who have outstanding ideas but never act on them and those who start and build successful businesses is the willingness and boldness to take risks.

In this passage, we see Nehemiah beginning to make his vision a reality by taking a risk. As a high-level servant of the king, he literally risked his life by appearing sad in the king's presence (vv.1-3). He also risked his position and his freedom by seeking to be released from his duties (vv.4-5). But he took these risks to pursue his vision, that of rebuilding the walls of Jerusalem. As a result, he was temporarily relieved of his responsibilities to commit himself fully to the project.

If you are ever going to have a successful business, you will need to take some risks. You will need to free yourself of other demanding or time-consuming obligations to commit and fully devote yourself to building your business. If you are only partially committed, you will most likely have a company that...

- fails to generate sufficient income for yourself and your family
- fails to create jobs for others
- fails to provide the services or products you should be contributing to your community or society
- fails to enable you to help the needy
- fails to enable you to give generously to take the gospel and God's Word to the world
- fails to fulfill your vision, dreams, and inner desire to be successful

Perhaps, you have started a small business in your spare time to supplement your income. This is an honorable venture. You are to be commended for starting a side business to help you better provide for your family, save for the future, or give more to the Lord's work. Indeed, a part-time business may be God's plan for you.

However, if you are stirred to build a growing, thriving business, at some point, you will need to commit yourself wholly to it. You will have to be bold enough to take some risks and devote yourself to fulfilling your dream. Most likely, you will need to invest everything you have in the business, or else recruit investors, or take out a loan sufficient to subsidize your business until it becomes self-sustaining. If you wish to be successful, you will have to do whatever it takes. You will have to commit yourself fully to the business.

b. **Being totally committed means** having to stay focused. You cannot allow yourself to be drawn away by, or into, other opportunities. Instead, invest your full attention and energy on your business (Ne.5:16). Nehemiah devoted himself wholly to the task of rebuilding the walls of Jerusalem. He and his officials had a definite task to achieve, and they were totally committed to completing it. In the process, he passed up other opportunities, such as acquiring land for himself. He focused solely on rebuilding the wall. He never diverted his workers' attention away from their jobs. He assigned each of them one task and one task alone: they were to work on the wall, not other projects, until the wall was finished.

Likewise, if you are going to achieve success in your company, you must stay focused and devote yourself wholly to building up your business. This is especially true in the early years of establishing the company. Other opportunities may arise, but until your business is established and stable, you need to invest your full attention and energy on making your vision for the business a reality.

c. **Being totally committed means** not being distracted or discouraged by adversity. Again, you need to stay focused (6:2-4). Like Nehemiah, you will face adversity. In his case, the adversity came from two sources: from individuals who fiercely opposed him and were determined to stop him from rebuilding the wall (2:10, 19-20; 4:1-23) and, from greedy business people who oppressed his workers (5:1-13).

Despite everything, Nehemiah stayed focused, refusing to be discouraged or distracted from his task (v.3). And so should you. Adversity is a part of life, and it is an unavoidable part of running or managing a business. Naturally, some trials or problems will be more difficult to handle than others; and, at times, you will face any number of trials simultaneously:

- financial shortages or other cash flow crises
- difficulty obtaining necessary financing
- increased payment amounts due to rising interest rates
- decline in sales
- economic downturns or recessions

- market changes
- changes in technology
- costly human or mechanical errors
- lawsuits
- equipment failure or maintenance issues
- employee conflicts or problems
- labor or government disputes
- unjust criticism or slander by a customer or competitor
- increased competition
- failure by others to fulfill their obligations
- disloyalty by a trusted associate
- increased government or industry regulations

These are just a handful of the countless issues or problems inherent to leading a business. Knowing this, we have to be strong and determined in facing our challenges. We have to be stronger in our commitment to our businesses or areas of responsibility than the difficulties that constantly rise up against us. This unshakable commitment can come only from the conviction that God has called us to our businesses or jobs and that what we are doing is important (v.3). Therefore, knowing that God has called you to be where you are, stay focused and committed to your work, refusing to allow adversity to distract, discourage, or defeat you.

"So, my dear brothers and sisters, be strong and immovable. Always work enthusiastically for the Lord, for you know that nothing you do for the Lord is ever useless" (1 Co.15:58, NLT).

CHAPTER 3

What You Can Do to Succeed in Your Business Operations

Contents

CHAPTER 3

WHAT YOU CAN DO TO SUCCEED IN YOUR BUSINESS OPERATIONS

1. *Build your business on the principle of loving your neighbor as yourself.*

> "Jesus said to him, ' "*You shall love the* LORD *your God with all your heart, with all your soul, and with all your mind.*" This is *the* first and great commandment. And *the* second *is* like it: "*You shall love your neighbor as yourself.*" On these two commandments hang all the Law and the Prophets' " (Mt.22:37, NKJV).

> "And this commandment we have from Him: that he who loves God *must* love his brother also" (1 Jn.4:21, NKJV).

Imagine what a different world this would be if all the businesses of the world would embrace and practice this commandment: love your neighbor—employees, associates, customers, suppliers, vendors, competitors, every human being—as yourself. Idealistic? Yes! But just because it is idealistic behavior does not mean we should not try. On the contrary, we should. Indeed, Christ's point is clear: we demonstrate our love for God by loving our neighbor as ourselves. This commandment, commonly called the *Great Commandment*, should be the foundation on which you build and operate your business. Paul referred to it as the *law of Christ* (Gal.6:2), and James called it the *royal law* (Jas.2:8).

How do we obey this commandment? How do we love our neighbors as we love ourselves? Jesus answered this question with what we refer to as the Golden Rule:

> "Do to others whatever you would like them to do to you. This is the essence of all that is taught in the law and the prophets" (Mt.7:12, NLT).

Everyone with whom you deal, no matter who they are, wants you to treat them just as you would like to be treated. Scripture tells us exactly how to treat others:

> **"Do nothing from selfishness or empty conceit, but with humility of mind let each of you regard one another as more important than himself; do not *merely* look out for your own personal interests, but also for the interests of others" (Ph.2:3-4, NASB '77).**

To summarize, we fulfill Christ's Great Commandment when we . . .

- treat others the way we want to be treated
- consider others to be more important than we are
- act in the best interests of others, rather than in our own best interests

Obeying Christ's commandment should be the underlying principle upon which you operate or manage your business. It should permeate all your policies, practices, and interactions, and it should extend to everyone with whom you are involved—your associates, employees, customers/clients, investors, suppliers, vendors, creditors, even your competitors. While the nature of your individual business will determine the specific ways you carry out this principle, consider the following practical examples of putting others' interests first:

- being impeccably honest in every detail of your business, never misrepresenting or overselling a product or service
- not making promises or commitments unless you are absolutely certain you can keep them
- saving your customers money whenever possible
- pricing your products or charging for your services fairly
- not pressuring customers to buy what they do not need or more than they need

- not pressing vendors to buy a quantity they cannot sell in a reasonable period of time
- presenting full information and options to customers, then letting them decide what is best
- setting fair profit margins
- recommending products or services with the customers' best interests in mind rather than what will make you the most money
- offering a variety of products or different levels of service to meet people's varying needs
- being considerate of others' circumstances rather than just your own
- working as efficiently as possible, especially when charging by the hour
- doing the best you can for your employees (paying them a fair and livable wage and offering the best benefits you are able to afford)
- being considerate of your employees' needs and showing genuine interest and care for them, not just thinking of them as a number or a means to an end
- not considering yourself better or on a higher level socially than your employees
- paying employees and suppliers before you pay yourself when cash flow is tight
- not putting down or speaking negatively about your competitors

When you build your business on Christ's Great Commandment, He will bless you. He has said that the greatest among us are those who serve others, and that those who humble themselves and serve will be exalted (Mt.23:11-12). When you serve others sincerely, Christ will exalt you, just as the Heavenly Father has exalted Him (Ph.2:5-11).

In addition, you will gain the admiration and loyalty of your customers, suppliers, and vendors. True, some can always be lured away by a lower price or by the promise of more for their money. However, most of your customers will stay with you through thick and thin when they know that you are impeccably honest and will always put them first. Suppliers will go out of their way to accommodate your needs when you have a healthy relationship and are faithful in paying them promptly. Your employees will respect you and stay with you. Even in trying times, most will be willing to make sacrifices because of the sacrifices they have seen you make for them. When you care about them and their families as Christ commands you, most of them will care about you as well.

When you conduct business according to God's principles, that is, treating people the way you want to be treated, you will be successful throughout life. And, perhaps most importantly, you and your business will be a strong testimony for the Lord Jesus Christ. You will be demonstrating how we ought to live with one another in this life and how we can build far stronger communities and societies throughout the world.

2. *Focus on developing a spirit of service in all things.*

> "Jesus knew that the Father had put all things under his power, and that he had come from God and was returning to God; so he got up from the meal, took off his outer clothing, and wrapped a towel around his waist. After that, he poured water into a basin and began to wash his disciples' feet, drying them with the towel that was wrapped around him. . . . When he had finished washing their feet, he put on his clothes and returned to his place. 'Do you understand what I have done for you?' he asked them. 'You call me "Teacher" and "Lord," and rightly so, for that is what I am. Now that I, your Lord and Teacher, have washed your feet, you also should wash one another's feet. I have set you an example that you should do as I have done for you. I tell you the truth, no servant is greater than his master, nor is a messenger greater than the one who sent him. Now that you know these things, you will be blessed if you do them'" (Jn.13:3-5, 12-17, NIV '84).

> **"Your attitude should be the same as that of
> Christ Jesus: Who, being in very nature God, did
> not consider equality with God something to be
> grasped, but made himself nothing, taking the
> very nature of a servant, being made in human
> likeness" (Ph.2:5-7, NIV '84).**

The most basic element found in every successful business is service—meeting the needs of others efficiently, happily, and to their satisfaction. Thus, every position at every level should develop a spirit of service within our companies. All employees should be taught to view themselves as servants.

a. **First,** how can we develop a spirit of service within our companies? How can we inspire every employee to adopt the attitude of a servant? In John 13, Jesus shows us the most effective way for owners, executives, or managers of companies to achieve this lofty goal. We are to set the example of service ourselves. We need to view ourselves as servants and demonstrate a servant's attitude to everyone else. This is exactly what Jesus did. He taught His disciples to serve by serving them. He, the very Son of God Himself, their Lord and leader, washed their feet— the lowest task of the lowest servant of a household (Jn.13:3-5, 12-16). Just as Jesus did, we should model the attitude of a servant toward every employee and every individual with whom our companies do business. We are to take on the very nature of a servant, embody it, and illustrate it on a daily basis (Ph.5:7).

b. **Second,** obviously, we should display a spirit of service toward our clients or customers. Our customers keep us in business, and we need to view ourselves as their servants. This should be what sets us apart from our competitors, the very quality that makes Christian-led businesses stand out. The majority of truly successful businesses are known for their excellent customer service. To achieve this enviable reputation, they go beyond the normal standard of service and usually surpass customers' or clients' expectations. They are not only willing but also eager to do whatever can be done to assure satisfaction. This means going a little further, giving a little more, providing a little extra, all while doing it happily and gratefully. This same spirit of service should permeate your dealings with everyone who is critical to your success—suppliers, vendors, and contractors as well as clients and customers—all with whom you interact as you go about the course of your work. Make their experience with your company outstanding, the very best they have ever had.

Another one of our major responsibilities as business leaders is to serve our coworkers in many ways. We serve them by providing fair, livable wages and helpful benefits, by compensating them as generously as we reasonably can. We serve them by providing the best working conditions possible, by understanding and accommodating their needs as much as possible, by caring about them and their families. In addition, we serve them by supplying what they need to be successful on the job—effective training, the best and most efficient tools, a positive and productive environment, practical and emotional support.

We can also find ways to serve them personally, by giving each employee individual attention, support, and help. If your business is small, you can easily do this yourself. However, if your business is large, then you will need to train your executives and managers to serve those under them in a personal way.

When you, the leader, model the spirit of Christ—the spirit of service—it will spread throughout your company. Your coworkers will not only seek to provide your customers and those with whom you do business with an excellent experience, but they will also seek to meet one another's needs, to help one another at every turn.

c. **Third,** Christ makes a firm promise: if we lead our businesses to follow His example and focus on service, we will be blessed (Jn.13:17). We will be blessed as the natural result or outcome of our attitude and actions. When we focus on serving others, we will be blessed with their loyalty. Clients or customers will come back repeatedly. Even more significant, we will gain new customers as satisfied individuals give us outstanding reviews and referrals. Employees will want to stay with us longer, and they and we will enjoy and benefit from the long-term relationships with one another as well as with our many other business clients and contacts. The Lord will shower His favor on us for obeying His command to serve others. And we will be blessed personally, with a sense of joy that money cannot buy. Serving others yields a measure and depth of joy that nothing in this world can match.

Remember what Jesus taught: the way to success is not through position, power, or authority, but through heartfelt service to others (Mt.20:26-27). We will be successful in life, in business, and, above all, in Christ's kingdom when we walk in our Lord's humble footsteps of service.

3. *Reject unethical advice and follow the counsel of God's Word.*

> **"Blessed is the man who walks not in the counsel of the wicked, nor stands in the way of sinners, nor sits in the seat of scoffers; but his delight is in the law of the LORD, and on his law he meditates day and night. He is like a tree planted by streams of water that yields its fruit in its season, and its leaf does not wither. In all that he does, he prospers" (Ps.1:1-3, ESV).**

In the course of doing business, you will constantly be exposed to all kinds of unethical or ungodly behavior. You will also hear, read, or receive a considerable amount of unethical or ungodly counsel, suggesting that you...

- cut back on the quality of the products or services you offer to increase profits
- show a higher retail price on a product or service when promoting a sale or reduced price

- keep your employee pay scale and as low as possible and offer as few benefits as possible (retirement and medical packages, sick and vacation days)

- charge an exorbitant price because your product or service is unique and no one else offers it.

- be as resistant as possible in accepting returned products or complaints without offending a customer

- undercut the price of smaller or financially weaker companies to eliminate competition

- try to secure *cost-plus contracts*—in particular when dealing with the government—so you can inflate your costs and increase your bottom line

- not hesitate to give *kickbacks*—under the table, secret money—to secure contracts, favorable inspections, rulings, or judgments

- do all you can to secure information on your competitors, even if it means getting it illegally or stealing from them

- ignore the working environment, conditions, and labor practices of your subcontractors, vendors, and suppliers (even if they are abusive sweat shops)

Because of the many businesses and their leaders whose only focus is growth and profit—no matter how they achieve it—the range of unethical advice you receive could be broad and long. These unscrupulous individuals have little, if any, personal concern for God or for building their businesses upon the principles of God's Word. Despite whatever temporary success they might achieve, dishonest practices are most unwise. If you truly wish to succeed in both life and business, you will do so with your integrity intact by following the keys spelled out in the Scripture above:

a. **Refuse to be influenced** by those who live ungodly lives (v.1). A successful person associates with and follows the right kind of people. As mentioned above, you are regularly exposed to ungodly counsel. In board meetings, conferences, seminars, television and internet programs, and journals and books, ungodly advice abounds. To be truly successful from God's perspective, you need to reject all advice that disagrees with God's Word, instead choosing to make decisions and to lead your business according to the principles of Scripture. To do this requires a significant measure of faith. It requires trusting God enough to choose His counsel over the advice of many who are successful from the world's perspective. It requires standing by God's wisdom instead of the prevailing wisdom of the day, however appealing it may be.

As you prayerfully differentiate between godly and ungodly advice, it is essential to remember this fact: to their shame, not all professing believers are godly. Be very careful about following an individual's counsel just because he or she professes to know Christ. Likewise, not all who do not know the Lord in a personal way are ungodly. Many unbelievers have high morals, sterling values, strong ethics, and impeccable integrity. Many follow the moral and ethical principles set forth in God's Word in their business practices, and they have wisdom that is worthy of your consideration. What is critical is that you know God's Word sufficiently to reject counsel that is contrary to His commands and principles.

b. **Refuse to walk in sin;** never depart from God's commands (v.1b). As you handle the operations of your business or job every day, you will face the temptation to disobey the commands and principles of God's Word. But you will be successful if you follow the Lord and resist such temptations as being less than completely honest with a customer, failing to mention pertinent information, or acting in your own best interests at the expense of a customer, supplier, or vendor. You need to suppress the urge to speak angrily to an employee, to be impatient with a nagging customer or client, or to lower your standards to the level of those who profit by dishonorable tactics. You need to guard against straying from the path of God's commands—refuse to walk in the sinful ways of this world.

c. **Guard against the influence** of those who question or scoff at God's Word (v.1c). In every walk of life, those who scoff at God's Word will pressure you to accept the world's path of dishonesty, unfairness, immorality, and other sinful practices. This is certainly no less true in the corporate world. Scorners of God's Word will attempt to compel you to compromise your integrity and values. However, if you want God's presence and help—His treasures, His prosperity—you have to stand strong and do what is right, regardless of the cost and consequences. Refusing to compromise God's principles may require you to swallow your pride. It may cost you a significant amount of money or cause you to lose a contract or promotion. Indeed, if you do not follow the order of a superior who is directing you to do something contrary to God's Word, it may even cost you your job. But God promises to bless you when you obey Him, and He cannot lie. You may suffer a severe setback, but eventually—in God's good time—He will make you successful. Never forget a vital truth: we forfeit God's blessing when we succumb to the pressure of those who scoff at God's holy commands.

d. **Be devoted to God's Word.** Instead of following ungodly advice, the wise business leader heeds the counsel of God's inspired Word. Instead of veering off the right path and following the wrong or sinful way, the wise leader walks in obedience to God's commands. Instead of caving in to the pressure of those who scoff at Scripture, the wise leader refuses to compromise God's principles. If you desire to be truly successful, that is, to achieve success honestly, you will . . .

- *take great delight in God's Word* (v.2a). You will read, study, and apply God's Word to all of your decisions and business practices. You will obey it in your day-to-day affairs.

- *meditate on God's Word continuously* (vv.2-3). Biblical meditation is nothing like the popular techniques taught in Eastern religions in which people are given methods of emptying their minds. To the contrary, to meditate on Scripture is to go over it continually in your mind. It is to commit a verse or part of a verse to memory, or to jot it down and read it repeatedly, mulling it over again and again. As you meditate on some portion of God's Word, ask His Spirit to guide you to its full meaning and to teach you how to apply it to your life and work. The Lord will show you what to do as you make the critical decisions and steer your company. As you lead your business day by day, many voices vie for your attention. How can you identify which voices or counsel should be ignored and which should be heeded? The answer is, by meditating on God's Holy Word. Through meditation you will learn to recognize ungodly counsel and reject it. Meditating on God's Word also strengthens you to resist sinful temptation and it protects you from being influenced by those who scoff at God's commands (v.1).

e. **Keep this fact in mind:** if you shun ungodliness and devote yourself to God's Word, you will prosper in all that you do (v.3). You will be fruitful—productive, effective—like a carefully planted, well-watered tree. You will be planted, firmly fixed. Like a deeply-rooted tree, you will be stable when crises and difficulties arise (Ep.3:17; Col.2:7). When the market changes, God will show you how to change with it. When you lose a key associate or employee, God will guide you to his or her replacement. When an economic downturn strikes, you will be strong enough to survive it. When you encounter labor disputes, the wisdom of God's Word will lead you to a resolution.

Business professionals usually associate prosperity and success with profits, growth, increased market shares, and rising value or stock prices. Along with these indicators, many would add intangible results such as customer and stockholder or owner satisfaction.

Prosperity certainly includes these things, but always remember a critical truth: God's richest blessings have nothing to do with material blessings. Scripture speaks of a far more valuable prosperity, the prosperity of the soul (3 Jn.2). True prosperity and success in our lives and businesses consist of far more than the bottom line, financially speaking, as important as it is. True prosperity and success...

• is providing adequately for yourself and your dear family (see Mt.6:33).

• is having a sense of purpose, fulfillment, and satisfaction in your work as you labor day by day.

• is bettering the lives of others through providing a needed or beneficial product or service.

• is providing meaningful employment to others whereby they can support themselves and their families and find significance in their own lives.

• is helping those who struggle to better themselves through additional training so they can succeed in securing and keeping gainful employment.

• is showing others the love of Christ by the way you treat and deal with them.

• is conducting business in a way that points people to the light of the gospel, to the salvation and satisfying life found only in Jesus Christ.

• is having a significant part in sending the gospel to the ends of the earth, in enabling God's faithful ministries to take His Holy Word to the people of every nation.

• is in feeling satisfaction in your soul from having used what God has given you—your abilities, opportunities, time, resources, business—to do far more than merely enrich yourself and fulfill your own selfish ambitions.

• is glorifying God by fulfilling His purposes for you and your company or job.

4. *Manage your time wisely, making the most of every minute.*

> "Look carefully then how you walk, not as unwise but as wise, making the best use of the time, because the days are evil. Therefore do not be foolish, but understand what the will of the Lord is [for every day]" (Ep.5:15-17, ESV).

On any given day, you have more that needs to be done than can be accomplished in the time you have. Of course, your business or job demands a significant portion of your time, in most cases, the largest share of the 168 available hours each week. But, humanly speaking, you are far more than just a business owner, executive, or manager. You are also...

- a part of a family—a spouse, a parent, a grandparent, a son or daughter, a brother or sister
- a friend to others
- a member of, and most likely a leader in, a church
- a believer equipped with spiritual gifts that God expects you to use through service in your church and other ministries
- a leader in your community who is sought after to participate in and support various causes, activities, and events
- a human being who requires rest, renewal, relaxation, and recreation

As a leader with many vital roles, relationships, and responsibilities, God reminds you to pay careful attention to how you walk, that is, how you spend your time. You are to make the best use of the time He has given you. Remember that our most valuable commodity is time. Unlike nearly every other asset, it cannot be recovered.

a. **First, God cautions us** to not be like the unwise: those who are unthinking and careless in the use of their time (v.15). The unwise give little thought to what they should or should not do. They simply arise in the morning and go to work or go about their daily routine with little thought as to how they can best use their time. Living a careful, disciplined, controlled life is unimportant to them. They do not prioritize, plan, or create a schedule. They do not consider whether an opportunity is a wise use of their time, nor do they realize that many of the things they do are a waste of their time. They never try to discern what *God* wants them to do, how God wants them to spend their time.

b. **Second, God encourages us** to be wise, to make the best use of our time (v.16a). If we are truly wise, we will think through the activities of the day. We will do all we can to become increasingly productive and to achieve more, both in and out of the workplace.

This is the key to making the best use of time: plan your day. One of the most important decisions you make every day is how you will spend the hours and minutes of that particular day. As you establish your priorities and create your schedule, seek God's guidance and will. Ask Him to help you as you plan, go to work, and carry out your daily responsibilities.

c. **Third, God encourages us** to make the best use of our time for a specific reason: because the days are evil (v.16b). This refers to all the evil that confronts us as we walk day by day—so much evil that we have to stay alert to keep from failing and falling. The evil can range from a mild temptation to a brazen solicitation to do something that could destroy your business, career, family, or entire life. In fact, if you surrender to the temptation to do evil, you will suffer the consequences at some point in time. The consequences could range from minor to major, for instance, from a financial setback to total bankruptcy, from a minor squabble to complete loss of trust, resulting in dissolution of a business or the end of a marriage. Without question, the evil of the world—both small and great—is ever before us. Using your time wisely—keeping busy with productive pursuits—will help protect you from falling into temptation.

Sadly, in our day and time, we have more opportunities than ever to waste the precious time God has given us. So many things compete for our time and attention, many of which appeal to our fleshly nature. Your task is to make the best use of whatever time God has given you. If you are not careful, you can inadvertently allow other things to devour your time—your valuable, irreplaceable hours. You can fail to spend your time as productively as you should, idly wasting hours, days, even weeks of valuable time. As a result, both your personal life and your business or job will suffer. To prevent this, do as God says, "Be careful." Be wise, not unwise. Make the best use of your time—the time God has given you throughout this day.

5. *Make wise, informed decisions.*

> **"Now if any of you lacks wisdom, he should ask God, who gives to all generously and without criticizing, and it will be given to him" (Jas.1:5, HCSB).**

> **"Trust in the LORD with all your heart, and lean not on your own understanding; in all your ways acknowledge Him, and He shall direct your paths" (Pr.3:5-6 NKJV).**

One of the most critical responsibilities of a business leader is to make wise decisions. On any given day, you have to decide what to do about a multitude of matters. Relatively speaking, many of these decisions will seem to be minor. Nevertheless, each is important, because every decision you make affects the welfare and success of your business, division, or department.

On the other hand, some decisions you face are truly major, decisions that will make a significant impact on your company and the people involved in it. Establishing priorities, hiring and firing personnel, assigning personnel, allocating resources, taking risks, going in debt, entering new markets, beginning and discontinuing product lines, enacting policies—these are only a few examples of the critical decisions you face, depending on your specific business.

Every decision you make has consequences and, typically, the larger the decision, the larger the consequences. But be encouraged: God has not left you alone to evaluate and choose. He promises to guide you. In fact, He reveals exactly what you need to do to make the right decisions. Note the following steps from God's Word:

a. **Ask God for wisdom (Jas.1:5).**

Obviously, knowledge about a subject is vitally important when making decisions. Therefore, you need to gather all the information you can pertaining to your subject. Knowledge alone is not sufficient to guide you, though. You need more than a head full of facts. What you need is wisdom. What does the Bible mean by wisdom? It is not merely having the facts, but also seeing and knowing *what to do with* the facts. It is knowing *what to do* about any given situation.

As a business leader who truly follows God, if you lack this kind of wisdom—if you do not know what to do—then there is one sure way to get the wisdom you need: ask God for it. He promises to give you the wisdom you need. All you have to do is ask.

b. **Seek the counsel of others:** consult all the knowledgeable people you can.

> **"Where there is no guidance, a people falls, but in an abundance of counselors there is safety" (Pr.11:14, ESV).**
>
> **"Without counsel plans fail, but with many advisers they succeed" (Pr.15:22, ESV).**

No one person in any business should make all the decisions alone. A number of wise advisers help ensure safety and success for any organization. Wise owners, executives, and managers will seek the help of other wise people in guiding their companies and making important determinations, for they know they do not have all the answers. They also know that their perspective on any matter is not the only perspective, and they recognize the importance of considering many viewpoints. For these reasons and more, they regularly consult with others to seek their advice. Consequently, they are usually successful in their endeavors. Those who fail to consult with others are more likely to fail in their endeavors.

If you want to be the most effective leader possible, you will seek the advice of others and then consider their counsel objectively without regard to your own personal desires. You also need to ask God to help you discern between wise and unwise counsel.

c. Seek God's will.

> **"Therefore do not be unwise, but understand what the will of the Lord *is*" (Ep.5:17, NKJV).**

> **"Don't act thoughtlessly, but understand what the Lord wants you to do" (Ep.5:17, NLT).**

The God of the universe cares deeply about you and your business or job. What a blessed thought! He has a plan for you, and He is so concerned about you that He wants to help you with even the smallest decisions. In His infinite wisdom and love, God knows what you ought to do in every situation, and He wants to reveal His will to you *if you will just seek Him.*

How, then, can you discern God's will for the specific decisions you have to make? How can you know His will about allocating resources, taking a risk, hiring the right personnel, dealing with a difficult or unproductive employee, responding to a dissatisfied customer, entering a new market, purchasing equipment, entering into a contract or partnership, choosing a supplier, or any number of other decisions you face? Note three steps from Scripture:

First, follow the leadership of God's Spirit:

> **"But when He, the Spirit of truth, comes, He will guide you into all the truth; for He will not**

> **speak on His own initiative, but whatever He hears, He will speak; and He will disclose to you what is to come" (Jn.16:13, NASB '77).**
>
> **"For all who are led by the Spirit of God are children of God" (Ro.8:14, NLT).**

When you received Christ as Savior, the Spirit of God began to dwell in you (Jn.14:17; Ro.8:9; 1 Co.3:16; Ga.4:6). Now, as you journey through life, He is your Divine Helper. He will lead and guide you, showing you where to go and what to do. It is God's Spirit who teaches us what God wants us to know and shows us what God wants us to do.

Even when you struggle with crucial decisions, God's Spirit will lead you to the right conclusion. Just ask for His guidance; ask Him to show you exactly what you should do. And He will answer. This is His promise (Jas.1:5; Pr.3:6).

Second, seek guidance from God's Word. Remember what the Bible says:

> **"All Scripture is inspired by God and is profitable for teaching, for rebuking, for correcting, for training in righteousness, so that the man of God may be complete, equipped for every good work" (2 Ti.3:16-17, HCSB).**

God guides you not only by His Spirit but also by His Word. Scripture is inspired by God (2 Ti.3:16-17). Literally, this means that it was *breathed out* by God. It is what God has to say to you, and it is profitable for you—useful, beneficial, helpful—both in your personal life and your professional life. How is Scripture useful to you? How does it help you make the right decisions?

- It *teaches you* (v.16a). The Bible gives the principles and rules by which you are to conduct your life and your business. It gives you the doctrines and foundations of life.

- It *rebukes you* (v.16b). When you are headed in a wrong direction or leaning toward a wrong decision, God's Word convicts you.

- It *corrects you* (v.16c). Scripture not only stops you in your tracks when you are headed in the wrong direction but also turns you around and sets you on the right path. It shows you what you need to do, what God wants you to do, what is right.

- It *trains you in righteousness*—in what is right (v.16d). God wants you to know the right thing to do or to say in every situation you face, every choice you make. By studying God's Word diligently and faithfully, you will learn what God approves, and you will learn how to apply the truths and principles of Scripture to your life and work (2 Ti.2:15).

- It *makes you complete*—mature, fully developed (v.17a).

- It thoroughly *equips you* for everything God wants you to do (v.17b).

As you seek what you should do by reading and meditating on God's Word, God's Spirit will guide you into the truth (Jn.16:13). He will bring to memory commands, principles, and guidelines from Scripture that apply to your situation (Jn.14:26). And He will speak to your spirit, guiding you to the right decision.

"For the LORD gives wisdom; from His mouth come knowledge and understanding" (Pr.2:6, HCSB).

Third, pray fervently about your decision. Prayer is essential because major, far-reaching decisions can be a source of serious stress in your life. They can easily distract you during the day, keep you awake at night, and affect your demeanor—keep you from being the person you ought to be with your family, associates, employees, and others.

God's charge to you when dealing with stress and worry is clear: *do not be anxious about anything.* You are not to worry, fret, or be stressed about a single thing, including crucial decisions you must make. Then, God tells you exactly what you *are* to do when caught in the clutch of anxiety. Rather than worrying, God instructs you to come directly to Him:

> **"Be anxious for nothing, but in everything by prayer and supplication, with thanksgiving, let your requests be made known to God; And the peace of God, which surpasses all understanding, will guard your hearts and minds through Christ Jesus" (Ph.4:6-7, NKJV).**

Turn to God in prayer. Bring your concern to Him and seek His help, and He will do a wonderful thing for you: He will bring peace to your heart (Ph.4:7). How can you know when you have God's peace about a matter? This is a challenging question to answer, for, as Scripture states, the peace of God transcends all our understanding. Therefore, it is difficult to define and explain. However, while the peace of God is unexplainable, it is also unmistakable. When God gives you *His* peace, you will know it. It will sweep over your spirit, giving you a sense of assurance and confidence about what you should do. It will give clarity where there was confusion. It will replace doubt with faith. This marvelous peace, the peace of God, will guard your heart and mind, keeping you from making the wrong decision and assuring you of the right thing to do.

But note a critical truth: God's peace comes only through fervent prayer. As you show your total dependence on the Lord by bathing your decision in prayer, He promises to answer you by giving you His unmistakable peace.

6. *Learn all you can about your business or position.*

> **"A wise man will listen and increase his learning, . . . " (Pr.1:5a, HCSB).**
>
> **"I applied my mind to seek and explore through wisdom all that is done under heaven . . . " (Ec.1:13a, HCSB).**

Wise businessmen and businesswomen will continue to grow and learn. To become or stay successful in your field, you too should seek to learn everything possible about the business you are in and/or the position you hold. You should never be satisfied or complacent with the amount of knowledge you have attained. Rather, you should continually look for opportunities to grow. Why? Because the world around you is progressing and changing at a lightning pace. New technologies, equipment, and ways to handle operations are being developed every day. You need to be wise and stay abreast of them. Always remember, a wise person is eager to seek *guidance* and to learn from others. So, continue to increase your learning, add to your knowledge, and improve your skills.

We are, indeed, living and working in a remarkable time, an era of progress unprecedented in world history. Interestingly, God revealed that this time would come (Da.12:4). People have greater knowledge than ever before, and the amount of knowledge to be gained is increasing at a mind-boggling rate. As a result, business and industry have expanded beyond imagination, creating opportunities previously undreamed of. This means that keeping up with the latest advancements and practices just in your area of business or job is more crucial—and more demanding—than ever before.

Subscribing to the best trade journals, participating in associations or guilds, attending seminars or conferences, and networking with others should be a part of your routine. In addition, you need to analyze your own methods and processes continually, studying reports and evaluating every facet of your business or area of responsibility. These practices will not only increase your company's productivity and profits, but, as you study, God may reveal a new method or invention to you. He may show you an area for change or improvement. He may show you a more cost-effective way of operating or give you a breakthrough idea that propels you to the top of your field or industry. Ultimately, He may enable you to do far more than you ever dreamed. If you truly follow the Lord and seek His wisdom, He will help you as you carry out your responsibilities day by day.

On the other hand, if you do not continue to learn or stay up to date, you *will* be left behind. Even worse, you and your company will risk becoming obsolete. You risk losing business to your competitors who operate more efficiently, doing things faster, better, and cheaper. Or, you might be replaced in your position by someone who knows and embraces the most current practices and technology. More than ever before, if you are going to become and *remain* successful, it is essential that you keep up to date in your business or profession. You need to be a *lifelong* learner.

7. *Organize your business or management area efficiently.*

> "Not slothful in business; fervent in spirit; serving the Lord" (Ro.12:11, KJV).
>
> "For God is not a God of disorder but of peace...." (1 Co.14:33a, NLT).
>
> "But let all things be done properly and in an orderly manner" (1 Co.14:40, NASB '77).

The Lord instructs us to be organized and orderly in a variety of areas. In like manner, you should be highly organized in your affairs and areas of work. You should also require this of all your associates and employees.

From *Genesis* to *Revelation*, God's Word highlights numerous accounts of God's orderliness in His works. It also highlights effective leaders who accomplished great tasks through diligent organization. Consider the following examples:

- God's orderly creation and precise operation of the universe—the ultimate example (Ge.1-2; Jb.38-41; Co.1:17; He.1:3)

- God's detailed instructions to Noah for the building of the ark (Ge.6:14-21)

- Joseph's administration of the storage and distribution of grain in Egypt (Ge.41:46-57)

- Moses's organization of the Israelites into manageable divisions under capable leaders (Ex.18:21-26)
- God's meticulous plan for building and operating the tabernacle (Ex.25–31)
- Solomon's administration of the temple's construction (1 Ki.5-7)
- Nehemiah's management in rebuilding of Jerusalem's walls (Ne.3)
- The Holy Spirit's purposeful distribution of spiritual gifts and placement of gifted individuals in the church (1 Co.12)

The Lord requires you to be a faithful steward (manager) over everything He has committed to your care (1 Co.4:2). If you are not organized in your business, division, or area, you will fail to meet God's expectations as well as those of your superiors, your Board of Directors, and your stockholders. Disorganization results in wasting valuable resources, both time and money. The under-utilization of employees and facilities, low productivity, low efficiency and effectiveness, frustrated employees, dissatisfied customers, suppliers, and vendors—these are just a few of the by-products of disorganization. Your business or area will not run smoothly, and chaos and conflict—as opposed to productivity and peace—will rule the day.

Ultimately, disorganization results in lower revenues and profits. Being organized requires discipline, and if you cannot become disciplined in this area, it will likely lead to the decline of your business or career. But if you are diligent about being orderly and organized, you will likely experience growth in your business or your personal career.

Benjamin Franklin reportedly said, "For every minute spent organizing, an hour is earned." Organization is one of the keys to success, and you and your business or area of management will not move forward without it. Therefore, as you seek to grow and improve in your business or career, heed what God teaches: give attention to orderliness and organization. Be the model for others in your business or management area.

8. *Seek God's leadership for new and revolutionary ideas.*

"Behold, the former things are come to pass, and new things do I declare: before they spring forth I tell you of them" (Is.42:9, KJV).

"Behold, I will do a new thing; now it shall spring forth; shall you not know it? I will even make a road in the wilderness, *and* rivers in the desert" (Is.43:19, NKJV).

"You have heard; now see all this; and will you not declare it? From this time forth I announce to you new things, hidden things that you have not known" (Is.48:6, ESV).

These verses declare an important truth, one that is extremely relevant to you as a leader in the business world. What is this truth? That God knows all things, including the future; and, in accordance with His will and purposes, He will give you whatever knowledge and understanding you need to help accomplish His will and purposes.

In fact, throughout history, many of the great discoveries and advancements that have revolutionized the world and improved life for humanity have come through men and women who believe, worship, and serve God. God's people have been behind much of the progress in science, medicine, agriculture, industry, and technology. True, God often chooses to give knowledge to those who do not know Him. But God wants to use *His* people. He wants to bless His people with knowledge and subsequently bless the world *through* His people. Ultimately, though, all true wisdom and knowledge come from God, even the knowledge of people who deny God (Ec.12:11).

God may choose to use *you*, to give you an idea for a new product or an improved process, or insight into new technology. He may especially select you if your heart is right and your motives are pure and honoring to Him. He may choose you if your true desire to be successful in business is not to become rich or famous but, rather, to serve God and humanity through...

- creating jobs and income for other people
- improving the quality of people's lives
- helping the helpless, those in desperate need in your community and throughout the world—the hungry, the suffering, the diseased, the orphans, the homeless, the uneducated, the disadvantaged
- taking the gospel and God's Word to the world

Out of His boundless compassion and love for *all* human beings, the Lord is concerned about the individual needs of *every* human being. He gives abundantly to those *who will use His gifts* to meet the fundamental needs of others. Above all, God is concerned for humanity's greatest need: the spiritual need, the need for a relationship with Him, the need for forgiveness. It was *this* need that compelled God, out of His immeasurable love for humanity, to give *His* Son as the sacrifice for our sin (Jn.3:16; Ro.5:8). Therefore, among those who know Him—genuine believers—God is seeking individuals whom He can trust with abundant resources to take the gospel and His life-changing Word to the world.

Consider this commonly acknowledged fact of life: many people who do not believe in the Lord are compassionate and generous. Many who do not truly know the Lord and some who do not even believe in God give selflessly to help meet the physical, intellectual, and social needs of others in their communities and throughout the world. They establish and support organizations that supply food, water, medicine and medical treatment, educational institutions, social programs, housing, job and skills training, and a host of other valuable services and programs.

Even so, *only* those who know the Lord personally—who have genuinely experienced the power of the gospel and God's Word to change lives, who know that people have no hope *in* this life and *after* this life without Jesus Christ—will invest their resources to take the gospel to the world. It is only believers, with very few exceptions, who support churches, missionaries, and ministries that are laboring to fulfill the Great Commission (Mt.28:18-20).

This is not to say or suggest that you as a believer should not give generously to causes that meet people's physical, intellectual, and emotional needs. Christ declared that such ministry to others is ministry to Him, and it is one proof of genuine faith (Mt.25:34-46; Jas.2:14-16). But, as one who has received the gospel and God's Word, you have a special responsibility to share it with others. You are to do what you can to win people to Christ and to send and support others to do so where you cannot. *You are a stakeholder* in the ministry of reconciling people to God (2 Co.5:18-21).

If you are faithful with what God has already given you, He may choose to bless you with more (Mt.25:21, 23; Lu.16:10). He supplies seed to the sower, promising that those who sow generously will reap generously (2 Co.9:6-11). With this in mind, you should . . .

- seek God for knowledge and insight; ask Him to make you innovative, to give you a breakthrough idea that can be profitable or can be used for His purposes and kingdom
- think and work your hardest, studying and laboring to come up with a product or process that the Lord will bless and use for the greater good of humanity
- invest in research and development, experiment and try new things
- follow God's leading in taking carefully calculated risks

You should pray fervently and faithfully for God to show you what you can do to have a greater impact on peoples' lives, to help more people, to provide more jobs, or to invest more of yourself in the work of spreading the gospel. As the point above says, seek God for new and revolutionary ideas that will thrust you forward in your life and business. Do so for the cause of Christ, that of ministering to the needy and hopeless of the world and reaching the lost for Christ.

9. *Hire executives and managers with excellent character and values.*

> "I will refuse to look at anything vile and vulgar. I hate all who deal crookedly; I will have nothing to do with them. I will reject perverse ideas and stay away from every evil. I will not tolerate people who slander their neighbors. I will not endure conceit and pride. I will search for faithful people to be my companions. Only those who are above reproach will be allowed to serve me. I will not allow deceivers to serve in my house, and liars will not stay in my presence" (Ps.101:3-7, NLT).

Leadership positions in business are always the most critical for management to fill. Executives and managers obviously have greater responsibilities than others in the company. Consequently, they impact the success or failure of the business more directly and significantly.

David realized this crucial truth, and he identified the types of individuals he would select to assist him in leading Israel (Ps.101:3-7). The word *companions* in verse 6 refers to David's inner circle of associates, his closest advisors and top leaders who would work directly with him. He made a commitment to select faithful people for these important positions. *Faithful* (aman) describes those who are . . .

- trustworthy and dependable
- constant and stable
- loyal and dedicated
- proven and can be counted on to do what is right
- honorable and have solid reputations and backgrounds

Simply stated, David pledged to choose only people of integrity to serve most closely under him. He would appoint only those who had a record of demonstrating excellent character and values. While God's Word does not give a specific list of qualifications for business leaders, it does cite a number of traits that good leaders should possess, whether in government, business, or any other area. Sprinkled throughout both the Old and New Testaments, these attributes are summarized in the qualifications given for church leaders (1 Ti.3:2-10). Granted, these standards are issued specifically for *church* leaders, not business leaders. They apply uniquely to those who lead God's people spiritually. Nevertheless, they express attributes important in *all* leaders, regardless of the setting. While God does not *command* you to hire executives and managers with this character, as He does churches, it is still wise to choose men and women...

- who live above reproach, meaning they do not engage in behavior that will bring shame to or cast doubt on your company (v.2a)
- who have high morals and are faithful to their spouses (v.2b)
- who exercise self-control, meaning they are not hot-tempered, impetuous, self-indulgent, or reckless (v.2c)
- who live wisely, meaning they are sensible, prudent, and make sound decisions (v.2d)
- who have a good reputation and are well-respected (vv.2e, 7, 8a)
- who are hospitable, meaning they are willing to serve and help others (v.2f)
- who are able to teach, meaning they can train and give direction (v.2g)
- who are not heavy drinkers or abusers of any substances (vv.3a, 8c)
- who are not violent (v.3b)
- who are gentle in their dealings and interactions with others (v.3c)
- who are not quarrelsome (v.3d)
- who are not greedy or covetous (vv.3e, 8d)
- who are proven, meaning they are experienced, not novices (vv.6, 10)
- who have integrity (v.8b)

These are high standards, and, again, God's Word does not dictate them as qualifications for business leaders. But you will eliminate a lot of problems if you hire executives and managers with these character traits. For example, take a moment to look through this list again and think about the problems you *could* have with individuals who do not possess these qualities.

By hiring leaders with these worthy attributes, you will help create and maintain a culture of very high standards in your company. This will have a positive impact not only on the people who work there, but also on those with whom you do business. Leaders with these values will both model and promote the values throughout your company. And they will help build a sterling reputation for your business in your community as well as in the segment of the business world in which you operate.

10. *Keep accurate records and track all results.*

> **"Be diligent to know the state of your flocks,** *and* **attend to your herds" (Pr.27:23, NKJV).**
>
> **"And he made the Most Holy Place. Its length, corresponding to the breadth of the house, was twenty cubits, and its breadth was twenty cubits. He overlaid it with 600 talents of fine gold. The weight of gold for the nails was fifty shekels. And he overlaid the upper chambers with gold" (2 Chr.3:8-9, ESV).**
>
> **"Next to him Ezer the son of Jeshua, ruler of Mizpah, repaired another section opposite the ascent to the armory at the buttress. After him Baruch the son of Zabbai repaired another section from the buttress to the door of the house of Eliashib the high priest. After him Meremoth the son of Uriah, son of Hakkoz repaired another section from the door of the house of Eliashib to the end of the house of Eliashib" (Ne.3:19-21, ESV).**

To operate a successful business (as represented by *flocks* and *herds*), you need to know what condition your business is in at all times. Staying up-to-date on the status of your company, regardless of the size, should be a top priority. The only way you can do this is by keeping accurate and thorough records and by tracking results. Large companies generally have the personnel and resources—sometimes whole departments—to keep thorough records; whereas, the record keeping in small businesses is often relegated to a part-time position for a few hours a week. In either case, though, the lack of accurate records can lead to serious problems, problems ranging from lost sales or delinquent taxes all the way over to bankruptcy.

For this reason, God says "be diligent to know the state of your [business] flocks;" in other words, keep accurate records and track your results. God has given us two prime examples of this principle in the Scripture above. Perhaps the two greatest construction projects of ancient history were the building of the temple, led by Solomon, and the rebuilding of Jerusalem's walls under Nehemiah's leadership after the Babylonian invasion. The scriptural accounts of these projects reveal that these wise leaders kept thorough records of the various aspects involved and tracked their progress. For example, Solomon kept painstaking records of the materials used in the construction of the temple (2 Chr.3:8-9). Nehemiah tracked precisely *what* was accomplished as the wall was rebuilt and *who* accomplished it (Ne.3:1-32).

Keeping records and tracking results provides the vital information you need to monitor your business, adjust its course, and create strategies to expand its progress. The data provided by records...

- shows you where to cut costs and where to increase the investment of resources
- reveals which customers or markets are profitable and which ones are not
- shows which advertising venues are effective and which are not
- identifies the strengths and weaknesses of your business
- provides crucial input into evaluating employees, managers, and departments

- enables you to manage cash flow carefully and accurately
- aids you tremendously in securing credit and repay-
  ing debts.

These are just a few ways that accurate data can help
you make your business more profitable. In fact, thorough
records and reports are a crucial lifeline to the *survival* of
a business, and even more so to its success. Yet, as pointed
out above, it is an aspect of business that is easy to neglect,
especially in small businesses and individual proprietor-
ships.

Never forget that your business, division, or department
is a trust committed to you by God. If you are going to be a
faithful steward, you should always know its status. Keeping detailed records, tracking results, and compiling the
data into informative, usable reports is key to overseeing
or managing your business. It is also key to making wise
decisions on behalf of your business and to avoiding the
pitfalls that happen to the ill-informed.

11. *Secure legal advice whenever needed, but especial-*
ly in all contracts.

**" . . . a man of understanding will acquire wise
counsel," (Pr.1:5b, NASB '77).**

A person of *understanding*—one who is discerning
and has good judgment—recognizes that they will benefit greatly from the expertise of others. In fact, seeking
counsel in legal matters is one of the most critical areas in
which a business leader should get help. Having a knowledgeable, trustworthy attorney, particularly one who spe-
cializes in corporate or commercial law, is one of the most
valuable resources you can have.

Many areas of business call for the services of a qualified
attorney. These professionals can help you ensure that your
employee practices and policies fall within the requirements of the law. In the United States, federal law dictates

labor standards that businesses are required to follow, and many other nations do the same. Failing to comply with these regulations can carry severe consequences within most countries. You may also need legal counsel when terminating employees and drafting severance agreements.

Securing sound legal advice and representation when dealing with liability matters and in keeping up to date with commercial laws and regulations is important for your business. However, the most critical area where you should get skilled legal assistance is perhaps in drafting and evaluating contracts. Regardless of a company's size, having solid contracts is essential to conducting and safeguarding your business. Various agreements are needed with suppliers, customers, clients, and employees as well as lease arrangements that involve property and equipment. These and numerous other business relationships necessitate the formulating of carefully-constructed contracts that define and govern expectations, conditions, compensation, performance of duties, and other essential details.

Whether you are just launching a business or are continuing to operate one, you would be most wise to engage the services of a qualified attorney. Make certain...

- that you understand all local and national laws
- that every required document is filled out
- that every agreement is worded clearly and correctly
- that nothing pertinent has been omitted
- that your best interests are represented
- that an attorney always represents you in writing contracts and, if needed, in negotiating them

In selecting an individual lawyer or a law firm, remember that the wise person does not follow the counsel of the ungodly (Ps.1:1). You will be best served by an attorney who shares your values, philosophy of business, and basic principles. But even then, you should always weigh the legal counsel against the teachings of God's Word, regardless whether your attorney is a professing Christian or not.

This proverb says specifically that the person of good judgment (understanding) will *acquire* wise counsel. The Hebrew word for *acquire* means to buy or purchase—to pay a price for. If you are a business owner or executive, especially of a small or struggling business, you may feel you cannot afford to pay an attorney. However, it may cost you much more *not* to use the services of an attorney than it does to consult one. Wise leaders do not plunge headlong into action without first obtaining all pertinent information available. They do not presume to be knowledgeable about things outside their area of expertise. They understand the value of wise legal counsel and are willing to pay the price needed to obtain it.

12. *Establish an environment of wise and righteous behavior within your company.*

> **"But if you have bitter envy and selfish ambition in your heart, don't brag and deny the truth. Such wisdom does not come from above but is earthly, unspiritual, demonic. For where envy and selfish ambition exist, there is disorder and every kind of evil. But the wisdom from above is first pure, then peace-loving, gentle, compliant, full of mercy and good fruits, without favoritism and hypocrisy. And the fruit of righteousness is sown in peace by those who cultivate peace" (Jas.3:14-18, HCSB).**

In the business world, envy and selfish ambition are too often the rule rather than the exception. As a result, turmoil and evil practices abound. Business leaders and employees alike can be ruthless and stab one another in the back. Naturally a business wants to grow and increase profits. And its employees want to be rewarded with pay increases and promotions and more retirement security. But it is most unwise for a business to develop a culture of destroying the competition and clawing its way to the top by stepping on whoever or whatever gets in its way. From a worldly perspective, business leaders who lead their company down such a path are often considered shrewd and successful. And far too many of them boast about what they have done and deny the truth about their practices (v.14). But note what God's Word says about this culture, this way of thinking (v.15):

- It is not from above—not from God.

- It is earthly—focused on corruptible, unrighteous conduct, not on the good and ideal conduct that God and the righteous of society desire.

- It is unspiritual—natural, sensual, carnal, immoral, unjust.

- It is demonic—demon-like, provoked by devilish thoughts.

Business leaders who consider envy and selfish ambition to be wise behavior are wrong. A person who wants to be truly wise seeks God's wisdom, the wisdom found in the instructions of God's Holy Word. And God's wisdom—the wise behavior He spells out—stands in stark contrast to the wisdom of this world. As a business owner or executive, you should strive to follow God's wisdom in all your relationships. If you will establish a culture based on God's wisdom in all your company's dealings, you can have a forceful impact on everyone with whom you interact, from your employees to your competition.

What is the wisdom of God? What is this wise behavior that is so superior to the wisdom of this world? Scripture says it is eight things (v.17).

a. **True wisdom is first of all pure.** If you are wise, you will make sure your heart is pure, not driven by envy and selfish ambition, when dealing with fellow workers, suppliers, and competitors. You will be fair, honest, and just in all your relationships.

b. **True wisdom is peace-loving.** The wise business leader seeks to build and maintain a peaceful spirit among all people. When murmuring, grumbling, conflict, or division arises, you will seek to restore peace and reconciliation immediately. Indeed, you will always seek to bring people closer together.

c. **True wisdom is gentle** as opposed to harsh. You achieve far more for your business if you are not harsh with people. Demonstrate a gentle spirit by being courteous, patient, and kind, and by taking time to inform, instruct, correct, and work with people. A spirit that is gentle and considerate will strengthen your company.

d. **True wisdom is compliant** or reasonable. This means you are to be willing to listen to reason and appeals, willing to change when you are wrong. It is the opposite of being stubborn or hard when giving or receiving instructions, suggestions, or correction. You are to be reasonable—never unreasonable—when dealing with others and in carrying out your daily responsibilities.

e. **True wisdom is full of mercy.** This means to have feelings of empathy, compassion, and kindness toward others. Wise business leaders show genuine interest and care in all who cross their paths throughout the day. A genuine spirit of kindness and concern (care) strengthens your reputation and your company's image, showing that you truly serve the public and are trustworthy and reliable—worthy to receive the communities' business.

f. **True wisdom is full of good fruits.** A wise person's wisdom is like good seed: when planted and looked after properly, it bears good results. As a business owner, executive, or manager, one thing you always want is good results. If you are truly wise, you will consistently do what is right in your personal behavior. You will also demonstrate the leadership that produces the best product and service you and your employees can deliver to the people you serve. Living right and serving the public as you should will go a long way toward making you successful.

g. **True wisdom is without favoritism.** So much injustice exists in the business world—and society as a whole—due to partiality. True wisdom mandates equality and fairness, not favoritism or discrimination. As you walk about making management decisions and dealing with people day by day, if you are truly wise, you will consider every individual important, never being unjust or show-ing favoritism toward anyone.

h. **True wisdom is without hypocrisy.** It is sincere, with-out deceit or guile, without pretension, genuine to the core. A wise business leader never attempts to deceive people—not business partners, associates, clients, cus-tomers, suppliers, subcontractors, family members, or anyone else.

Now imagine the effect of this kind of wisdom, God's wis-dom, sweeping throughout society. We would have a world of righteousness, a world where every individual does what is right (v.18). But note how this righteousness is brought about: by making peace. People living righteously—living as they should and treating each other and God as they should—can never come about unless a culture of God's wisdom overtakes the selfish culture of the world.

You personally can make a difference by demonstrat-ing and expecting a culture of wise decision-making and righteous behavior in your business, as well as in all your dealings as a business leader. You can make a difference in the lives of your associates, your employees, your custom-ers/clients, your vendors and suppliers—everybody you touch. If enough business owners and executives would counteract the world's philosophy by following God's wis-dom, they could ignite a movement, a mighty movement that would change society and the world.

13. *Set the example for a calm and quiet spirit in the workplace.*

> "Make it your goal: to live a quiet life, . . ." (1 Th. 4:11a, NLT).

There is a proper way and an improper way to live and to do your job. Likewise, there is a right way and a wrong way to manage people. The right and proper way to man-age or oversee others is, first, to seek a quiet spirit within your own heart and, second, to seek the same within the workplace for which you are responsible. By a quiet life,

God means living with a peaceful, confident, and controlled spirit. If you are quiet, you are not loudly seeking attention. You are not verbally abusive or divisive. You do not roam around the workplace looking for problems or conflicts with others, nor do you raise issues unless genuinely necessary. You do not lose control of your emotions—being disruptive, yelling, disrupting, correcting, and threatening those around you—whether employees, suppliers, vendors, customers, or anyone else for that matter. On the contrary, you seek to keep a quiet and serene spirit within yourself while maintaining the calmest atmosphere possible in the workplace among others.

Even when you must correct an employee, or customer, or some other business associate, God instructs you to be quiet—controlled and calm. A quiet spirit will lead you to take the erring person off to the side, where you can correct the individual without embarrassment or disruption. A business leader with a quiet spirit would never deliberately humiliate a person or cause a disturbance within the workplace. Maintaining a calm and peaceful atmosphere will make your company a place where people enjoy working. Furthermore, it will lead to higher levels of production and growth than will an atmosphere that is contentious, stressful, and intimidating.

As a business owner, executive, or manager, you should strive to obey this instruction from God and make leading a quiet life one of your daily goals. A quiet and peaceful spirit helps to build a healthy atmosphere in the workplace as well as in your home and throughout society.

14. *Do not interfere in other people's affairs.*

"Make it your ambition . . . to mind your own business" (1 Th.4:11a, NIV '84).

Can you believe the Word of God says this? God actually tells you to "mind your own business." Why? Because too many people are busybodies. What is it that causes a person to meddle in other people's business or personal affairs?

- Some people meddle because it is their very nature or disposition to gossip, murmur, or grumble. Through the years, they have criticized, murmured, and talked about others so much that meddling is now a way a life for them. They have become busybodies by nature.

- Some people meddle because they fail to see their own shortcomings and failures. Complainers and busybodies are always looking for faults (specks of sawdust) in other people when they have very serious faults (beams) of their own (Mt.7:3-5).

- Other people meddle because they prefer interfering in the affairs of others rather than looking after their own affairs as they should. They neglect their own responsibilities and the work God has given them to do. Instead of meddling, though, they should be developing and enhancing their own lives.

- Still others meddle because they do not have enough work, not enough to keep themselves busy or to occupy their time and energy while on the job.

The Lord's instruction is clear and strong: "Mind your own business." You should not be a busybody, not meddle or interfere in the business of others. Commit your time and energy to your own business, your own work and responsibility.

If you do not have enough work to keep you busy and productive, you should approach the proper person to ask for more work or expanded responsibility. You should also be striving to improve your job performance, to be more efficient and effective. Failure to do so . . .

- negatively impacts the company's production and/ or services to the community

- lowers or fails to build your own self-esteem, interest, and feelings of satisfaction from having done a good job. (It is human nature to feel good when you do your best. Your ego and self-esteem are boosted.)

If you are able to take on more work and responsibilities, your request will likely thrill those in authority over you. You could receive an increase in pay or a bonus, or, in time, even be promoted as a result of your taking the initiative to do more work. In addition, when you work to the maximum of your ability, you are more productive and gain a far greater sense of purpose and fulfillment in both your work and your life.

15. *Accept the authority of those over you, even if they are unreasonable or overbearing.*

> **"You who are slaves [employees] must accept the authority of your masters [employers] with all respect. Do what they tell you—not only if they are kind and reasonable, but even if they are cruel. For God is pleased with you when you do what you know is right and patiently endure unfair treatment" (1 Pe.2:18-19, NLT).**
>
> **"All slaves [employees] should show full respect for their masters [employers] so they will not bring shame on the name of God and his teaching" (1 Ti.6:1, NLT).**

If you are an executive or manager who works for a good and considerate business owner or higher-level executive, you are very fortunate. You are even more fortunate if your employer is a genuine Christian. Under a true Christian owner or executive, you will usually be treated not only justly and fairly but also in a brotherly or sisterly spirit.

Realistically, though, you have no guarantee a workplace environment will be so positive. Some business owners and executives are neither considerate nor good. Nor are they just and fair. Nevertheless, God's instruction to you is clear: as a Christian employee, you are to accept the authority of your employer even if he or she is unreasonable, overbearing, or harsh. Why would God demand such a thing of you? First Timothy 6:1 gives one simple reason: God does not want you to bring shame on His name or on the teaching of His Holy Word.

God does not want you failing at your job—not in a single duty assigned to you. Nor does He want you failing to be a living testimony of the triumphant life He gives His followers, a life filled with the fruit of His Spirit: love, joy, peace, patience, kindness, goodness, faithfulness, gentleness, and self-control/discipline (Gal.5:22-23).

God wants you to live a godly life in the workplace so your coworkers will see Christ in you and be attracted to Him and the great salvation He offers. Therefore, even if your employer is unfair or cruel, you are to accept his/her authority. This may be a difficult command to follow; and yet, it is what God calls for. Never overlook this critical fact: if you do not ...

- work with the right attitude
- do what your employer asks of you
- give a full day's work for a full day's wage

... you dishonor the name of Christ. You disobey God's clear instruction given in 1 Timothy and 1 Peter. Moreover, if you are lazy, unproductive, or disrespectful in the workplace, your employer considers your Christian status or profession meaningless. Why? Because Christ has made no obvious difference in your life. Your professed faith in Christ has made no impact on your work ethic. Sadly, you bring shame to the name of God and to the teaching of His Holy Word. For this reason, and many more, you are to obey God's instruction to accept the authority of your employer—even if he or she is unreasonable, overbearing, or harsh.

As 1 Peter 2:19 says, God is pleased with you when you obey His instructions while being treated unfairly. God will use your endurance of unfair treatment either as a testimony to reach your employer or to bear witness against him/her in the coming day of judgment.

CHAPTER 4

What You Can Do to Ensure Excellent Financial Management

Contents

CHAPTER 4

WHAT YOU CAN DO TO ENSURE EXCELLENT
FINANCIAL MANAGEMENT

1. *Spend wisely and control costs.*

> "Jesus told this story to his disciples: 'There
> was a certain rich man who had a manager han-
> dling his affairs. One day a report came that the
> manager was wasting his employer's money. So
> the employer called him in and said, "What's
> this I hear about you? Get your report in order,
> because you are going to be fired"'" (Lk.16:1-2,
> NLT).

Reduced to its simplest, most basic definition, business
is the activity of taking what you have—money, goods, an
ability or skill, an idea, a commodity—and using it to make
money. Indeed, making money—generating a profit—is a
fundamental objective of business.

Remember that the earth and everything in it belong to
the Lord (Ps.24:1; 89:11;1 Co.10:26). If you own a business, God has entrusted the business to you. Therefore,
He expects you to use the resources wisely (Mt.25:14-27).
If you are a company executive, then the owner(s), stockholders, and investors of the business you work for expect
you to manage their resources wisely and to produce the
largest profit possible.

In Luke 16:1-13, the subject of Jesus' parable was a
manager who had wasted his employer's money, so much
so that the employer decided to fire him. *How* the manager
had squandered funds is not revealed, only that the owner
was displeased. Why? Because, instead of using his money
for its intended purpose—whether for savings, reinvest-
ment, supplies, salaries, or anything else—this manager
wasted it. He failed to spend wisely and to control costs.

As a business leader, you too have a responsibility to
spend money wisely, to use funds committed to you on

that which is necessary to generate profits. It is your duty, either directly or indirectly, to be sure no money is wasted. If your business is small, you might be able to review and approve every expenditure personally. In larger businesses, others will share the responsibility of purchasing and of spending company funds. Therefore, spending and cost control measures need to be implemented throughout the business.

Among other things, controlling costs effectively includes:

- careful planning and budgeting
- accountability—establishing a system of checks and balances
- regular evaluation of expenditures, checking for unnecessary spending
- routine analysis of methods, practices, and procedures
- finding innovative ways to cut expenses
- upgrading equipment
- periodically bidding or getting other quotes on supplies and services
- comparison shopping
- buying in bulk when practical by joining an association where purchasing power is multiplied
- hiring only when necessary and hiring the most productive people available
- utilizing every employee in the most effective way possible
- cross-training employees
- using space efficiently

When business is good and cash flow is plentiful, it is easy to become lax toward controlling costs. However, it is important to motivate yourself and your staff to get the most for every dollar spent by focusing on the purpose(s) of your business. Never forget that making the most money possible is not an end in itself. You are not in business for the purpose of hoarding wealth. To the contrary, increased profits enable you to do more for your loyal employees, more for your community, more to help the needy, and more to help spread God's Word around the world. Higher profits can also be reinvested, producing even more income that can be used toward these noble purposes.

2. *Prepare for emergencies ahead of time.*

> **"Now listen, you who say, 'Today or tomorrow we will go to this or that city, spend a year there, carry on business and make money.' Why, you do not even know what will happen tomorrow. What is your life? You are a mist that appears for a little while and then vanishes" (Jas.4:13-14, NIV '84).**
>
> **"A prudent person foresees danger and takes precautions. The simpleton goes blindly on and suffers the consequences" (Pr.22:3, NLT).**

Without question, the business world is filled with uncertainties and risks, but nothing is more uncertain than the future. This passage reminds you, the business leader, of a truth that is easy to forget, especially in prosperous times: tomorrow holds no promises. *If* tomorrow comes, it may or may not be as profitable as today.

You may already have your business plan laid out for the coming year, five years, or even ten years. You may have every intention to expand and enter a new market successfully, as did the overly confident individuals addressed in Scripture above.

But you have no guarantee that things will go according to your plan, either that you will expand or that profits will increase. In fact, you have no guarantee that you will even be able to maintain your business at its *current* level. At some point, you may very well face an economic crisis. Any number of challenging issues could happen overnight, changing your financial situation drastically. For example:

- the market and demand for your product or services could sharply decline

- a labor dispute or strike might suddenly throw everything into turmoil
- a disgruntled customer or employee could file a lawsuit against your business
- new technology might force you to make costly upgrades or else be left behind
- expensive equipment might have to be repaired or replaced
- illness or some other personal crisis might prohibit you from leading the company

The list of potential crises, calamities, and catastrophes that could batter your business and devastate your cash flow is endless. In addition to all these things, history has proven that recessions and economic downturns do eventually reoccur. It is not a matter of *if*, but *when*. Moreover, government leaders who are not favorable to businesses or who do not understand how to build an economy could come into power, affecting businesses throughout the nation. No company is completely insulated from the effects of difficult, sometimes devastating, economic conditions.

What can you do to prepare your company for the possibility of future adversity? Always remember Scripture's valuable lesson from the ant: prepare for the coming winter while it is summer (Pr.6:6-8). In busy or productive times, when your services are in demand or sales are heavy and cash flow is strong, you need to set aside funds. The time will come when business is slow and cash is limited, or when a crisis or financial emergency strikes. It is during those times that you and your associates and employees will be very thankful for your having planned ahead. A wise person anticipates adversity and takes precautions against its consequences (Pr.22:3). If you have not already done so, you should begin as soon as possible setting aside a cash reserve for emergencies. Be faithful to add to it consistently, even if you cannot contribute much. Resist the urge to spend profits right away by expanding too quickly, giving large bonuses, or making unnecessary purchases. Instead, plan wisely and spend cautiously until your emergency fund is well-established.

As the owner or executive of a business or manager of a division, always be conscious of the fact that your management decisions affect not only you but also many others. Keep your employees and their families, your suppliers, your customers or clients, and your vendors in mind as you think about the future of the business. For their sakes, as well as yours, God encourages you to prepare for life's uncertainties. Make setting aside funds a priority today. It will help sustain you through whatever adversity tomorrow may bring.

3. *Avoid borrowing money or stretching your debt to the limit.*

> **"The rich rules over the poor, and the borrow-
> er *is* servant to the lender" (Pr.22:7, NKJV).**

God's Word does not forbid borrowing money, but it clearly warns and advises against it. This proverb points to the major reason we should avoid going into debt if we possibly can: at some point, we may not be able to pay what we owe. In biblical times, people who could not repay their debts either became servants to their lenders or were sold into slavery to satisfy their unpaid obligations (Ex.21:2-7; 2 Ki.4:1; Mt.18:24-25). In today's world, you may not *literally* become your lender's slave, but *figuratively* you will be. The money you earn will go to your creditors, rather than to you. In reality, you will work for your lenders rather than for yourself. Until you repay what you owe in full, you will be bound to the debt and to the creditor to whom you owe it.

Debt causes all kinds of pressure for people, including some of the most agonizing tension imaginable. You may not lose your freedom if you do not have money to pay your debts, but you can be left destitute, unable to provide food or housing for yourself and your family. This is especially true for small business owners, who often end up mortgaging everything they have, including their homes, just to secure loans. The stress of being in debt can cause all kinds of health problems, such as ulcers and high blood pressure, strokes and even heart attacks. In addition, the pressure of debt and financial difficulties can create all kinds of friction at home and at work. It can rip families and friendships apart.

For many businesses as well as individuals and families, borrowing money is a normal function, a regular part of day-to-day life. However, you would be wise to follow a different course. Operating on a cash basis is obviously the best policy, and you should do so as much as possible. Paying cash requires discipline and patience, two virtues that pay off not only in dollars but also in peace of mind. Nevertheless, launching or expanding a business usually requires a large investment of funds, far more than most people have on hand or readily available. And there are occasions when time is of the essence, when waiting to act will mean a lost opportunity. In such circumstances, you should still consider all options available before rushing to borrow. One example might be to seek investors who would own a percentage of your company in return for providing the capital you need.

Nearly all businesses, especially those that are seasonal in nature, go through periods when sales or production or demands for service are slow and cash flow is restricted. The best way to survive such challenging times is to *borrow from yourself*; that is, establish a reserve fund, draw upon it when necessary, and repay the drawn funds as soon as possible (see pt.2, p. 86, also ch. 1, pt.2, p. 5). Obviously, if you have just started your business, you will not have the funds available, but you should start to build up reserves just as soon as you are able.

If you have no other choice than to borrow money, then borrow as little as necessary for as short a term as possible. Do not obligate yourself to a monthly payment you cannot make, and do not extend the term of a loan for the sake of taking home extra money. In most cases, your best option for short-term loans is to secure a line of credit with a local institution. Avoid unsecured debt, such as loans guaranteed only by a signature or borrowing from your credit cards. These usually have exorbitant interest rates, and most are designed to keep you making payments for as long as possible. Repay the loan as quickly as you can, making whatever sacrifices are required to free yourself from the bondage of the debt.

Credit cards should only be used as a convenience, never for credit. If you use a credit card, you should pay the balance in full every month. It is *always* unwise to fall into the trap of revolving debt. Many individuals and inexperienced business people build up high balances on credit cards, believing they can get everything they need or want upfront and pay it off over time. The problem is, they usually need their monthly income or receivables to pay for their current and immediate needs. Therefore, they have no choice but to pay the minimum balance due on the card(s) each month—piling up the interest and never paying on the principle—then continue to charge necessary expenditures, placing themselves in continuous bondage at an extremely high rate of interest.

If you are sustaining your business by borrowing funds over and over again, you have fundamental problems you need to confront and address. And you will need to make some difficult decisions to resolve these issues. When all is said and done, there are basically two ways to increase cash flow without increasing your debt: reduce expenses or increase income. Cutting costs can be very painful. You may be forced to temporarily lay off loyal employees or to release them altogether. It might be necessary to reduce compensation or to downsize your operation or to make tremendous personal sacrifices. The one thing you cannot do is continue to accumulate debt. If you do, your business will eventually collapse, costing you all you have invested in it and leaving everyone involved unemployed.

One of the riskiest elements of owning or operating a business is going into debt. God's Word is forthright and warns us earnestly of its perils: we should do everything possible to avoid it.

4. *Pay all that you owe when it is due.*

> **"Pay to all what is owed to them: taxes to**
> **whom taxes are owed, revenue to whom revenue**

is owed, respect to whom respect is owed, honor to whom honor is owed. Owe no one anything, except to love each other, for the one who loves another has fulfilled the law" (Ro.13:7-8, ESV).

"The wicked borrows but does not pay back, but the righteous is generous and gives" (Ps.37:21, ESV).

God's Word is clear: you are to pay whatever you owe, and this includes paying your debts when they are due (Ro.13:7-8). This very practical instruction applies to businesses of every size as well as individuals. It also applies to debt (bills, payments) of any size. No person or company, no matter how big or important, is exempt from this clear command. Obviously, this does not mean you can use whatever means you choose to pay your debts. Using devious tactics to make payments (floating checks, for example) is not an acceptable method of paying your debts.

At first glance, verse 8 seems to be saying that the believer is never to borrow or become indebted to anyone. However, while God's Word advises against borrowing, it does not forbid it. Extending credit was a part of life for God's people both in the Old and New Testament periods of history, and it is part of the business world today. Credit is often extended and accepted for convenience sake, as in the establishing of monthly accounts. On the other hand, debt is sometimes necessary, such as when constructing a building or purchasing expensive equipment.

The point of God's Word is simply this: if you establish a monthly account with a supplier or a line of credit or long-term loan with a lending institution, you are to make your payments on time, keep all accounts current. The same would be true if you use a credit card. You should not be late or fall behind in your payments. As Scripture says, "let no debt remain outstanding" (v.8, NIV '84). When you sign a loan agreement, specific repayment terms are spelled out. You do not owe the money *until* the payment is due, but you do owe it *when* it is due. If you do not pay *what* you owe *when* you owe it, you are clearly violating the terms of your agreement with the lender. But even more critical, you are disobeying God. With that in mind . . .

- you should never borrow for a purchase unless it (the purchase) is *absolutely necessary,* nor should you borrow for that purchase if you have another means to pay for it.
- you should never borrow for a purchase unless you can meet the obligation of paying for it. If you are not sure you can make the payments, then you should not make the purchase. If the purchase is a necessity, then you should seek repayment terms that you can meet, even if it requires a longer payment term or a higher rate of interest.
- you need to make all payments faithfully as scheduled, even if doing so requires cutting back elsewhere in your business or making personal sacrifices.

5. *Be cautious when extending credit to those whose business decisions are unwise.*

> **"Get security from someone who guarantees a stranger's debt. Get a deposit if he does it for foreigners" (Pr. 20:16, NLT).**

Extending credit is a necessary part of carrying on most businesses. The extension of credit is based on trust: you are trusting the other party—one or more individuals or a company—to pay you for the goods or services you provide when payment is due. But note Scripture's warning about trusting people to pay you at a later time, especially when they have a history of making bad business decisions.

The bad decision cited specifically in this verse is cosigning for another person's debt. Scripture repeatedly warns against pledging or guaranteeing the debt of another person (Pr.6:1-5; 22:26). It is even unwise to guarantee a loan for someone you know well, such as a relative, neighbor, or friend (Pr.17:18). But to guarantee a loan for a *stranger*—someone outside the family of Israel, a foreigner—was the height of folly in Old Testament times (Pr.11:15).

With this understanding, the principle of Scripture becomes clear: if you decide to extend credit to a person who has a record of making risky business decisions, always require collateral or security. It is not an insult to demand collateral or a deposit from a person, especially from someone who does not always display sound judgment. It is simply a good, wise business practice. Those who act insulted by the request for collateral are usually not trustworthy. Honorable, ethical people understand this requirement and have no problem complying with it. So, when doing business with a person who makes questionable decisions, you need to protect yourself by insisting upon a tangible assurance of payment.

Another lesson is implied in this proverb: you should gather as much information as possible about an individual or company before extending credit to them. In the above verse, the person requesting a loan had earlier made a very poor business decision: he had guaranteed the debt (the loan) of a stranger. A very foolish thing to do! The lesson is clear: you should make every effort to learn all you can about those who are asking you for credit. You need to know if they have a history of poor business practices. In industrialized societies, you can usually find this out by obtaining a credit report. But no matter what society you live in, you can always require references and check them thoroughly.

God blesses the wise in their decision-making and their business policies. We cannot expect the Lord to bless us if we disregard His counsel and make foolish decisions or have unsound business practices. Your business decisions need to be based on sound principles and prudent methods, not swayed by emotions or personal feelings, even when dealing with family members. We should never indulge nor give license to (encourage) unwise decisions, for they can only harm and undermine our own credibility.

6. *Be careful when lending money and cosigning or guaranteeing a loan.*

> "My child, if you have put up security for a friend's debt or agreed to guarantee the debt of a stranger—if you have trapped yourself by your agreement and are caught by what you said— follow my advice and save yourself, for you have placed yourself at your friend's mercy. Now swallow your pride; go and beg to have your name erased. Don't put it off; do it now! Don't rest until you do. Save yourself like a gazelle escaping from a hunter, like a bird fleeing from a net" (Pr.6:1–5, NLT).

Putting up security refers to underwriting or cosigning another person's debt (v.1). Throughout Scripture, God encourages you to be generous and giving, even to lend to others when you can. But there is one thing God advises you against doing: you should not go into debt for someone else. From time to time, friends, associates, and even children or other relatives may ask you to cosign a loan for them. Or you may receive a business proposal requesting that you guarantee a loan with the promise of interest or a share of potential profits. Scripture strongly cautions you not to act unwisely by taking on the debt of others.

Why would God's Word be so forceful in discouraging this practice? The reason is simple: if you guarantee another's debt, you are equally responsible for it; it becomes your debt as well (v.2). You can put yourself in bondage for years to come by securing someone else's loan. Just like a bird caught in a net, you can become trapped with no way out.

What happens if the person whose note you cosigned makes a bad decision or acts irresponsibly, or has an accident, health problem, or other crisis? Or, what if the individual becomes unemployed or takes a pay cut due to a company's downsizing? Insurmountable problems do happen. Consequently, when you cosign a note, you are jeopardizing your own security, and you are jeopardizing your health with the potential for added stress. This is especially true if your finances are limited and you cannot survive the loss if the worst happened.

God's counsel is firm to those who enter into such pledges thoughtlessly: free yourself from this foolish commitment. Deliver yourself from this trap (v.3). Do not delay in taking corrective action (v.4). Go to the person whose debt you secured and to the creditor immediately, the same day. Do not put it off until tomorrow. Do not sleep until the matter is settled and you have done all you can to be released from the debt. Securing your release from a foolish obligation may require a price, but it is better to assume a smaller loss than to risk your financial security and perhaps your health through worry and anxiety.

Many good-hearted people have placed themselves in financial bondage to help others, in particular, family members and close friends. A wise business person recognizes that God does not command nor does He expect you to place yourself in financial bondage for any reason. In fact, you may be hurting others more than helping them by enabling them to go into debt. You may be *indulging or giving them license* for irresponsible behavior. If people are unable to secure loans or to buy things on their own, they should probably forget the loans and the goods they seek and reevaluate their financial situation. God's wise instruction is clear: you should not cosign or guarantee a loan for someone else.

7. *Be honest and fair in setting prices and establishing sales policies.*

> "You must not have two different weights in your bag, one heavy and one light. You must not have two differing dry measures in your house, a larger and a smaller. You must have a full and honest weight, a full and honest dry measure, so that you may live long in the land the LORD your God is giving you. For everyone who does such things and acts unfairly is detestable to the LORD your God" (Dt. 25:13-16, HCSB).

> "**Differing weights and varying measures—both are detestable to the** LORD" **(Pr. 20:10, HCSB).**
>
> "**Providing for honest things, not only in the sight of the Lord, but also in the sight of men**" **(2 Co.8:21, KJV).**

God's Word prohibits any kind of dishonesty in business dealings. In many ways, a customer is always at the mercy of a merchant. Businesses can easily exploit and take advantage of their customers. But the Lord forbids all deceit in business.

The Scripture passages above cite the common practice of using two weights in measuring merchandise in the ancient world. It was easy for a merchant to use a larger weight to overcharge when selling merchandise and then to use a lighter weight to underpay when purchasing. This deceptive tactic, the most prevalent example of corruption in Old Testament times, represents all dishonesty in business. The principle from God's Word is clear: as a businessperson, you are to be honest in all your dealings, both in selling and in purchasing, whether merchandise or services. Note that two strong reasons are given for honesty in business dealings:

a. **First,** integrity in business affairs will assure the blessings of God (Dt.25:15). If you are impeccably honest, you position yourself where God can bless you, and God's blessing brings success and longevity. Of course, honesty is not the only criteria for business success, but your business will not survive without it. If you are dishonest, God will not bless you, and you should not be surprised when your business suffers and perhaps even fails.

b. **Second,** dishonest business dealings are detested by God (Dt.25:16; Pr.11:1; 20:10). Notice the harsh description of deceit: it is *detestable*—an *abomination*—to the LORD. God hates all sin, but Scripture reveals that some sins are especially disgusting and abhorrent to

Him. Dishonesty in business dealings is one of those sins. This is a strong warning to all who mislead or deceive their customers or clients: God will judge you unless you change your ways and begin to deal with people fairly and honestly.

Never waver from being honest in your sales policies and strategies. Your guiding principle should always be to treat your customers as you want to be treated (Mt.7:12; Lk.6:31). In setting profit margins and price markups, strive to be reasonable, but cautious. Do not overprice your goods or services, but do not underprice them either. Likewise, you should be sensible and competitive, but never greedy, charging enough to produce a fair profit for your business while not taking advantage of your customers. In all advertising, special offers, and sales, make every effort to attract and entice the customer, while at the same time being completely truthful and consistent.

Many business leaders and sales people rationalize their deceptive tactics as simply being *sales strategies that are not necessarily dishonest.* But any statement or method that misleads or discriminates against the customer is dishonest and, consequently, despised by the Lord. Consider these common deceptions:

- Misleading customers about profit margins, pricing, invoice prices, the amount you are making on sales.

- Exaggerating or lying outright about product performance, quality, or expectations.

- Telling customers they are getting the best price available, knowing that others receive lower prices.

- Taking advantage of customers because of their gender, age, lack of education, or any other factor.

- Lying about work needed, or telling customers they need repairs or services that are unnecessary.

- Some unscrupulous businesses go as far as secretly creating damage so they can repair it.

- Not doing all the work you promise to do.

- Pushing customers excessively to purchase unnecessary services. There is certainly nothing wrong with recommending helpful services to increase your sales, or with offering a discount on a bundle of services, but badgering customers to agree to extra services or penalizing them for not purchasing them goes too far.

- Deceiving customers about parts used, for example, using inferior or aftermarket parts when promising to use first quality or original manufacturer parts.

- Falsely inflating prices or value and then offering deep discounts to make customers believe they are getting a better deal.

- Misrepresenting competitors' prices and services.

These and other similar tactics are practiced so widely that many consider them normal and harmless. Deceitful businesses care little about doing what is right., little about helping to build a moral, just, and strong society. They lie, steal, and cheat to get what they want or when it is to their advantage. The dishonest will go as far as they can to better themselves or to get more money. Their only interest is in self and in putting more money in their pockets, regardless of whom they hurt.

Business leaders who cheat and deceive others need to remember the just character of God. Every unfair or dishonest business transaction, large or small, is witnessed by the Lord. Dishonest business leaders may profit for a time, but they will eventually pay for their deceitful ways. If the scales of justice are not balanced while they are living, God will undoubtedly balance them in eternity.

In contrast to dishonesty, the Lord delights in honest business practices, as represented by *an accurate weight* (Pr.11:1). You should always strive to conduct your business—every deal, every transaction, every ad or promotion—in a way that pleases the Lord. God commands you to be honest in all of your practices and policies, never deceiving or cheating anyone.

"Better is a little with righteousness than great revenues with injustice" (Pr.16:8, ESV).

"Making a fortune through a lying tongue is a vanishing mist, a pursuit of death" (Pr.21:6, HCSB).

"Behold, I strike my hand at the dishonest gain that you have made..." (Eze.22:13a, ESV).

8. Be honest and fair in all purchasing practices.

" 'It is good for nothing,' cries the buyer; but when he has gone his way, then he boasts. There is gold and a multitude of rubies, but the lips of knowledge *are* a precious jewel.... Bread gained by deceit *is* sweet to a man, but afterward his mouth will be filled with gravel" (Pr. 20:14-15, 17, NKJV).

God expects you to be honest and fair in all your purchases, just as in your sales. Paying an unfair price for supplies or services is just as wrong as selling your products or services at an unfair price.

The above Scripture highlights the buyer who misrepresents a product's value in order to negotiate a lower purchase price, but the lesson is applicable to all situations. All deceitful purchasing practices are condemned. Everybody loves a bargain, and everybody wants the lowest price possible for any purchase. In truth, purchasing wisely is crucial to surviving in business. Good management includes negotiating the best price possible for any purchase of supplies or services.

But just as you need your customers and vendors to pay a fair price for your products and services—enough to meet your expenses and allow for a reasonable profit— so do the companies who supply products and services to you. Once again, the Golden Rule applies: you should treat your suppliers the way you want your customers to treat you. You should be honest and fair with them...

- in every detail of your transactions
- in every statement you make in negotiations
- in pricing expectations
- in what you are willing to pay

In verse 15, the *lips of knowledge* belong to people who are factual and truthful in all their dealings, no matter which side of the business deal they are on. Whenever you are tempted to sell or trade your integrity to make more money, you need to remember this: truthful speech is far more valuable than gold and rubies. You cannot put a price on being truthful and fair, nor can you put a price on those who are truthful and fair with you.

Tragically, the business world is populated with dishonest sellers and deceitful buyers. Doing business with honest people is a rare treasure. Therefore, we should value our relationships with honest businesses and also be loyal customers, always paying merchants and suppliers fairly for the goods or services they provide us.

This passage concludes with a sharp warning: dishonesty in business carries severe consequences (v.17). The unscrupulous buyer bragged about the tremendous bargain he negotiated deceitfully (v.14). Indeed, dishonest people enjoy the fruits of their fraudulent practices (v.17). Their consciences are numb to the point that they feel no remorse or guilt (1 Ti.4:2). However, the sweet taste of what is gained through deceit will soon turn very bitter. What is so satisfying quickly becomes like a mouthful of gravel or sharp rocks. Crooked people may profit from their unethical business practices for a while, but some day they will pay a painful price for their greed. An unwaveringly just God will see to it that they reap the dishonesty they have sown (Ga.6:7-8). Ultimately, their dishonesty will destroy their businesses—and them, as well.

On the other hand, God blesses people who are honest and ethical. He blesses the businessperson who sells items for a fair price, giving customers good value for their money.

And He blesses customers who pay a fair price for their purchases, not trying to cheat merchants or suppliers out of the money they are due.

9. *Do not exploit people during disasters or catastrophes.*

> "The people curse him who holds back grain,
> but a blessing is on the head of him who sells it"
> (Pr.11:26, ESV).

Leaders in business who are willing to help others in times of need will be blessed for their generosity by both the Lord and the recipients. The setting for this proverb is a time of famine. When a famine struck, some who had grain would hold onto it instead of selling it. As the famine stretched on the situation became critical, because the people had little to no food. The hungrier they became, the more they were willing to pay for grain. By holding back their grain in the beginning, the greedy farmers made far more from it in the end—but at the expense of those who had no choice but to pay the unfair, inflated prices.

Note the principle of this proverb: businesses should not take advantage of others when catastrophes arise. They should not increase their profits by gouging those impacted by disasters, when customers are forced to purchase needed products or services due to circumstances beyond their control.

The law of supply and demand is one of the most basic tenets of economics. When a disaster batters a community—a hurricane, tornado, flood, wildfire, drought, or some other calamity—demand for certain goods and services suddenly increases, and supply becomes very limited. Unusually high demand pushes prices up. Many businesses take advantage of the situation by charging more for their products or services. They know that those affected by the disaster have no choice but to pay whatever they charge.

For example, consider a community devastated by a tornado. Trees are downed, and people who do not own chain saws must suddenly buy them. Houses and other buildings are damaged, creating a rush for building supplies and furnishings. Contractors who provide needed services are suddenly flooded with more work than they can handle.

If you are the leader of a business that provides these necessary goods/services, you have a choice to make. You can raise your prices in response to the sudden demand brought on by tragic circumstances, or you can maintain your regular prices. When you know that your volume is going to increase significantly, you can please the Lord by helping your neighbors and regular customers in their time of need. You might even choose to offer a modest discount to those affected by the disaster.

The message of this proverb will prove true in every case: businesses that exploit desperate situations will be despised and cursed by others. Conversely, merchants and contractors who are willing to sell goods or services at a fair price in such urgent times will be blessed by their neighbors as well as by the Lord. Those impacted by devastating circumstances will remember the businesses that helped them in their time of need, and they will certainly never forget the ones that tried to take advantage of their unfortunate circumstances. Sadly, some people have no sense of loyalty, but many others do, and they will be your devoted customers until the end. More important, the Lord will not forget your compassion for your neighbors, and He will reward you for your goodwill.

10. *Prepare and save for retirement years.*

> **"Go to the ant, you slacker! Observe its ways and become wise. Without leader, administrator, or ruler, it prepares its provisions in summer; it gathers its food during harvest" (Pr. 6:6-8, HCSB).**

The lowly ant teaches a priceless lesson that you should not ignore: in plentiful times, you should prepare for lean times in the future (v.8). The industrious ant works all summer, while food is available, to gather and store food for the coming winter. The ant understands the discipline of *saving* for the time when food does not grow. If a lowly insect recognizes the need to plan ahead and prepare for the future, how much more should we as human beings?

The lesson of the ant—preparing for the future—applies to saving for retirement years (Pr.6:6-8). If you live to a full life expectancy, a day will likely come when you will no longer be able to work to earn an income, or when it is best for your company that you step aside and turn over your position to someone else.

If you are wise, you will invest in the future by saving for the time when you and your spouse can no longer work. You should establish investment strategies and accounts for retirement and continuously build upon those with your current income. Failing to plan and budget for the future for any reason is most unwise—a clear indication of a lack of discipline and self-control.

In the early years of your career or when your business is young and struggling to get established, you may barely earn enough to meet your immediate needs. Still, your future requirements should always be on your mind, and, as soon as possible, you should begin investing money for retirement, even if it is only a small amount. As your income grows, so should the funds you set aside for the coming years when you might not be able to work. Do not delay, for the power of compounding interest is tremendous. Even small sums set aside in the early years of your career will multiply exponentially by the time you need to retire.

In addition, you would be generous and wise to provide some sort of retirement benefit for your employees if at all possible. A plan where you match some amount of an employee's contributions toward retirement motivates the employee to save. Offering a retirement benefit will also pay off for your company. By sowing into your employees' futures, you will reap a long-term family of loyal, grateful coworkers.

The winter of your life will come, and it will be here before you know it. If you are wise, like the disciplined, farsighted ant, you will prepare for it during the summer of your life—the years when you can still work to earn an income.

CHAPTER 5

What You Can Do to Cultivate Excellent Employees

Contents

CHAPTER 5

WHAT YOU CAN DO TO CULTIVATE EXCELLENT EMPLOYEES

A. HIRING AND DEVELOPING EMPLOYEES

1. *Develop clear-cut job descriptions, then hire qualified, trustworthy employees.*

> "But select capable men from all the people—men who fear God, trustworthy men who hate dishonest gain—and appoint them as officials over thousands, hundreds, fifties and tens" (Ex.18:21, NIV '84).

The qualifications listed above in Exodus 18:21 are essential for success with anyone you hire, no matter the generation. When seeking to fill any position, you would be wise to make the qualifications part of what you look for in potential employees. And note an important fact: the higher the position, the more crucial these specific characteristics become.

a. **First, you need to hire** people who are capable, who have the skills to do the job you need them to do. Note that this qualification is at the top of the list, the very first requirement. This placement emphasizes an important lesson: you may have an applicant of excellent character who glowingly meets the three vital qualifications that follow. But if he or she does not have the ability to do the job, you cannot expect that person to be successful. Character without capability will result in failure, the same as capability without character will fail, although in different ways.

To hire a capable person for any position, you must *first determine what skills* are necessary for success in that position and then include those skills in a written job description. This document should be detailed, stating clearly everything you expect from the employee in the position. As you interview candidates for the job, you would be wise to discuss the job description thoroughly, allowing the candidate to respond to its most essential items. Once candidates advance to the final step in your hiring process, you would also be wise to review your company policy and procedures manual with them, making sure they understand all pertinent requirements for employees *prior to* accepting the position.

Drafting a thorough job description is a crucial step, not only for you, but also for the person whom you ultimately hire. Hiring the wrong person will cost you precious time, money, and productivity. But it can be devastating for the individual who proves to be incapable of doing the job. Failing and being dismissed from a job wounds any person's spirit deeply, and it can be crippling to some. It can also hinder a person significantly from finding future employment.

Not only should you clearly communicate the skills necessary for a job, but whenever possible, you should also *test candidates* to see how they perform, if they can actually do the work. Of course, this is not possible for every position. But in most cases, you can find or develop a way to give applicants an opportunity to demonstrate their ability in key areas to do what you need them to do.

In some cases, you may choose to hire someone of exceptional character who lacks experience, training, or skills for the position. You may see in that person a strong willingness and the potential to learn the skills necessary to fulfill the role and become an outstanding employee. If you decide to go this route, you should offer employment only on a *trial basis*. Clearly communicate the situation to the prospective employee: be sure they understand that if they cannot develop the necessary skills in a reasonable period of time, the position will not become permanent.

b. **Second, you should seek** to hire people who live according to God's commands for humanity, who follow

God's Ten Commandments. They should be people whose ethics and values are righteous before God— exactly what they should be. This is what is meant by people who *fear God.* You want employees whose work ethic mirrors what God's Word says about laborers. In addition, you want workers:

- who are honest
- who will not steal from you
- who will give you an honest day's work for an honest day's pay
- who are faithful and take care of their families
- who help prevent workplace immorality, injustice, and disturbance
- who are respectful of other people and their property
- who are of a high moral character

Does this mean you should hire only Christians? No, it does not. Hiring an individual who professes to be a Christian does not guarantee you a diligent, honest employee. Tragically, some who claim to be Christians are lazy, unreliable, and dishonest—some even more so than individuals who do not know the Lord personally. Moreover, in many countries, it is illegal to treat applicants differently based on religious beliefs or practices.

Remember this, God has not written His laws only in His Word but also *on the heart,* the conscience, of every human being. Many people who do not know the Lord personally obey God's laws instinctively, because they know in their hearts that God's principles are right (Ro.2:14-15). These are the types of people you want to hire, whether they are professing Christians or not.

c. **Third, you should hire people** who are *trustworthy.* Literally translated, the phrase used in Scripture here is *people of truth.* This means people who are stable, dependable, faithful, loyal, genuine, and honest. To summarize it in one term, it speaks of people of integrity, people of proven character.

Discerning an individual's character is perhaps the most difficult part of the interview process. You cannot rely on your own instincts, regardless of how keen you think they are. Nor can you trust how well you or a friend of yours may know the individual. Looking into a candidate's past record and checking references thoroughly is probably the most critical thing you can do to establish whether that person is truly trustworthy, and it is a step you need to complete diligently and without exception.

Keep in mind that some governments—including that of the United States—regulate what you can and cannot do in investigating the record and character of potential employees. Consulting an attorney with a thorough knowledge of employment laws will assure that you understand all government guidelines. A skilled attorney can advise you how to obtain as much information as possible within the boundaries of the law.

Trustworthiness should be the most important trait you seek in all employees, and you should prioritize it over other qualifications. Individuals applying for positions may have outstanding skills and valuable experience, but if they are not trustworthy—if they lack integrity—the time will come when you will regret hiring them.

d. **Fourth, you should hire people** who *hate dishonest gain,* who are impeccably honest in their financial dealings. The love of money, or covetousness, is the root of all sorts of evil (1 Ti.6:10). A covetous person, especially one in a position of significant responsibility, may cause serious problems and do tremendous damage to your business. He or she may cut corners unwisely, take foolish risks, deceive customers, suppliers, or clients, jeopardize others' safety, take bribes or kickbacks, steal from you, and deceive you for his or her own benefit.

In hiring personnel, it is crucial to perform due diligence. Assuring that applicants are capable, trustworthy, and honest, people of integrity with strong ethics and high values, is of paramount importance. Again, as much as possible, you should investigate backgrounds and records, including performing background checks, obtaining available reports, checking multiple references, verifying information on résumés, and acquiring as much information from previous employers as legally permitted. If you do these things, you are far more likely to be pleased with your personnel and they are far more likely to be successful. This is exactly what God's Word teaches.

2. *Provide adequate training for all positions.*

> **"All Scripture is inspired by God and is profitable for teaching, for rebuking, for correcting, for training in righteousness, so that the man of God may be complete, equipped for every good work" (2 Ti.3:16-17, HCSB).**

Observing how God leads His people can teach us many valuable principles that also apply to business. This passage, perhaps the strongest in the entire Bible about the origin and purpose of Scripture, models one such principle, that of training. God trains us, His people, to live and serve Him in a way that is pleasing to Him. To accomplish this, He has given us a training manual—His Holy Word, the Bible—to teach us exactly how to live.

In like manner, you have a responsibility to train your employees to do the jobs you hired them to do. Providing adequate training is essential to leading a successful business, and it is imperative to help your employees as they seek to become successful. Never forget that God has designed us to find purpose and fulfillment in productive, meaningful work. By training your employees adequately, you not only help yourself and your company, but you also help the individuals whom God has committed to your stewardship. You help them to become what God has designed them to be: productive human beings with a deep sense of purpose and fulfillment. You do this through the meaningful work you have provided and trained them to do. If they fail in their jobs because you have not trained them adequately, you bear some measure of responsibility for their failure and their wounded spirits.

Just as God has given us His training manual—His Holy Word—so we can be thoroughly equipped for our assigned tasks, the training you provide for your employees should furnish them with every tool they need to perform their jobs effectively. The four steps of God's training process serve as an excellent model for training individuals in any business position:

- *Teaching*—instructing your employees; teaching them both what to do and how to do it; explaining and spelling out in detail everything you expect from them.

- *Rebuking*—this word sounds harsh, but it does not signify a mean, harsh spirit. Rather, it is patiently pointing out where a worker is falling short, where he or she needs to show improvement. If people do not realize where they need to improve, how can they do better?

- *Correcting*—setting the person straight or on the right path. This step goes hand-in-hand with rebuking. When you point out employees' shortcomings, you should simultaneously show them how to do the job correctly, how to make the necessary improvements.

- *Training*—the Greek word for training is the word used for cultivating, nurturing, and educating the young or inexperienced. It involves all three of the previous steps and includes implementing the discipline necessary to attain the stated goal.

It is essential that you train those who work with you not only in the skills required for their jobs, but also in other areas that are critical in today's work climate. For instance, clear guidelines (and disciplinary measures where appropriate) need to be spelled out regarding sexual harassment, discrimination, reporting of violations, safety procedures, and any other matters unique to your company. In fact, a thorough review of all company policies is recommended.

As you hire and prepare to train new employees, keep in mind that many young people have not been taught social and interactive skills by their parents. Tragically, many of the traits necessary for success in life—a strong work ethic, respect, perseverance, the pursuit of excellence—are simply not being taught at home or in schools as much as they once were. You can take one of two approaches toward this dilemma. First, you can refuse to hire or quickly fire individuals who display an obvious ineptitude for the job, and you certainly have the right to respond this way. Without question, training ill-equipped individuals will cost you precious time, money, and productivity.

On the other hand, you can choose to invest in people who have been robbed of the fundamental training parents and schools are supposed to provide. When you find a young person with a driving desire to succeed and a teachable spirit, you can provide training and mentorship in these vital areas. Look to those in your company who would be willing to invest their time and energy working with young people, helping them gain valuable experience. Doing so may cost you in the short run, but the Lord will surely bless and honor you when you use your business to build up other people, especially the disadvantaged of society.

The world around us is changing at a lightning-fast pace. Therefore, to survive in today's competitive market, it is essential for companies to provide ongoing training for their employees. You and the other leaders of your business need to find the best methods of training for the jobs you need done. In fact, if you want to continue to succeed, you will need to make training an ongoing priority in your company.

3. ***Train your employees to be thorough and to persevere until a job is done.***

> **"Poor is he who works with a negligent hand,**
> **But the hand of the diligent makes rich. He who**

> **gathers in summer is a son who acts wisely,**
> ***But* he who sleeps in harvest is a son who acts shamefully" (Pr.10:4-5, NASB '77).**

In this proverb, the person who deals with a slack or negligent hand is not one who refuses to work, but one who is sloppy and careless in his or her responsibilities. The diligent worker, on the other hand, is the exact opposite of this person.

Careless employees are half-hearted and have little interest in their jobs beyond their paychecks. For this reason, when you are hiring and training people and even during their employment, you need to remind your employees that those who are diligent and committed to doing quality work are the ones who will be prized and will advance.

In glaring contrast, those who are irresponsible about their work must be alert to the following:

- Cutting corners or presenting sloppy, inferior work is unacceptable and represents a serious failure in job performance.

- Continuing to do unsatisfactory work will lead to probation, a possible demotion, and, ultimately, termination.

- Being slothful will bring about dismissal and a disgraceful work record, often making a person unemployable, which, in turn, gives rise to poverty and dependence on other people or the government, and sometimes even a life of crime.

As the owner, executive, or manager, demonstrate your expectations by rewarding the diligent and responsible for their outstanding work. Compliment your coworkers as well. Set high standards and recognize those who excel or go the extra mile. Praise the ones who have worked their way up in the company. Establish goals and incentives. Everyone hopes to be rewarded for their outstanding efforts with bonuses, promotions, increased responsibilities, and higher compensation. Those prone to laziness need to be pointed toward employees whose hard work has paid off.

However, when you face economic downturns and lean times, you may not be able to reward your employees financially. When this is the case, find other ways to honor and show your appreciation for their loyalty and work well done. Yes, paying people their promised wages should be enough. But employers who make their employees feel valued and appreciated will usually reap increased production—the good will they themselves have sown.

Note that the Hebrew word for *diligent* is the same word that is used of a sharp, effective tool (Is.41:15; Am.1:3). Challenge your employees to excel, to develop themselves into the most qualified, skilled workers they can be. When possible, contribute to their growth by making additional training and development opportunities available to them. And when they excel or reach goals, reward them appropriately.

If you are an employer or an executive who is responsible for personnel, the one thing you want is to hire employees who work diligently. It is the diligent who recognize the importance of doing a job promptly—as soon as the opportunity presents itself—not procrastinating. The example in this proverb comes from farming, the most common industry in non-industrial societies. Crops must be harvested in the summer when they are ripe. They do not grow year-round; for this reason, farmers must reap the harvest and gather it into their barns when the crops are ripe. They may grow tired, and they may not feel like working every day, but they still get out of bed and do what needs to be done while it can be done. This is what disciplined, industrious people do. They get up, and they go to work when they are required to work in order to provide for themselves and their families. They do not come in late, skip work, go home early, or deceptively call in sick. In fact, they are willing to work extra hours within reason when needed by their employers. They keep on working, sticking to their tasks until the job is done. As a result, they thrive and succeed in their professions and make their families proud of them.

In stark contrast, those who sleep during the harvest—who will not work even when they are needed the most—

are a discredit to themselves and their families' names. They are lazy and undisciplined. They seldom push themselves or persevere until projects are finished. Sadly, they are an embarrassment to their parents and families! They bring dishonor upon their families again and again because the root of their problem is a matter of poor character, character that is deeply flawed and proves shameful in many ways throughout their lives.

What can you do to instill a strong work ethic in employees? Invest in them by challenging and training them to work hard, to be diligent and industrious. Even your best employees can become lax if they are not challenged and reminded to always do their best. Several suggestions follow (Col. 3:23-24) . . .

- *Remind them* that there is dignity and respect in working hard and doing a good job, but that there is shame in laziness and poor work.

- *Teach them* the importance of setting and keeping schedules, of prioritizing necessary tasks over other activities, of being prompt, and of not procrastinating.

- *Challenge them* to work hard, to be diligent and enthusiastic, giving every task their very best effort.

- *Remind them* that anything worth doing is worth doing right.

- *Inspire them* to show initiative—to be self-starters who go beyond doing the minimum their job requires.

- *Reward them* for outstanding work.

Undeniably, the most effective way you can teach these lessons is by living them out in your own life and in your work. As much as allowed, strive to establish a biblical philosophy and culture of work in your company. A biblical philosophy simply means that everyone should be taught to do what is right at all times both for and within your company. When careless employees are moved toward greater productivity through incentives such as better wages, benefits, bonuses, and promotions, this can have a positive effect on a segment of society that refuses to work at all, that is, those who are content to live on government assistance or to make money through illegal means. If all true believers—true followers of the Lord—worked with these principles in mind, work environments around the globe would be positively impacted and the economies of the world would be significantly strengthened.

4. Set the expectation and the example of following instructions in the workplace.

> **Slaves [employees], obey your earthly masters [employers] with deep respect and fear. Serve them sincerely as you would serve Christ. Try to please them all the time, not just when they are watching you. As slaves of Christ, do the will of God with all your heart. Work with enthusiasm, as though you were working for the Lord rather than for people. Remember that the Lord will reward each one of us for the good we do, whether we are slaves or free (Ep.6:5-8, NLT).**

Once you hire a person and provide training, the newly hired employee should follow your instructions. All employees should do what you tell them to do when it concerns their jobs and the welfare of the business that provides their livelihoods. God requires this of workers. By the same token, the Lord expects you—the executive or manager—to follow the instructions of your superiors in the company. Just as you are held accountable by those over you, you are to hold those under you accountable for their job performance. You are the owner, executive, or manager, the person responsible for the business or for a particular division, department, or area of the company. If you do not require job performance of your employees, who will?

Of course, this does not mean employees are to go along blindly with demands that are damaging to themselves, others, or the company, or that are contrary to the teachings of God's Word (Ac.5:29). On this note, you should never give such orders to those who serve under you. But it does mean that workers are to obey legitimate instructions, especially when they have been given jobs, given . . .

- the privilege of earning a living and providing for themselves and their families
- the privilege of doing purposeful work by helping to provide some product or service needed by society
- the privilege of becoming responsible citizens and helping to meet the needs of their communities and of the poor and helpless

As a business owner or executive, it is you who creates and provides jobs, products, and services for the public. Therefore, at the very least, you have the right to expect employees to follow your directives. In fact, the more attention your employees give to following instructions and performing their duties, the greater their production and service to the public. And, naturally, God wants the public—both believers and unbelievers—provided for.

Considering God's concern for people's welfare, you need to ensure that your employees carry out your instructions. (This requires that you provide them with well-defined and easily understood job descriptions. See pp.105-106.) God's Word even spells out the behavior you should expect from your employees:

a. **Employees are to respect you** enough to follow your instructions (v.5a). In addition, they should fear displeasing you lest you reprimand or possibly dismiss them for their failure. This kind of fear—the fear God expects employees to have—is not a slavish fear of management. To the contrary, it is a fear of consequences—an awareness that one's own misbehavior or rebellion against authority brings negative consequences such as a rebuke, strong corrective action, and ultimately dismissal.

b. **Employees are to be sincere** in following your instructions (v.5b). This simply means they are to work with purpose and focused attention, without pretense or hypocrisy. Earnest workers do not waste or misuse time. They are not *lazy*, nor do they merely pretend to be good workers. Rather, the sincere employee is a good, productive laborer. He or she follows your instructions wholeheartedly and does a commendable job. Note how important a *sincere heart* is to God. Employees are to obey you just as they would obey Christ (v.5).

c. **Employees are to follow your instructions** all the time, not just when you are watching them (v.6a). Sadly, some workers slow down or stop working altogether when their employer or manager is not looking and then speed up when he or she is looking. Some take undeserved and extended breaks, daydream, or even sleep. Others play games or handle personal affairs on their computers or cell phones. Some simply walk around and talk with others. Such people are lazy, dishonest, and inconsiderate. They are stealing from their employers by not earning the wages they are being paid. At the root of their behavior, these slackers lack initiative, purpose, and motivation. Such low work standards rob labor of its dignity and bring disrespect to the Lord's name.

No matter how diligently you try to hire employees with a strong work ethic, some will fall short of God's standard to be diligent in all that they do. As you seek to be the best steward possible for your company or for the department committed to your oversight, God will help you recognize those who are taking advantage of you and the company, those who need correction and encouragement to become productive workers.

d. **Employees are to work with enthusiasm,** as though they are working for the Lord Himself and not for people (vv. 6b-7). Working "with all your heart" actually means working enthusiastically—with focused interest and energy. It is the opposite of working out of routine, of being listless, sluggish, of having no energy or heart for one's work. Workers should always remember this fact: even if the boss is not looking, the Lord sees what kind of work they are doing. Therefore, they should work as though they are working for Christ. The very drive of every employee's heart should be to serve the Lord by doing a good job and by following their instructions with enthusiasm.

God promises to reward the employee who has a positive attitude toward you—his or her employer—and who works enthusiastically (v.8). These are the instructions of God Himself to all of us, no matter who we are, employees or employers. We should all ask ourselves one question at the end of the day: Have I pleased the Lord by doing my best today?

As an employer or manager of others, you should model this same work ethic for those who serve under you. You should fulfill the responsibilities of your position with this attitude and energy, showing respect for those over you in the company in addition to supporting their visions and goals. Even if you are the owner of the company and answer to no other human, you still answer to the Lord, who owns the earth and everything in it. In every aspect of your work, you should put forth your most diligent effort with a grateful heart to God, who has blessed you with the privilege and responsibility of owning a business.

Only when you work with this attitude and energy can you expect the same of those who work under you. As a leader, this is an essential part of your responsibility, to model this ethic and to teach it to all who serve in your company. Most will follow your example in their own job or position, and all of you can finish each day with the satisfaction that comes from knowing you have done a good job!

5. Establish a fair and legal disciplinary process for your employees.

> "A servant [employee] will not be corrected by mere words; For though he understands, he will not respond" (Pr.29:19, NKJV).

Nearly every company, regardless of size, has to contend with unsatisfactory employees from time to time. While some workers underperform, others behave in an unruly manner. When either of these happens, you need to quickly deal with the individual before the situation gets out of hand. But it is important to remember this truth when you do: as human beings, we are all imperfect. We all fall short of what we should be at times and fail to do what we should. Too often we act selfishly, even sinfully, both at home and at work. As a result, we need to be corrected, instructed, or encouraged to do better sometimes.

With the above in mind, it is crucial to establish a *legal* and *fair* disciplinary process to guide you and/or your company when dealing with such employees. Even if you are a single-person business operation now, when you are ready to add employees, you will need clear-cut job descriptions plus guidelines spelled out in a personnel manual. The manual may be only one or two pages long, but it will help protect you against lawsuits. Indeed, employees file thousands of lawsuits every year due to misunderstandings about work requirements and/or a disciplinary action that became necessary. You do not want this happening to you. In many cases, small businesses lack the finances to fight legal battles and are forced into bankruptcy. This is mentioned here because the vast majority of businesses in this nation, as well as throughout the world, are small. And the vast majority of workers are employed by small businesses. In most cases, you do not have the assets or reserves to handle legal battles. Thus, you need to protect yourself and your company by developing, or contributing to, a personnel manual.

Most employees genuinely want to perform well on the job, to succeed in their careers. Most desire to do excellent work, to earn their wages or salaries honestly, to be productive, to please their employers, and to advance. While such individuals will usually put forth their best effort and be diligent in following guidelines and policies, they will still make mistakes and still have room for improvement.

Other individuals, however, do not have such a strong work ethic. They want to do as little as possible and actually feel a sense of satisfaction in getting paid for their lax behavior. We have all seen employees and work crews who habitually arrive late for work, take extended breaks, take too long for lunch, then look for an excuse to leave work early. They are unreliable, untrustworthy, and unproductive unless constantly supervised. They arrogantly scoff at policies and behave however they choose, feeling a sense of pride in their rebellious nature. Many such people are disrespectful toward their coworkers, ridiculing and mocking them because of their hard work and loyalty to their employers and companies.

Both types of people need to be corrected at times. As their employer or manager, it is your responsibility to hold them accountable and to teach them to meet company expectations. The first type, those who seek to be excellent workers, will usually respond to gentle verbal correction and instruction. For the second group, the lax, indifferent workers, verbal correction and instruction are often not enough to produce proper conduct, as this proverb teaches. Certain people tend to push the limits as far and as long as allowed. When this happens, harsher disciplinary measures are usually needed.

Although employees may understand what is expected of them, if there is no penalty for poor work or unacceptable behavior, many will not perform their duties—not well or diligently or efficiently. Therefore, you need to establish clear, unmistakable guidelines for all workers and communicate those guidelines through a detailed personnel manual. The manual should plainly state and explain policies, procedures, expectations, standards of behavior, and consequences. By doing so, your employees will have a better understanding of what is expected of them and of the consequences of poor performance or unacceptable behavior. The manual should spell out a disciplinary process step-by-step, leading up to termination of employment. To protect yourself and your company from potential lawsuits resulting from disciplinary action or dismissal, you would be wise to seek legal counsel in developing this manual.

Certainly, you have a right and an obligation to expect your employees to behave appropriately, to be productive, and to perform quality work. When they continually fail in these areas, you have a right and a responsibility to your company to dismiss them. Throughout the disciplinary process, however, you should remember the commands of Scripture...

- to love others as yourself (Mt.22:39)
- to treat others the way you want to be treated (Lk.6:31)
- to humbly consider what is in the best interests of other productive employees (Ph.2:3-4)
- to try to help and strengthen the character of lax or indifferent employees (Ga.6:1-3; 1 Th.5:14)

To do these things, you may have to take strong disciplinary action. Many individuals will change when the consequences become more severe, but others will not. For some, being dismissed from a much-needed job may be just what it takes to turn them around. It could compel them to correct their behavior and work habits for the remainder of their lives. Tragically, other individuals will stubbornly refuse to change and scorn every effort to correct or instruct them.

As a business owner or executive, you should establish a fair and legal process for your employees. And in so doing, you should always establish the authority to hold workers accountable. This is the only way you can be truly successful in business and fulfill your God-given purpose, that of doing honest work that serves the public or private sector in some capacity while also providing gainful employment for other individuals.

6. *Reprimand employees who are insubordinate.*

> "Slaves [employees] . . . must not talk back."
> (Tit.2:9, NLT)

Wise, capable and trusted employees—the kind of employees you want working for you—will not talk back to you. When an employee is antagonistic, challenging you and refusing to accept your instruction, you have a problem. And if you fail to deal with the problem swiftly, it can have a very negative impact on the workplace. A person's talking back—whether to the owner of the business or a department head—can deeply affect the spirit of unity, enthusiasm, and sense of common purpose among other employees. It can pollute the whole atmosphere of the workplace and cut into production.

This is why God commands employees not to talk back to their superiors. Instead, God says employees are to go above and beyond their duty. They are to strive to please you in all things, including in their . . .

- attitude: they are to have an attitude of appreciation for the job and for the livelihood it provides them

- spirit: they are to show commitment and loyalty to you and the company as well as an eagerness and diligence in their work

- thoughts: they are to think constructively about their work, how to improve their performance and be more efficient

- speech and words: they are to speak positively and build up the company and the work it does

- relationships: they are to seek good relationships—a spirit of teamwork—with fellow employees and management

- work and labor: they are to be on time and give a full day of labor. They should seek to increase their own productivity and that of the whole workplace. They should help the company when extra effort or hours are needed and be willing to go beyond what is required.

In summary, employees are not to talk back or to contradict or defy you. They are to recognize and respect the need for orderliness and for levels of management or supervision to get the work done in the most efficient, effective way possible. Talking back to a supervisor, which is a spirit of rebellion, is totally unacceptable in the workplace. So, if employees display a reactionary spirit, you need to deal with them immediately, before any anxiety or unrest sets in and affects other workers and their production. This is God's clear instruction to us all.

7. *Correct employees wisely and constructively.*

> **"A wise correction to a receptive ear is like a gold ring or an ornament of gold" (Pr. 25:12, HCSB).**

> **"Do not let any unwholesome talk come out of your mouths, but only what is helpful for building others up according to their needs, that it may benefit those who listen" (Ep.4:29, NIV '84).**

When you need to correct an employee, approach the matter wisely and cautiously. Why? Because you want the correction to be well-received and heeded, and how you deliver it largely determines the outcome. Wise correction is kind, gentle, and constructive, not abusive. By approaching a problem with the right spirit, you will help yourself and your company as well as the worker who is falling short of expectations in some area.

Indeed, God's Word tells us plainly not to let any unwholesome—corrupt, abusive—talk come out of our mouths (Ep.4:29). With this in mind, you should correct employees in a way that...

- is *helpful*, not harmful
- *builds them up* rather than tears them down
- addresses what is necessary—*according to their needs*
- *benefits* them, resulting in changed behavior

Note the valuable lesson of this proverb: wise correction is like gold to a receptive ear. Wise people (the receptive) value correction, whereas the foolish (the unreceptive) hate it (Pr.12:1a). But being corrected is painful for everyone. It awakens every defensive tendency within us. Even those who understand the value of correction will resist or react if you are harsh, demeaning, or derogatory. If you are calm and careful when you offer correction, though, building them up instead of beating them down, those individuals will seldom become angry or defensive. Granted, some people foolishly refuse to accept correction, regardless how it is given (Pr.12:1b). But most will respond favorably to correction when you offer it in the right way. Wise correction helps...

- to save the employee's job
- to stir the employee to be more productive
- to increase the company's production, income, and profit
- to build up the spirit of teamwork within the company
- to strengthen both the company and the community that the company serves

When correction is given wisely and well-received, it is a beautiful thing, *like a gold ring or ornament.* And, like fine gold, it is exceptionally valuable. Thus, you should always correct your employees carefully, not hastily or rashly. Weigh and choose your words deliberately. You cannot control how a person will receive your correction, but you can control how you deliver it. Pray and ask God to guide you and to help you display the right spirit.

8. Minimize conflict in your work environment.

"Do all things without complaining and disputing." (Ph.2:14, NKJV).

> **"These people are grumblers and complainers, living only to satisfy their desires. They brag loudly about themselves, and they flatter others to get what they want" (Jude 1:16, NLT).**

No work environment is immune to people who complain, criticize, and cause division. As a business leader, you will at some point have to deal with disgruntled people. If you fail to address the problem and allow the criticism, fault-finding, and gossip to go on, a spirit of divisiveness can take over. And division within will damage your business, most notably, the effectiveness and production of your workers (Mk.3:24-25). What can you do to minimize conflict within your business?

First, acknowledge the reality that some people are going to complain. Certain individuals are simply that way by nature; no matter what happens or what you do, they will find fault and complain. They are just grumblers. Other complainers are troublemakers with evil motives. It is the troublemakers who usually stir up others to help them get their way (Jude 16).

Still others complain when they become frustrated or dissatisfied or perceive something to be wrong or unfair. In many cases, their complaints are legitimate. No business is perfect, and situations or circumstances will arise that cause employees to become upset. If things do not change, even the most compliant people will eventually vent their feelings.

With this being true, it is wise to adapt policies and procedures for expressing concerns and grievances. Encourage employees to go to the appropriate person to discuss their concerns and identify the appropriate person for various departments or situations. For this process to be effective, you need to build a team or family environment within and throughout your company—a "we" atmosphere as opposed to an "us" and "them" culture. Teach employees to be respectful and constructive in their comments. Likewise, company leaders—supervisors, managers, executives—need to be approachable and fair. Many employees will not speak with leadership about an issue for fear of retribution or of being viewed unfavorably. It is important to assure them that this will not be the case. Once a concern has been discussed, leadership needs to follow through with addressing it and subsequently communicate with the employee about any action that has, or is going to be, taken.

It is important to properly train people at every level to handle issues or grievances that arise. Then, the process of airing and addressing concerns needs to be promoted regularly and enforced consistently—a key to developing a spirit of team or family within your company. The company policy should include disciplinary steps for those who fail to follow it. When these steps are carried out, you will eventually have the grounds to terminate any employee whose divisiveness warrants it, as well as any supervisors or managers who discriminate against or mistreat any employee who follows the proper procedure in lodging a complaint.

As the business owner or executive, your desire should be not only to squelch all complaining, but also to deal with every legitimate concern. If unfair conditions or situations exist, you should sincerely seek to correct them. Eliminating them makes both you and your company stronger.

Creating a culture in which every individual is valued, where every voice is heard, and where all work together for the good of the business and one another, is the foundation for preventing complaining and disputing. Some people will never fit into such an environment; therefore, drafting applicable policies and procedures will give you a fair and legal process for removing them if it becomes necessary. You will never eliminate all complaining and criticizing, but you can certainly minimize it by confronting the reality of it and offering a way for concerns to be aired and addressed.

B. Managing and Rewarding Employees

1. Treat your employees as you expect them to treat you.

> "And masters [employers], treat your slaves [employees] in the same way. Do not threaten

them, since you know that he who is both their Master and yours is in heaven, and there is no favoritism with him" (Ep.6:9, NIV).

"So in everything, do to others what you would have them do to you, for this sums up the Law and the Prophets" (Mt.7:12, NIV).

What a difference this principle would make in labor-management relationships if it were genuinely practiced by both parties! God gives two clear instructions that are to govern how you treat the employees under you.

a. **You, the business owner,** executive, or manager, are to set the example for all employees (Ep.6:5-9). You are...

- to serve the company (both those above and below you) with deep respect and fear (v.5a). This attitude is necessary lest you cause so much grumbling and displeasure among your employees that it results in lost productivity and/or sales, the loss of your job, or possibly even the collapse of your business.

- to be sincere as you labor day by day, working with purpose and focused attention, without any pretense or hypocrisy (v.5b).

- to work diligently throughout the day, not only when your employees or an executive who may be above you is watching (v.6). God instructs you to do exactly what you want your employees to do: to work hard. For that reason, you need to set the example by working hard always.

- to work with enthusiasm, as though you are working for the Lord Himself—serving Him with focused attention and energy (v.7).

Every business owner and manager wants their employees to work as the above four points spell out: with deep respect, sincerity, diligence, and enthusiasm. Set the example for them. Your example is the strongest motivation they will ever receive.

b. You are not to threaten or mistreat your employees (v.9). This does not mean that you cannot correct or release a worker if the individual is not diligent or loyal. God does not tolerate laziness, irresponsibility, indulgence, or rebellion. To the contrary, God warns and then disciplines us when we misbehave and disobey His commands (He.12:5-6; Pr.3:11-12).

God does not want you to be overbearing or to react in anger when correcting an employee. Stern measures—like issuing warnings or firing someone—are to be taken only after all other corrective measures have failed. Every person, no matter how unproductive, is worth saving for the workforce of our communities and nation if they are willing to heed correction. If possible, every unproductive worker needs to be rescued and developed into a conscientious employee.

Granted, it is not always possible to salvage every lazy or unskilled worker. Some are simply unwilling to work, to be productive, or to contribute to society. But when they are willing to listen and to change their work habits, you need to rescue and develop them.

Once again, note God's instruction in the Scripture about threatening your employees (v.9b). You must guard against unwarranted threats. Why? Because *you* too have a Master—a Master in heaven—the Lord Jesus Christ. And He has no favorites. Just as you hold every employee accountable to you, so the Lord holds you accountable to Him for the way you treat your employees. Therefore, you should always issue warnings firmly, but also courteously and carefully.

Furthermore, when firing or taking corrective action against an employee, you need to protect yourself by keeping written or recorded documentation of all meetings and actions. This is critical for future reference, in the event that a scorned employee retaliates against you by making false charges or taking legal action.

In summary, as a business owner or executive, you hold enormous authority over the lives of your employees. How you treat them affects the relationship between you and them. In addition, it significantly influences the workplace environment and the level of production in your company as well as the home and social lives of everyone involved. Your treatment of employees reflects heavily on your Christian testimony and your effectiveness in setting a dynamic example for others. God is clear: you are to treat your employees just as you want them to treat you.

2. *Build a spirit of enthusiasm and teamwork.*

> "Then I said to them, 'You see the trouble we are in: Jerusalem lies in ruins, and its gates have been burned with fire. Come, let us rebuild the wall of Jerusalem, and we will no longer be in disgrace.' I also told them about the gracious hand of my God upon me and what the king had said to me. They replied, 'Let us start rebuilding.' So they began this good work" (Ne.2:17-18, NIV '84).

> "Eliashib the high priest and his fellow priests went to work and rebuilt the Sheep Gate. They dedicated it and set its doors in place, building as far as the Tower of the Hundred, which they dedicated, and as far as the Tower of Hananel. The men of Jericho built the adjoining section, and Zaccur son of Imri built next to them.... Next to him, Malkijah, one of the goldsmiths, made repairs as far as the house of the temple servants and the merchants, opposite the Inspection Gate, and as far as the room above the corner; and between the room above the corner and the Sheep Gate the goldsmiths and merchants made repairs (Ne.3:1-2, 31-32, NIV '84).

> "So we rebuilt the wall till all of it reached half its height, for the people worked with all their heart" (Ne.4:6, NIV '84).

To this very day, Nehemiah stands as an exemplary model of leadership. Stirred to action by an overwhelming burden for his homeland, he led a relatively small group of people to return to Jerusalem after the Babylonian Captivity. What they accomplished was truly amazing! They achieved the mammoth task of rebuilding Jerusalem's war-ravaged walls in less than two months, an incredibly short timeframe (Ne.6:15).

One of the secrets to Nehemiah's remarkable success is that he inspired the people. He created a spirit of enthusiasm and teamwork among them. This should be a top priority for you as you lead your business or area of responsibility. Whether you have a handful of employees or hundreds, it is imperative that you keep the concept of teamwork in mind as you seek to inspire your people. Pulling them together to work wholeheartedly and as a team is a critical component to your company's success.

The following three points reveal valuable insights into building a spirit of enthusiasm and teamwork in your company, division, or department:

a. **First, rally your people** around the purpose or goal of your business (Ne.2:17-18). Note that Nehemiah did not emphasize the intimidating task at hand—rebuilding the wall—but the purpose behind the task, that of restoring their beloved homeland. It was the *purpose* that energized the people to take on the task and put their hearts into their work.

   Likewise, you need to define your business's purpose and always keep it before the people who work with you. In recent years, organizations of all types have created *mission* or *purpose statements*. These declarations convey the organization's purpose clearly and concisely and are usually stated in just one extended sentence. Adopting a carefully-worded mission statement will, among other things, give your co-laborers a brief summary of your company's purpose on which they can focus.

   Whether you manufacture a product or provide a service, the tasks involved can sometimes become mundane or meaningless in and of themselves. Therefore, everyone in your business needs to understand and embrace your company's purpose, *why* you do what you do, *what* each team member's dedication and hard work accomplishes, and *how* it contributes toward improving people's lives and society in general. Grasping the company's purpose or goal will help give meaning to each individual's job and help inspire your team to work wholeheartedly and as one. Periodically, encourage personnel to remember the company's mission or purpose, especially when they are facing problems or merely having a bad day.

b. **Second, acknowledge** that every job is important, every worker is significant (Ne.3:1-32). Nehemiah did a remarkable thing: he listed the names of those who repaired the wall along with the sections of the wall where they labored. By doing so, he made a powerful point, one that is crucial to the success of any business: acknowledging that every job is important and that every individual is significant to the company's success. People who labor with you will only work with enthusiasm and as a team when they feel valued, needed, and an essential part of the business.

Regardless of title, pay scale, and duties, all employees need to do their jobs effectively for your business to be successful. From the lowest entry-level position to the CEO, every individual contributes to the company's success. Jerusalem's wall was completed only after every worker or division of workers had finished construction of their individual sections. Likewise, your company accomplishes its tasks or goals through a collective effort, through teamwork, through each worker or department or division performing its appointed duties.

Your company is made up of individuals, but it is *one* company, *one* business. It accomplishes its mission when everyone works together under the direction of the company's leadership. In light of that, every individual is important and every individual is a key component to your company's success, regardless of position or pay level.

When you, like Nehemiah, genuinely demonstrate a deep commitment to your company's purpose and acknowledge every individual's value openly, you will build a team of workers who are loyal, diligent, and effective in their jobs. And you will build a spirit of enthusiasm and teamwork in your business.

c. **Third, give** your co-laborers credit for what your business accomplishes (Ne.4:6). At the halfway point of the mammoth rebuilding project, Nehemiah paused to emphasize the progress that had been made. Notice what he said, "So *we* [emphasis ours] rebuilt the wall." Then, note the reason he gave for this accomplishment: "for the people worked with all their heart." Like any wise and effective leader, Nehemiah did not grab the glory for what had been done. Instead, he attributed the project's success to the wholehearted dedication of the workers. No doubt, this acknowledgement encouraged the laborers to persevere in spite of vehement opposition and to press on until the job was completely finished (Ne.6:15).

In most cases, it will be your initiative and leadership that drive the progress of your company or division. But you need to be humble enough to recognize that you do not work alone; your company's accomplishments are the result of a team effort. In addition, you should always express your gratitude to the people who have a part in making you or your business successful. You need to freely recognize and give them the credit they are due. When you do, you inspire your people to a greater spirit of dedication, productivity, and excellence. The spirit of enthusiasm and teamwork will usually prevail when you, the leader of the team, give your co-laborers the credit for success.

3. *Do not micromanage—trust responsible people.*

> "Now his master saw that the LORD was with him and *how* the LORD caused all that he did to prosper in his hand. So Joseph found favor in his sight, and became his personal servant; and he made him overseer over his house, and all that he owned he put in his charge. And it came

> about that from the time he made him overseer in his house, and over all that he owned, the LORD blessed the Egyptian's house on account of Joseph; thus the LORD's blessing was upon all that he owned, in the house and in the field. So he left everything he owned in Joseph's charge; and with him *there* he did not concern himself with anything except the food which he ate. Now Joseph was handsome in form and appearance" (Ge.39:3-6, NASB '77).
>
> "Then they entrusted it to the men appointed to supervise the work on the LORD's temple. These men paid the workers who repaired and restored the temple. . . . The men did the work faithfully. . . " (2 Chr.34:10-12a, NIV '84).

As a business leader, you know well that much of a company's success depends upon its employees. Therefore, your goal should always be to hire capable, skilled people, but you also want people who are dependable, honest, and loyal to the business. In a word, you need people who are *trustworthy*. The higher the position, the more crucial this quality becomes.

Once you have selected and instructed trustworthy individuals, trust them to do their jobs or to lead their divisions or departments. You need to give them the authority to do what you expect them to do, and then allow them to do it. Simply stated, you should not micromanage your business and associates. Once you have set goals and expectations together and established reporting and accountability measures, you should then let them do their jobs and simply communicate with them regularly and clearly.

Sadly, some people in leadership do not quite grasp this principle. They operate by the old saying, "If you want something done right, do it yourself." Wise executives and managers know that this is not necessarily true. Similarly, many business leaders have a natural tendency to think that the more closely we watch our workers, the better they will do. But if we have capable, trustworthy individuals, micromanaging is not necessary; in fact, it may do more harm than good.

The dangers of micromanagement have been discussed and documented in countless business articles and books. Without question, you will have some individuals within your business or department who are not trustworthy, who do not have a strong work ethic, or who will work hard only when closely supervised. Those who *are* trustworthy, though, will almost certainly become frustrated if you do not have confidence in them to do their jobs. And, they will likely move on to other departments or even other companies if the opportunity arises. If you are a micromanager, you stand the chance of losing your best talent. So, make yourself aware of this tendency and work on correcting it. Consider asking one or more people to help keep you aware of it. You should strive to hire people who are both capable and trustworthy, then trust them to do their jobs. They will help you become more and more successful as you seek to serve your community through the products or services you offer.

4. Be just and fair with all employees.

> "Masters [employers], be just and fair to your slaves [employees]. Remember that you also have a Master—in heaven" (Col.4:1, NLT).

As a business owner or executive, you hold authority over the lives of your employees while they are working. They labor for hours every week for a variety of reasons, but how you treat them is of vital concern to the Lord. Note the Scripture above: it is a command from God, not a suggestion. God demands you, as a business owner or executive, be just and fair with your employees. You are to be just and fair in . . .

- wages
- work assignments
- production schedules
- expectations and demands
- promotions
- corrections and warnings

Scripture clearly states the reason for the command: you too have a Master—a Master in heaven. Even if you are the sole owner of your business, you are not its highest authority. Just as your employees must answer to you, you must answer to God. Never forget that the Lord God sees everything you do. Whether fair or unfair, just or unjust, nothing escapes God's eye. God commands you to be fair, and therefore, you need to give careful attention to dealing justly with your employees at all times and in all things. God holds you accountable for your actions.

5. *Do not cheat your employees and contractors.*

> **"Look! The wages you failed to pay the workmen who mowed your fields are crying out against you. The cries of the harvesters have reached the ears of the Lord Almighty. You have lived on earth in luxury and self-indulgence. You have fattened yourselves in the day of slaughter" (Jas.5:4-5, NIV).**

As a business leader, owner, executive, or manager, you have both the ability and the opportunity to help supply jobs for others so that they, in turn, can earn a living to provide for themselves and their families. Your creation of jobs, along with the money that flows throughout communities from those jobs, helps to build stronger families and societies. Therefore, you have a responsibility to pay your employees and contractors adequately and promptly for the work they perform. God's Word clearly commands us not to take advantage of our workers, and part of that command includes paying full wages on time. If we fail to do so, we stand guilty before God and will face the coming judgment (v.5; 24:14-15).

Sadly, this passage addresses a common problem in society, that of employers living selfishly and extravagantly while failing to adequately pay their workers. Many business owners and managers cheat, deceive, and steal from their employees and contractors by . . .

- not paying fair or adequate wages
- not paying a full hour's or day's wage
- not paying for all work done
- not withholding (taxes, fees, etc.) accurately or honestly
- not paying in a timely fashion
- not evaluating work fairly or truthfully
- not honoring contract or employment terms

The list could go on and on. Such behavior is totally unacceptable. It is even more deplorable, though, when the employer is wealthy (v.5). We sometimes hear reports of CEOs who have multiple homes, excess vehicles, extravagant possessions, and all the pleasures money can buy, yet they are cheating employees by misusing retirement funds, providing poor working conditions, working underage children, or any number of other devious schemes. These executives have enough money to last several lifetimes, yet they refuse to pay their employees enough to live modestly and meet their families' most basic needs.

Without question, it is perfectly fine for business leaders to enjoy the fruits of their labor. Nowhere in Scripture does it teach that lower level employees and top executives be paid equally. But, as stated above, those who live luxuriously while failing to pay employees adequately, fairly, and promptly, stand guilty before God. Do not set yourself up to fall under God's strong judgment.

Note what usually happens when employers defraud their workers: those who are cheated cry out because of the injustice (v.4). When they cry out to God, He hears them. He promises to help the poor, the disadvantaged, and the oppressed who truly trust and live for Him. But this is not all. God will also deal firmly with the dishonest employers, either in this life or in the coming day of judgment (v.5).

Scripture has much to say about cheating people out of their due wages or dealing dishonestly with employees and contractors, thereby oppressing them:

a. **If you seek** to become wealthy through dishonest means, you are seeking death, perhaps an early death.

> **"Making a fortune through a lying tongue is a vanishing mist, a pursuit of death" (Pr.21:6, HCSB).**

b. **If you trick** or take advantage of others, expect to meet a day of severe need.

> **"Oppressing the poor to enrich oneself, and giving to the rich—both lead only to poverty" (Pr.22:16, HCSB).**

> **"Like a partridge that hatches eggs she has not laid, so are those who get their wealth by unjust means. At midlife they will lose their riches; in the end they will become poor old fools" (Je.17:11, NLT).**

c. **If you build** your estate by defrauding your workers, God warns that He will bring fierce judgment upon you.

> **"Woe to him who builds his house by unrighteousness and his chambers by injustice, who uses his neighbor's service without wages and gives him nothing for his work" (Je.22:13, NKJV).**

> **"Then I will draw near to you for judgment. I will be a swift witness against the sorcerers, against the adulterers, against those who swear falsely, against those who oppress the hired worker in his wages, the widow and the fatherless, against those who thrust aside the sojourner, and do not fear me, says the LORD of hosts" (Mal.3:5, ESV).**

d. **If you cheat** others, God will not forget or overlook your dishonest works.

> **"Listen to this, you who rob the poor and trample down the needy! You can't wait for the Sabbath day to be over and the religious festivals to end so you can get back to cheating the helpless. You measure out grain with dishonest measures and cheat the buyer with dishonest scales. And you mix the grain you sell with chaff swept**

from the floor. Then you enslave poor people for one piece of silver or a pair of sandals. Now the LORD has sworn this oath by his own name, the Pride of Israel: 'I will never forget the wicked things you have done!' " (Am.8:4-7, NLT).

6. *Reward deserving employees.*

"Let the elders [leaders] who rule well be considered worthy of double honor, especially those who work hard at preaching and teaching. For the Scripture says, "You Shall Not Muzzle the Ox While He Is Threshing," and "The laborer is worthy of his wages" (1 Ti.5:17-18, NASB '77).

"'Well done!' the king exclaimed. 'You are a good servant. You have been faithful with the little I entrusted to you, so you will be governor of ten cities as your reward' " (Lk.19:17, NLT).

God's instructions on management of the church again serve as a model for business leaders. God's Word decrees that *His* employees—the elders or pastors of churches—who labor hard and perform outstanding work are worthy of *double honor*, or extra compensation.

All of us want to feel appreciated, to know that our efforts and contributions are noticed and valued. Your dedicated and trustworthy employees are a true treasure. If you are wise, you will let them know how much you value them. The verses above suggest three ways you can reward deserving employees.

a. **The most obvious way to reward deserving employees is with additional compensation (1 Ti.5:17-18).** When employees perform outstanding work, exceed expectations consistently, give extra time, make sacrifices, or go beyond what is required of them, you are wise to show your gratitude in a tangible way. Virtually all employees appreciate a raise or bonus. And everyone likes to make more money, whether they need it or not, because extra compensation can be used for whatever the recipient chooses. When you are financially able, this is one of the best ways to reward a deserving employee. If you do not have the funds to give a raise or bonus, find other ways to reward an outstanding team member, such as giving extra time off with pay.

Some employers have the attitude that the agreed-upon wage or salary is all they owe their workers, and that employees should not expect anything more. Essentially, this is true. But when employees consistently go beyond what you expect or require of them, you should compensate them appropriately. Moreover, showing your appreciation for outstanding work and faithful service in a tangible way motivates good people to do even better. It conveys how much you value exceptional employees and generates even more loyalty from them.

b. **You should always reward deserving employees with praise and recognition (Lk.19:17).** God's Word specifically states that God will evaluate His people, and that He will reward the faithful by recognizing and praising them (1 Co.4:5). Every genuine believer longs to hear the Lord say, "Well done, good and faithful servant" on that day (Mt.25:21).

Likewise, your dedicated employees desire to hear similar words from you. Everyone needs affirmation; conscientious people want to know that they are doing a good job, that you are pleased with their work.

Sadly, many business leaders fail miserably in this area, only letting their employees hear from them if their work is unsatisfactory. What a disheartening way to deal with those who labor diligently to please their superiors! Furthermore, it is a direct violation of God's command to encourage and build up others through edifying words (Ep.4:29).

In addition to frequently praising outstanding workers, you should also have special occasions when you recognize them before the company or a division of the company. Awards such as plaques, certificates, and gifts may be mere tokens of your appreciation, but they will be treasured by devoted employees.

c. **When the opportunity arises, you should reward deserving employees with promotions (Lk.19:17).** One of the clear teachings of Scripture is that a laborer who is faithful in little will be faithful in much (Lk.16:10). When a position opens in your company, you should seriously consider promoting someone from within. You eliminate many risks and uncertainties by moving someone to a position of greater responsibility whose character, ability, and work ethic you already know. You also reward a faithful and deserving employee. At the same time, you will need to guard carefully against promoting an individual to a position beyond his or her ability.

Opportunity for advancement is important to many career-oriented individuals. For this reason, you risk losing outstanding team members if your company cannot offer such opportunities. If you have no positions available, you can still reward aspiring and valued employees by giving them higher titles or some measure of increased responsibility, accompanied by a pay increase. Whatever you choose to do, make it as meaningful and significant as possible, for rewarding deserving employees is a necessary step in operating a successful business.

7. *Provide at least one day off a week for your employees to rest and worship.*

> **"Remember the sabbath day, to keep it holy" (Ex.20:8, KJV).**

> **"And he said unto them, The sabbath was made for man, and not man for the Sabbath" (Mk.2:27, KJV).**

Work, rest, and worship—all three are essential for a truly fulfilling life. You and your employees need all three because God made you this way. This is what the Sabbath is all about. God Himself set the seventh day aside for humanity because He loves and cares for us; He knows what we need. Every human being needs a full day of rest every week, a day set aside for relaxation and worship—so much so that God made it one of the ten great laws that are to govern human life (Ex. 20:8-10). And as Jesus said, *the sabbath was made for man.*

However, in our industrialized and technological society, a number of businesses operate seven days a week. In some cases, factories cannot shut down their huge furnaces, boilers, or machines without damaging them mechanically. They have to be operated continually, requiring thousands upon thousands of people to work on Saturdays and Sundays. The same is true with various service industries as well as other types of businesses. As a result, countless people *are required to* work on Saturdays and/or Sundays, the day their religion sets aside for worship and rest.

If your business has to operate seven days a week, you need to be sure that your employees who have to work on the Sabbath or Sundays have another day off for rest and worship. Of course, most of these employees have a weekday off, but usually this does not give them the opportunity to worship corporately with their church, synagogue, or other religious body. What can you do to help accommodate your employees who wish to join in corporate worship?

In largely Christian societies, Sunday is the day that affects most of your employees. If possible, consider operating at a reduced capacity on Sunday, using only as many employees as is necessary.

Look for a "both/and" solution: one that permits your employees to work when you need them but also allows them to be off when you do not need them so they can attend worship services. One option is to work with your employees to accommodate their preferences. For example, a Jewish or Seventh-Day Adventist employee would most likely prefer to work Sunday rather than Saturday, allowing an employee who worships on Sunday to work on Saturday instead. Or, if the nature of your business allows, employees could work at different times on the weekends according to the worship schedule of their individual churches. Quite a few churches now offer multiple services on Sunday, and some offer Saturday evening and other weekday services as well. Employees who attend such churches could be encouraged to be more flexible toward a "both/and" solution.

Another alternative would be to arrange the Sunday work schedule so as many employees as possible can worship at their church's service. For example, most churches offer services on Sunday morning. Instead of working a normal schedule on Sundays, you could begin the work day in the early afternoon. Or perhaps more employees could work shorter shifts.

You might choose to create a rotating schedule, where employees do not have to work *every* week on their day of worship. Different groups or shifts of employees could work every other Sunday or once a month or quarterly, depending on your business needs.

The point is, you have options. Be flexible and open to new ideas. Try to help your employees who genuinely wish to worship with their churches or other religious bodies from week to week. As Christians, the Lord has expressly commanded us not to forsake meeting together with other believers for worship and encouragement (He.10:25). And you should have the same consideration for employees of other faiths. While this will require some extra effort by those who plan your company's schedule, it can be done in most cases.

Finally, prayerfully consider whether your business *truly* needs to be open on Sundays. While it may not be popular to say so, the majority of businesses that operate on Sunday do not *have* to do so. If you are open on Sundays because you feel you need the sales from that day or because you do not want to forfeit that day's business to competitors who are open, trust, instead, that God will bless and honor you for honoring Him. Trust, instead, that He can send enough business in six days to make up for what you forfeit on the seventh. Thousands of Christian business owners can testify to God's faithfulness in this area.

God gave the fourth commandment for our good: we are to remember, and keep, the Sabbath day holy. Without the Sabbath rest, our bodies would soon break down. We would be physically drained, constantly exhausted. Productivity would soon decline. This has been proven time and again in dictatorial nations and slave markets that demand almost continuous work with no rest for its labor force. Productivity—as well as health, physical strength, mental alertness, and ability—declined sharply.

Resting from work one day a week is essential for the overall wellbeing of the human body and mind. Business and labor leaders, government officials and private citizens—we must all protect our bodies and minds. By doing so, we protect productivity in our society as well as the economy. As a Christian business leader, you have the added concern for your employees' souls, their spiritual needs. This gives you an even stronger incentive to help enable them to gather for worship. You may have to be creative to make this work for your business, but God will honor you for doing everything you can to honor His holy commandment: "Remember the sabbath day, to keep it holy" (Ex.20:8).

CHAPTER 6

What You Need to Do When Dealing with Critical Business Matters

Contents

CHAPTER 6

WHAT YOU NEED TO DO TO WHEN DEALING WITH CRITICAL BUSINESS MATTERS

A. LAWSUITS

1. *Determine if God wants you to defend yourself or to settle out of court.*

> "You have heard the law that says the punishment must match the injury: 'An eye for an eye, and a tooth for a tooth.' But I say, do not resist an evil person! If someone slaps you on the right cheek, offer the other cheek also. If you are sued in court and your shirt is taken from you, give your coat, too" (Mt.5:38-40, NLT).
>
> "Do not be overcome by evil, but overcome evil with good" (Ro.12:21, NKJV).

Matthew 5:38-40 is one of the most misunderstood and misapplied passages in all the Bible (Mt.5:38). It is often interpreted to mean that we should *never* defend ourselves or our property when we are attacked or when sued. However, as with all of God's Word, this passage can be understood accurately only when interpreted both in context (setting) and in light of other Scripture.

Note that the context deals with retaliation, as indicated by Jesus' reference to the Jewish law. The people were given the right to seek exact retribution—perfect justice—against those who wronged them. The context also deals with loving our enemies by doing good toward them rather than evil (vv.43-48). However, when balanced with the overall teaching of Scripture on the subject, God's Word says there *are* occasions when we should defend ourselves and our property or possessions.

Christ's point strikes at the heart of the matter. As business leaders who follow Christ, we are not to be consumed with fighting over property and disputing rights. We are

147

not to retaliate just because we have the legal right to do so. We are not to focus on self, on our possessions and rights, but on displaying a spirit of Christlikeness by doing good to those who do evil against us. We should have a nature of reconciliation, not retaliation.

With these thoughts in mind, our Lord teaches a very important lesson: as the owner or leader of a business, there are times when you should respond to a claim against you by making concessions and giving the other party at least a portion of their demands. Practically speaking, this is often the best thing to do for a number of reasons:

- It is often cheaper to settle a suit than it is to fight it. It may cost you less to repurchase or regain whatever is in dispute than to fight to retain it.

- Settling out of court spares you the negative publicity of being sued.

- Settling demonstrates an admirable spirit on your part as a business leader, that, above all else, you want those with whom you do business to be satisfied and to feel that they have been treated fairly; that you are willing to suffer a personal loss in order to guarantee that they do not feel wronged or cheated.

- It may actually change the heart of the other party, even causing them to feel ashamed of their behavior.

- Most importantly, it shows that you have a Christlike spirit, that you are willing to give up your rights for their benefit. It leaves a good testimony with the other party, and it may even play a part in that person's coming to know Christ as Savior.

Jesus Himself set the example by spending His earthly life combating evil and injustice. He did not always turn the other cheek (Jn.18:22-23), and neither did Paul (Ac.22:25; 23:2-3; 25:8-12). Indeed, God's Word commands us not to indulge nor give license to do wrong to anyone, and God is strict in His command. For example, if a man does not work because he is lazy, he should not eat (2 Th.3:7, 10).

What determines whether we should accept a wrong committed against us or defend ourselves? The governing principle for the believer is clear: "Do not be overcome by evil, but overcome evil with good" (Ro.12:21, NKJV). If a person sues you unjustly and wins, he or she will be encouraged to repeat the evil behavior. If allowed to continue, the evil of profiting from unjust claims against businesses will prevail and become even more widespread in society.

Sadly, this happens often in today's materialistic society. Unprincipled people are always looking for easy opportunities to get money without working for it. One way to secure large sums is by suing others. Driven by their own love of money, greedy lawyers solicit the business of such opportunists by instigating class action suits and producing advertisements that promise large settlements or awards. In many of these unjust and frivolous cases, the defendants settle because it is their cheapest and most logical option. Fighting it would cost far too much time, money, and manpower. The result of settling, though, is both sad and tragic: evil and deceit overcome truth and honesty. Meanwhile, other dishonest individuals and unscrupulous attorneys are emboldened to do the same.

When you or your company is sued, you need to seek God's guidance as to how you should respond. In some cases, the Lord may lead you to settle according to Christ's teachings in this passage. In other cases, the Lord may lead you to stand against injustice and unrighteousness by refusing to allow others to take advantage of you. You may feel led to take a stand and set a precedent on an issue. Or, you might help establish new guidelines or laws to ensure that righteousness prevails over evil, not allowing evil to overcome good. In determining what to do, you should recall or search out the entire teachings of God's Word on the matter, then ask God for wisdom and direction for your specific situation (Jas.1:5; Ps.32:8).

As you make your decision, you should also remember your responsibility as a steward. You, your business, and all your assets belong to God. He has entrusted everything into your keeping, for your management. In fact, one of the major reasons you and your business exist is to accomplish God's purposes in your life and to help build His kingdom on earth. Therefore, you should prayerfully consider whether God wants you to take resources that could be used to help others and instead give them to the unjust and ungodly. God may show you that you can better advance His purposes and kingdom by giving the other party at least some of what they want. At other times, however, you may serve the Lord's kingdom better by taking a stand against injustice and fighting for righteousness.

Whatever the Lord leads you to do, you can rest in Christ's promise:

> **"But seek first his kingdom and his righteousness, and all these things [material needs] will be given to you as well" (Mt.6:33, NIV '84).**

If the Lord leads you to give the other party what they want, He will give you back what you have given up for His kingdom. If He leads you to fight for righteousness in court, He will supply the resources you need.

2. *Settle disputes or lawsuits outside of court whenever possible.*

> **"Settle matters quickly with your adversary who is taking you to court. Do it while you are still with him on the way, or he may hand you over to the judge, and the judge may hand you over to the officer, and you may be thrown into prison. I tell you the truth, you will not get out until you have paid the last penny" (Mt.5:25-26, NIV '84).**

> **"Do not go hastily to court; for what will you do in the end, when your neighbor has put you to shame? Debate your case with your neighbor, and do not disclose the secret to another; lest he who hears *it* expose your shame, and your reputation be ruined" (Pr.25:8-10, NKJV).**

When another business or an individual pursues a lawsuit against you, you should do everything possible to settle the case before it proceeds to court. The reason is clear: once the case goes to court, you have no control over the outcome. You risk a more severe judgment against you than what you might reach in a settlement, and you will be bound by the decision of the court.

In Jesus' day, a defendant who could not pay the full amount of a judgment would be imprisoned until the last penny was paid. The lesson is obvious: allowing a claim to go to court could cost you far more than a settlement would, not only in dollars, but in other damaging ways as well. Note the Scripture above, how a lawsuit can hurt far more than just your bank account (Pr.25:8-10):

- You might suffer the shame of losing the case (Pr.25:8).

- Your dispute with the other party will become public knowledge (v.9). Nothing is confidential once a case proceeds to court. It is far better for the dispute and all its details to remain between you and the other party. With this in mind, it is wise to insist on confidentiality as a condition of the settlement.

- Word about the dispute will spread and both your personal and business reputation could suffer irreparable damage (v.10). Others will talk about you and the case, and they will not always relay accurate information. Even worse, the news media might decide to report on the case, making the details known instantly throughout the community.

As mentioned in a previous point, you also have a Scriptural responsibility to consider: you are not to indulge nor give license to evildoers who unjustly accuse and sue other individuals or businesses (Ro.12:21). So, when facing legal disputes or lawsuits, you need to prayerfully consider what God would have you do. However, whenever possible, you should do all you can to settle outside of court. The Lord calls you to have a spirit of reconciliation, to pursue peace with others as much as humanly possible (Ro.12:18). The time for reconciliation is while some openness still exists between you and the other party. As Jesus emphasized, you should attempt to reconcile with the other party immediately, before anger and bitterness have a chance to bear their poison fruits (Mt.5:25; He.12:14-15). Scripture actually counsels you to settle all disputes with others *the same day* they arise (Ep.4:26). Disputes can usually be resolved if dealt with quickly, before they are allowed to fester.

When someone with whom you work or do business—a customer, supplier, vendor, fellow associate, or employee—has an honest dispute with you and is a reasonable individual, your displaying a humble, conciliatory spirit can usually bring about a change his or her attitude (Pr.15:1). Regardless, you should always show a willingness to make right any errors or shortcomings on your part. Even if there is a misunderstanding or you feel strongly that you are in the right, you and your business will both be winners when the other party is pleased with the outcome.

3. Avoid settling a dispute with another believer by going to court.

> "When one of you has a dispute with another believer, how dare you file a lawsuit and ask a secular court to decide the matter instead of taking it to other believers! Don't you realize that someday we believers will judge the world? And since you are going to judge the world, can't you decide even these little things among yourselves? Don't you realize that we will judge angels? So you should surely be able to resolve ordinary disputes in this life. If you have legal disputes about such matters, why go to outside judges who are not respected by the church? I am saying this to shame you. Isn't there anyone in all the church who is wise enough to decide these issues? But instead, one believer sues another—right in front of unbelievers! Even to have such lawsuits with one another is a defeat for you. Why not just accept the injustice and

> **leave it at that? Why not let yourselves be cheat-
> ed? Instead, you yourselves are the ones who
> do wrong and cheat even your fellow believers"**
> **(1 Co.6:1-8, NLT).**

Upon first reading, this instruction for settling legal disputes seems shocking. But just keep reading, and God's
reasons for giving it will become clear. Civil courts exist to
settle disputes. When your business has an unworkable
dispute with another individual or business—be it a customer, supplier, service provider, or any other person or
entity with whom you interact—you have the recourse of
going to court and allowing a judge or jury to decide the
case. However, if the person with whom you have the dispute is a fellow believer, God's Word plainly says that you
should not take the individual to a civil court. Note three
important observations from this passage:

- This passage deals *only with disputes between true
  Christians.* It says nothing about going to court
  against unbelievers.

- This passage appears to address taking another *individual* to court, not necessarily another *business.*
  However, when the owner or principal leader of the
  other business is a believer, the truths expressed in
  the teachings of this passage should apply. As Christians, we should be able to resolve the dispute with
  God's help and that of other believers rather than
  going before a secular court for a legal judgment.

- This passage speaks about civil disputes, not criminal offenses. God has expressly ordained that law
  enforcement and government authorities deal with
  criminal acts (Ro.13:1-7). Those who harass, abuse,
  endanger, defraud, steal, or break any other laws,
  are to be punished by civil authorities. No Christian business leader, or any believer for that matter, should use this passage to allow anyone who
  is abusing or harming others—whether physically,
  mentally, emotionally, verbally, or financially—to
  continue in their destructive behavior. They should

report the person's lawless and abusive behavior to the proper authorities.

In this passage, Scripture advances from question to question, building reason upon reason, until the concluding principle is stated straightforwardly: as a believing business leader, it would be better to accept the injustice and suffer the loss rather than run the risk of doing wrong by suing another believer in a secular court (vv.7-8).

At the same time, this statement does *not* mean that you have no recourse against another believer, that you must tacitly accept the wrong done against you and the resulting financial loss. As stated in previous points, we are not to allow unrighteousness to prevail by indulging or giving license to anything that is wrong or unjust. But when the individual who has wronged us is a fellow believer, we are not to turn to the world's courts for justice. As believers, we are to settle our disputes with other believers within our own Christian society. We should be governed by the life of Christ and the law of God, not by the world's standards. In God's eyes, it is wrong for *believers* to go against each other before the world's judges. There are at least three reasons it is wrong...

a. **Believers who** settle differences before the world reproach and damage the name of Christ, their own reputations, and their witness for Christ. There is no escaping this tragic reality: when believers *carry their differences* before the world, it always hurts the name of Christ.

b. **When we as believers** settle differences before the world, we fail the Lord miserably. How? We fail to govern our affairs according to God's Law and the example of Christ. Instead, we choose to go before unbelievers who may not govern by these same standards. Christ tells us that we are the salt of the earth and that we are to permeate the world, not the other way around. God has called us to follow His Holy Word as the standard of life rather than to accept and live by the standards of the world.

c. **As believers,** we have both the Holy Spirit and Christ-centered leaders to help us determine God's wisdom. The Spirit of God indwells and counsels every genuine believer. We also have qualified leaders within the body of Christ who can give us spiritual counsel by applying God's wisdom to our situations. When we have a conflict with other believers, it is always God's will for us to seek the guidance of His Spirit along with the sound biblical counsel of qualified advisors.

In addition, God has specifically called certain believers to be attorneys, judges, and magistrates. Many business disputes revolve around conflicting understandings and interpretations of *civil* laws. Therefore, a judgment is needed from someone trained and skilled in applying these laws. You actually have a legal recourse for settling disputes without going to court; you can seek to resolve the matter through mediation or binding arbitration. You and the other party can retain the services of a mutually-agreed upon legal expert who is also a committed believer, a trained man or woman, or organization devoted to Christian mediation. Look for mediators who have the spirit of Solomon—who seek wisdom from God in making judgments (2 Ki.3:9-10). Such individuals can judge the matter according to both civil laws and God's laws. The matter can also be handled without harming the testimony of Christ by making the dispute a matter of public knowledge and record. In fact, in many places, associations and ministries exist for this very purpose. Involving a mutually-respected spiritual leader or organization in the process may help apply Scripture to the matter.

In binding arbitration. you and the other party both agree to accept the decision of the arbiter as final. Many business leaders today—both believers and unbelievers—are including a provision in contracts to settle any disputes through arbitration rather than by going to court. This saves both time and money, and it protects the reputations of the businesses involved by keeping private disputes from becoming public knowledge. For Christian believers, it offers a way for disputes to be settled justly while obeying God's command not to take each other to court.

4. *Remember God's warning when considering legal action against the needy.*

> "Do not exploit the poor because they are poor and do not crush the needy in court, for the LORD will take up their case and will plunder those who plunder them" (Pr.22:22-23 NIV '84).

The Hebrew word for *poor* in this verse describes people who are needy due to circumstances beyond their control. Through no fault of their own, they find themselves in vulnerable or unstable situations. The word does not refer to people who "work the system," that is, those who take advantage of others' kindness or who abuse social programs designed for the truly needy. Nor does it necessarily speak of those who are poor because of their own sinful or unwise choices.

As you consider how you should treat the poor and what action you should or should not take against them, keep this in mind: the Lord is the champion of the poor. Never forget what God says in these verses: *He* will rise to defend the needy if you deal harshly with them (v.23). *He* is the attorney or advocate who will plead their cause. Although the disadvantaged may not receive justice in human courts, they will certainly be vindicated in the heavenly court. If you are unmerciful toward the poor, God warns that He will overpower and devastate you in the same fashion that you have devastated them. Your heartless, immoral actions will not go unpunished.

Two offenses against God are listed in these verses: taking advantage of the struggling poor and crushing them through legal action (v.22). Remember this: just because something is *legal* does not mean it is *moral* or right. In many cases, you will have a *legal* standing to take action against an individual. However, even when your position is supported by the law, there is much more to consider. If you are a true follower of Christ, you should think about the impact that such a judgment would have on the offending party. Someone who is already struggling to survive could be completely devastated by a judgment against them.

The Bible teaches that there are times when you should suffer the wrong committed against you rather than take legal action (1 Co.6:7). Perhaps you are facing one of those times. If so, the Lord would want you to extend mercy to those who are genuinely struggling and in need due to circumstances beyond their control. You are to be generous and compassionate toward them.

You have options when someone owes you a debt. Among these options are extending the payment time, reducing the payment amount, not charging interest, working out an alternative method of payment, forgiving all or a portion of the debt, and any number of other creative, compassionate solutions.

As you work through each situation, take into consideration the individual's circumstances and character. You will deal with some who are struggling because of their poor choices. You will encounter others who habitually buy things they cannot afford or who sustain their lifestyle by taking advantage of other people. Seek God for wisdom as to how you can be made whole in the matter while, at the same time, best help the offending party. Never forget that being compassionate toward some individuals only enables them to continue their ill-advised ways. In such cases, we should never indulge nor give license to irresponsible behavior.

While taking all of these factors into account, be mindful that God will judge you if you are cruel toward sincere and responsible people who are genuinely struggling. And He will reward you if you are compassionate toward them.

B. FINANCIAL CRISES

1. *Turn to the Lord for help when facing a financial crisis.*

> **"One of the wives of the sons of the prophets cried out to Elisha, 'Your servant, my husband, has died. You know that your servant feared the LORD.**

> Now the creditor is coming to take my two children
> as his slaves.' Elisha asked her, 'What can I do for
> you? Tell me, what do you have in the house?' She
> said, 'Your servant has nothing in the house except
> a jar of oil.' Then he said, 'Go and borrow empty
> containers from everyone—from all your neigh-
> bors. Do not get just a few. Then go in and shut the
> door behind you and your sons, and pour oil into
> all these containers. Set the full ones to one side.'
> So she left. After she had shut the door behind her
> and her sons, they kept bringing her containers,
> and she kept pouring. When they were full, she
> said to her son, 'Bring me another container.' But
> he replied, 'There aren't any more.' Then the oil
> stopped. She went and told the man of God, and
> he said, 'Go sell the oil and pay your debt; you and
> your sons can live on the rest'" (2 Ki.4:1-7, HCSB).

What can you do if you cannot meet your financial obligations? In this historical account, the widow of a minister
found herself unable to pay her debts and faced the worst
consequence possible. Her story gives insight about what
to do if you cannot meet your obligations. Note the following steps:

a. **First, pray.** Lay out your problem before the Lord. Ask
   Him to help you find a way to meet your need. In desperation, the widow went to Elisha—the prophet through
   whom the Lord spoke and worked at that time—to appeal for help (vv.1-2). As simply as she could, she explained her circumstances, how desperately she needed help to pay off her debts and to keep her sons from
   being enslaved by the creditor. In like manner, you can
   take your financial need to the Lord, crying out to Him
   for direction, wisdom, and help. If you are a genuine believer, God's Spirit lives within you, and the Lord will
   lead and speak to you through His indwelling Spirit.

b. **Second, seek help** from others. With a heart full of
   compassion, the prophet told the widow to seek the
   help of her neighbors, from whom she borrowed containers for the miracle God was going to perform (v.3).

Similarly, God may lead you to seek help from others. Of course, you can seek to borrow from a friend or family member, if the Lord so leads. However, there are other ways people might be able to help you generate the funds you need. For example, depending on the nature of your business and the size of your need, you can contact regular customers or vendors and offer them a higher-than-usual discount if they purchase from you within a specified time. Or you can offer a high volume of inventory at a drastically-reduced price. This could motivate some to purchase goods or services that they had not planned to purchase, *if* they are offered a good enough price. Some who value their relationship with you may go ahead and place an order that had been scheduled for a future date. By thinking, praying, and being creative, you might find other ways that people can help you apart from borrowing from them.

c. **Third, do all you can** with what you already have. Note that the widow did not sit back and wait for God to do something miraculous. Instead, she and her sons began working, personally doing all they could to meet their desperate need (v.4). She did exactly what the Lord—through the prophet—had directed her to do. The miracle came when the destitute woman started pouring the oil into the borrowed containers, when she took *what she had* and put it to work. God met her need when she *did what she could do.* Certainly, God could have sent someone with the money she so desperately needed, and God can do the same for you. But more often it seems He works *through us,* expecting us to do what we can with what we have.

Earnestly ask God to show you what you can do to generate the needed income to meet your obligations. The Lord may show you that you need to make drastic changes to your business plan or model, or sell a certain asset, or bring in a partner, or take some unusual short-term action. Be willing to do whatever is necessary. Work the extra hours; make the necessary sacrifices; put forth the required effort; reduce your profit margin to gain additional business; ask your associates and employees to sacrifice temporarily for the immediate need. Do whatever the Lord directs you to do.

Most of the time, God does what *He* can when *we* are doing all *we* can. It is *then* that He contributes His miraculous power. It is *then* that He directs someone your way with an unusually large order. It is *then* that He unexplainably multiplies your sales. It is *then* that He touches someone's heart to loan you the needed funds with little or no interest. It is *then* that He sends someone to purchase a piece of property or other asset from you. It is *then* that someone unexpectedly invests in your business or enters into a partnership with you, providing the funds you so desperately need.

d. **Fourth, trust God** to help you as you seek to meet the need. This is exactly what this poor, destitute widow did. She trusted the Lord to meet her need and believed what God had spoken through Elisha. She then did exactly as the prophet instructed (v.5). She took the little bit of oil she had in a small jar and began to pour it, believing that God would multiply the oil until all the jars were full. Imagine the great faith this took!

Likewise, you must believe God, trusting that He will help you. Believe His promises and obey His Word. When you follow Him, He will hear and answer your prayers. Remember the encouraging, doubt-defying words of Jesus:

> "I assure you: If anyone says to this mountain, 'Be lifted up and thrown into the sea,' and does not doubt in his heart, but believes that what he says will happen, it will be done for him" (Mk.11:23, HCSB).

God can remove your mountain—meet your desperate need—if you will do what this widow did: seek Him and do what He leads you to do, trusting Him as you do so. Even if you face the worst possible outcome, that of losing all you have and going bankrupt, God will sustain you through it all. He will work all things out for your good because you love Him and are a true follower (Ro.8:28).

2. *Seek to make arrangements with your creditor for debt you cannot pay on time.*

> "Therefore, the kingdom of heaven is like a king who wanted to settle accounts with his servants. As he began the settlement, a man who owed him ten thousand talents was brought to him. Since he was not able to pay, the master ordered that he and his wife and his children and all that he had be sold to repay the debt. "The servant fell on his knees before him. 'Be patient with me,' he begged, 'and I will pay back everything.' The servant's master took pity on him, canceled the debt and let him go" (Mt.18:23-27, NIV '84).

What should you do if you cannot pay a debt or make a payment when it is due? Like the debtor in Christ's parable, you should speak to the creditor, express your earnest desire to pay what you owe, ask for patience, and seek to work out an agreeable arrangement for repayment.

a. **First, you should take the initiative** and voluntarily communicate with your creditor (vv.24-25). Note that the debtor in Jesus' parable did *not* do this. He owed the king an exorbitant amount of money and was in default on the loan. Because the king had not heard from him, he assumed the man had no intention of paying. Therefore, the king had the debtor brought before him, and he exercised his right to have the man's family sold into slavery to repay the debt. It is obviously far better to contact your creditor first, before your creditor is forced to contact you.

b. **Next, express your sincere intention** to pay what you owe (v.26). Without making excuses, explain your circumstances honestly, stating what has affected your cash flow so drastically much that you are unable to stay current on your obligations.

c. **Ask your creditor for patience,** for more time to pay what you owe (v.26). Propose an agreement based on what you *can* do to repay the debt, a repayment schedule that you are confident you can keep. While you should do everything you can to catch up on your account as quickly as possible, you should also be realistic about what you can do. It is far better to make smaller payments over a longer period than to obligate yourself to a larger payment and find yourself in default once again. You can always make larger payments and pay off the balance sooner, and you *should* do so if you can. This is the right thing to do whenever possible, because you are already behind on your obligation.

Your creditor's response will largely depend on your past record and your relationship with him or her. The creditor may agree to your proposal, offer a counter proposal, or ask for a penalty or additional interest. On the other hand, he or she may be unwilling to extend your time for repayment. If this is the case, you will have to find an alternate way to come up with the payment or else face the consequences. This could mean facing a lawsuit, being turned over to a collection agency, incurring damage to your credit rating, suffering repossession of property, or some other harmful action.

Any time you cannot make a payment on time, you should follow the above process. *Always* contact your creditor first to seek an agreement for repayment. By doing so, you convey to your creditor that you are honest and that you are not trying to avoid your obligation to pay what you owe. If you do not take the initiative to reach out to your creditor, he or she will reasonably assume that you are reneging on your contract and will likely turn over your account to a collection agency or take other action against you. You will then find yourself in the same position as the debtor in Jesus' parable: begging for mercy.

3. Declare bankruptcy only as a last resort.

> "At the end of every seven years you shall grant
> a release. And this is the manner of the release:
> every creditor shall release what he has lent to
> his neighbor. He shall not exact it of his neigh-
> bor, his brother, because the LORD's release has
> been proclaimed" (Dt.15:1-2, ESV).

> "About this time some of the men and their
> wives raised a cry of protest against their fellow
> Jews. They were saying, 'We have such large fam-
> ilies. We need more food to survive.' Others said,
> 'We have mortgaged our fields, vineyards, and
> homes to get food during the famine.' And oth-
> ers said, 'We have had to borrow money on our
> fields and vineyards to pay our taxes. We belong
> to the same family as those who are wealthy, and
> our children are just like theirs. Yet we must
> sell our children into slavery just to get enough
> money to live. We have already sold some of our
> daughters, and we are helpless to do anything
> about it, for our fields and vineyards are already
> mortgaged to others' " (Ne.5:1-5, NLT).

One of the most controversial subjects in today's business
world is that of bankruptcy. Is it all right to declare bankruptcy? Is it moral? Is it ethical? Is it biblical? If so, under
what circumstances? These are not easy questions to answer. Opinions vary widely among sincere Bible scholars
and ministers as well as among business professionals, attorneys, and society in general.

Again, the issue is both controversial and complicated,
and there is no clear answer as to whether bankruptcy is
right or wrong. No one simple answer applies to all. Because
circumstances differ from case to case, the variable factors
naturally add to the complexity of the issue. For example...

- Who caused or contributed to the downfall or distress of the business? Were the leaders unwise or irresponsible in hiring, purchasing, or spending? Was
  there a lack of accountability?

- Did management fail to pay attention to the day-to-day finances and simply let things get out of control? Was the business harmed by oppressive lenders or unjust regulations? Or, did predatory lenders solicit and entice the already troubled business with offers not in their best interest?

- What effect does bankruptcy have upon the owners of failing businesses? Small business owners and individual proprietors are usually devastated financially, emotionally, and otherwise when their businesses fail. Sadly, at the other extreme, many wealthy business magnates and giant corporations consider bankruptcy to be a normal part of doing business.

- What other factors caused the business to fail? Changing markets or business conditions? Formidable competition from mammoth retailers or multinational conglomerates? Economic downturns or recessions? Stifling government regulations? The list of possibilities is endless!

In addition to all these, every business venture carries a degree of risk. Because of the risk, some people feel that lenders and suppliers should also assume a share of that risk and bear the consequences of their decision if a business fails.

Unquestionably, knowing what to do would be much easier if the Bible simply said, "You should (or should not) file for bankruptcy." But it does not. However, God's Word does address the subject of debt and debt relief. Without going into the specific ramifications and circumstances involved, the passages above illustrate that in Old Testament times, debt relief was offered through God's law as a protection for those in extreme financial distress.

Today, a number of countries regulate debt relief as well as the duties of both distressed borrowers and their creditors through bankruptcy laws. These laws vary from country to country and might be identified by terms other than bankruptcy, such as insolvency, receivership, or liquidation. In the United States, there are different types of bankruptcies for different situations. Some types allow for the restructuring of debt, while others regulate the liquidation of failed businesses.

If you are in extreme financial distress, you should exhaust every possible measure before even considering bankruptcy. If, as a last resort, you are forced to contemplate bankruptcy, you should sincerely seek God's will as to whether He would have you take this step. You need to consider your specific circumstances and weigh them prayerfully against what God's Word says. And you should seek counsel, not only from your pastor or another spiritual leader, but also from seasoned business professionals. In a matter like this, where godly, sincere people have differing opinions, you would be wise to seek the advice of several qualified individuals. Remember, "in an *abundance* of counselors there is safety" (Pr.11:14, ESV, emphasis added).

As you earnestly seek what God would have you do, Scripture offers the following principles to guide you in your decision:

- First, God commands you to obey the laws of the nation in which you live and work (Ro.13:1-5; Tit.3:1; 1 Pe.2:13).

- Second, many laws are for your benefit (Ro.13:4). Scripture does not prohibit you from taking advantage of the laws—even bankruptcy laws—that benefit you as a citizen. The Bible records occasions when Paul exercised his rights as a Roman citizen to his advantage (Ac.22:22-29; 25:6-12).

- Third, you are never to use any liberty or right as an opportunity for self-indulgence but, rather, to serve others in love (Ga.5:13). Love does not seek what is in one's own best interests, but what is in the best interests of others (1 Co.13:5; Ph.2:4).

- Fourth, God commands you to pay what you owe, to owe no debt to anyone but the debt to love them (Ro.13:8). Furthermore, Scripture states plainly that it is the wicked who borrow and do not repay (Ps.37:21).

- Fifth, God expects you to be impeccably honest in all matters (2 Co.8:21; He.13:18).

- Sixth, you will give an account to God for everything you do (Ro.14:12; 2 Co.5:10).

- Seventh, you are always to be conscious of how your actions impact others, especially those who do not know Christ (Ac.24:16; Ro.14:13; 1 Co.8:9).

If you decide to file for bankruptcy, it should only be after you have exhausted every other option and made every effort to work out an agreement with your creditors (see ch. 4, pt.3, p. 87). Bearing in mind what Scripture says, filing for bankruptcy may be an appropriate course of action if your purpose is to work out a way to repay—not escape—what you owe. Filing for bankruptcy can help you restructure your debt and secure court approval for a plan making it possible to repay your debts. It can also give you some relief from constantly increasing costs charged by certain lenders when your account is overdue (higher interest rates, paying interest on interest, exorbitant fees and penalties). Scripture forbids these types of practices that further oppress those in financial distress (Ne.5:7; Pr.28:8; Ezk.22:12), and man-made laws may offer you a measure of protection from them.

If you are the owner of a business that has filed for bankruptcy, you should also consider your personal responsibility to your creditors. If your business is incorporated, the law usually protects your personal assets from being seized to repay business debt, unless you have pledged certain assets as collateral for a loan. If your company fails completely and closes, and there are not enough assets remaining to cover the debt, bankruptcy laws may discharge you from any further responsibility. However, you need to weigh whether it is right for you to keep what wealth you have accumulated while those whom your business owes suffer loss.

Neither God's laws nor most man-made laws expect you to become destitute if you file for bankruptcy. They do not expect you to do without the necessities of life nor to forfeit the resources you need to recover and reestablish yourself and/or your business (Ex.22:26; Dt.24:6; Jb.24:3; Am.2:8). In fact, bankruptcy laws are designed to prevent this from happening. On the other hand are owners who file for bankruptcy on a failed business while continuing to live luxuriously on assets they earned during the company's profitable years. Or, wealthy owners of multiple businesses sometimes file bankruptcy on one business that fails while living exorbitantly off the profits of other businesses, investments, and income.

God's Word is clear: if you are able, you are to repay what you owe. Even when man-made laws say otherwise, God's Holy Word is the final authority (Ac.5:29). Those who continue to live luxuriously while their creditors suffer loss will surely answer to God.

In contrast, most small business owners lose everything when their businesses fail. Even when incorporated, most will put everything they have into trying to turn the business around. Many will use their personal savings to pay bills or to keep loyal employees as long as possible. Some will even take out mortgages on their homes to pay business expenses. If this is your case, know that God will bless and honor you if you do everything you can to pay your creditors. It may take you years paying in small amounts, but if you let your creditors know of your intentions, some may graciously forgive and cancel your debt (Mt.18:27). Others might allow you to repay them on more flexible terms. Regardless, in the process of doing so, you may accomplish something worth more than all the money in the world: you may point them to Christ.

Every situation has its own unique set of circumstances. If you are facing possible bankruptcy, evaluate your circumstances in light of the principles of God's Word. Seek Him through prayer and fasting. If you genuinely desire to please and obey Him, He will guide and direct you in what you do (Ps.25:9; 32:8; Ph.4:6-7).

C. DEBT COLLECTION

1. *Seek God's guidance in handling unpaid bills and outstanding debt.*

> **"I will instruct you and teach you in the way which you should go; I will counsel you with My eye upon you." (Ps. 32:8, NASB '77)**

When customers or clients neglect to pay you after repeated notifications, you have a difficult decision to make: What action should you take next? Before doing anything else, the course of wisdom is to seek the Lord's counsel. Ask Him to show you how to proceed. As this assuring verse promises, the Lord will show you the right path to follow. He will guide you step by step as you handle the problematic account. Thankfully, we are not simply left on our own when it comes to making business decisions. God promises to provide sufficient instruction and guidance for every decision we have to make, for every action we should take. (See ch. 3, pt. 5, pp.55-60.)

In the matter of pursuing an overdue payment, you need to consider every case on an individual basis. Of course, the larger your business the more time-consuming this is. It is obviously much easier in a large business to have firm policies in place that have already been thought through and written in a *Policies and Procedures Manual*. These policies spell out exactly how delinquent accounts are to be dealt with and make them less complicated to handle. But even if you are a small or one-person business operation, you would be wise to think through the steps you should take when people fail to pay. Being prepared is always more professional and it will make your efforts that much more successful. At the same time, God's Word teaches that there are different ways you should respond to different people and situations. Therefore, considering each case individually is a necessary part of obeying God in this area. You may need to assign this responsibility to an employee who understands God's Word and your desire to obey Him.

First, consider your customer's circumstances. If the non-paying customer does not come to you about the matter, contacting him/her about the account gives you the opportunity to learn why payment has not been made. Understanding the customer's situation requires wisdom, an honest look at all the factors involved, including your very own nature and tendencies. For example, if you have a tender, trusting heart toward others, you may be too lenient toward someone who is lying or taking advantage of you. On the other hand, if you have a skeptical nature, you may not extend the compassion God expects toward someone who is genuinely in need. Thus, when considering a customer's circumstances, ask God for the wisdom to judge rightly, and He will give it to you (1 Ki.3:7-14; Jas.1:5).

Once you have sincerely prayed about the matter, you need to apply God's Word to the individual's circumstances. God instructs you to be compassionate and patient toward those who are genuinely in need (see section A, pt.4, pp. 156-157). At the same time, the Lord expects you to be firm with those who take advantage of—and, in reality, steal from—honest businesses. In many such cases, it may be easier, less time-consuming, and even cheaper, to drop the matter, write off the unpaid balance as a loss, and move forward. When this is true, you need to consider the teaching of Scripture commanding you to do what is in the best interests of *others* (Ph.2:3-4). If you let the dishonest customer get by with not paying what is due . . .

- Is it in the best interest of your other customers who will have to pay higher prices to compensate for the loss?

- Is it in the best interest of the offender him- or herself, who will be emboldened to continue the deceitful practice?

- Is it in the best interest of other businesses who must deal with the same people?

However you decide to handle non-paying customers, treat them in such a way that you serve as a shining light pointing them to the Savior. Even when you must be firm, you should always strive to be kind. If the Lord leads you to show individuals mercy, let them know it is because Christ has been merciful to you. Or, if they are genuinely in need, share Scripture that expresses the Lord's love and care for them.

Once again, it is crucial that you seek God for guidance, for if you are compassionate toward people whose hearts are open, your kindness may be just the thing that brings them to Christ. On the other hand, it you show mercy to the hard-hearted, they may scoff at your grace—and God's— and leave more determined to continue in their sinful ways (Pr.26:5).

These are difficult decisions, decisions that require an investment of time and effort that may exceed the amount of money involved. But you must always keep in mind that you are in business for far more valuable purposes than money. People are more important than profits. Souls matter more than sales. As you sincerely strive to follow the Lord and to build His kingdom through your business, remember the above Scripture, "His eye is always upon you." God will keep His Word. He will instruct and counsel you, show you what to do.

2. Confront and hold accountable customers who do not pay you.

> "Take heed to yourselves. If your brother sins [does wrong] against you, rebuke him; and if he repents, forgive him" (Lk.17:3, NKJV).

A problem common to nearly all business leaders is slow-paying or non-paying customers. What does God's Word tell you to do when a customer does not pay as agreed? Jesus' command concerning forgiveness reveals the first step to take in resolving this problem, as well as many other problems business leaders face.

If a customer fails to pay for a product or service you or your company provided, you should confront and hold the customer accountable. You should seek to settle the account.

Many people misunderstand what Jesus said about forgiveness. They think that the Lord commands us to automatically forgive others for every offense they commit against us, regardless of their attitude toward what they have done. But that is *not* what our Lord commands. Certainly, Christ's instruction in Luke 17:3 centers on forgiveness, which means that a spirit of love and compassion should exist. But note Jesus' *full statement:* He commands us to forgive *after* we have confronted those who offend us and *after* they have repented of their wrong. In the case of delinquent customers, repentance on their part is paying what they rightfully owe. It is not merely saying, "I am sorry; I cannot pay." Simply put, true repentance is honoring their agreement either through immediate payment or working out an arrangement that is agreeable to you. At this point, the Lord instructs you to forgive—not to forgive the debt, but to forgive the debtor by no longer holding the delinquency against the person.

There may be times when understanding is called for. Some people encounter genuine, unforeseen circumstances—loss of income, a sickness or medical emergency, an unexpected home or car repair—that hinders them from paying you as promised. In such cases, God's Word teaches that you should respond with compassion and patience by working with the suffering customer to satisfy the debt. Or, the Lord may even lead you to forgive part or all of the debt.

People of integrity who owe you money will usually *contact you* when they cannot pay as expected. Or, if they genuinely need the service or product you provide and know they cannot pay you immediately, they will inform you of their situation and seek to work out an agreement for payment *before* purchasing anything else. When individuals with such character truly need your product or service, the Lord will bless you for helping them in whatever way you choose. You could consider offering a special reduced price, extended payment terms, or some other creative gesture that helps the customer while protecting your business interests at the same time.

However, the sad reality is that many people live beyond their means, and many others spend money on unnecessary things while claiming not to have enough money to pay their bills. Always remember an important truth: you are not helping such individuals by tolerating their refusal to pay or by forgiving their debt. Rather, you are emboldening them to continue in their dishonest ways. In addition, you are harming other business operators and customers who must pay more for products and services because of your debtors' dishonesty.

For this precise reason, Jesus commands us to correct those who do us wrong. To not hold delinquent and dishonest customers accountable is to indulge them and to give them license to sin, and this is the last thing God wants.

> **"The wicked borrows and does not repay. . ."** **(Ps. 37:21a, NKJV).**

> **"And we exhort you, brothers: warn those who are irresponsible, comfort the discouraged, help the weak, be patient with everyone."** **(1 Th.5:14, HCSB).**

3. *Be neither cruel nor ruthless when dealing with those who owe you.*

> **"A kindhearted woman gains respect, but ruthless men gain only wealth. A kind man benefits himself, but a cruel man brings trouble on himself"** **(Pr.11:16-17, NIV '84).**

These two proverbs stress the importance of being kind and merciful to others. When we are kind, others will take notice and gain respect for us. But, if we are cruel or ruthless, we will quickly lose people's respect. We might also bring unnecessary and costly problems into our lives— problems both personally and professionally. This principle certainly applies to every area of life, meaning that we should always treat others kindly. However, the second half of verse 16 places these proverbs within a business or financial setting. The Bible is not suggesting that we let others take advantage of us, but that we not be heavy-handed in making a demand for payment. Instead, we should be kind and show understanding to those who owe us money.

When an individual or another business does not pay what it owes you, it places you in a difficult position. How you handle the situation speaks volumes to all those involved in the process. Obviously, the business you own or manage needs money to pay its debts and to meet other financial obligations. Nevertheless, you need to weigh each situation on an individual basis and consider each debtor's circumstances and character. Even when you feel you must take strong action by being direct and forceful, you should still be kind and gracious. The Scripture clearly says that trouble comes to those who are cruel and ruthless. So, if you conduct business in a harsh manner that might hasten repayment of a debt or secure a higher profit for you, that is all the good you will gain. You will simultaneously develop a reputation for ruthlessness and be despised, or even feared, by clients, customers, colleagues, and your community.

Never forget that people are more important than profits, and if you mistreat your clients or customers, you will lose out both personally and from a business standpoint. You will not get repeat business or referrals from others, nor will you earn the respect, admiration, or friendship of any people involved. In contrast, business people who treat others kindly and fairly reap a community's respect and loyalty and all the things that money cannot buy.

Keep another fact in mind when you show kindness to those who owe you: you can bring additional problems upon yourself if you develop a reputation for being too lenient. Some may take advantage of your perceived leniency and cause financial setbacks for you through theft, excessive product returns, false claims, or dishonest reviews. You could be forced to raise your prices to cover the loss—a price that could make you non-competitive, or perhaps send you teetering toward the brink of bankruptcy. For this reason, your acts of kindness toward debtors need to be tempered with responsibility. Considering all circumstances, you could . . .

- Work out a mutually agreeable payment plan and set up a schedule for it.

- Work out a mutually agreeable exchange of goods or property and write up a contract stating the details.

- Work out a mutually agreeable schedule of services to be provided at low or no cost to you. You could utilize the debtor's skills or availability of time as a means of repayment (IT skills, legal assistance, grounds maintenance, for instance).

Establishing a payment plan helps prevent the debtor from becoming irresponsible, from sponging off others or exploiting them. A reasonable payment plan is also more likely to recover the money owed.

Remember, the Bible does not suggest that we let others take advantage of us, only that we avoid being heavy-handed or cruel in our demand for payment. We are to treat others the same way we would want them to treat us if we were going through a hard time. As you contemplate what measures to take toward a person or business in your debt, remember that none of us knows what tomorrow may bring. At some point, you too may find yourself needing understanding and kindness from a person with whom you do business.

CHAPTER 7

What You Can Do to Overcome Problems and Difficult Situations

Contents

CHAPTER 7

WHAT YOU CAN DO TO OVERCOME PROBLEMS AND DIFFICULT SITUATIONS

1. *Consider all trials as opportunities for personal growth.*

> "Consider it pure joy, my brothers, whenever you face trials of many kinds, because you know that the testing of your faith develops perseverance. Perseverance must finish its work so that you may be mature and complete, not lacking anything" (Jas.1:2-4, NIV '84).

The assuring message of this passage is that you can be triumphant no matter how severe the trial or challenge you are going through. How? By viewing all trials as opportunities for great growth in the Lord. Note exactly what God's Word says:

a. **First, you will face** many trials and challenges in life, including in the daily operation of your business (v.2). But if you trust God and ask for His help, He will work in your life and will use the trials for a good and beneficial purpose. You will become stronger—more focused, more determined, more steadfast, and more confident. Your leadership skills will become more refined and sharpened by the experience. This refinement process strengthens your character, making you a better and more resilient leader. Furthermore, it enables you to set an example for others in the workplace, showing them how they, too, can face and overcome challenges.

b. **Second, you are to face** trials and challenges with a spirit of joy (v.2). How is this possible? How can you be joyful—as opposed to desperate and hopeless—when facing great adversity or serious problems?

There is only one way to face trials or trouble with a spirit of joy: you have to *change your way of thinking*—turn your attitude about the situation completely around. You have to stop focusing on the negative and concentrate on the positive. In the words of Scripture, you must *know* something, and you must *do* something.

You need to *know* that trials develop perseverance (v.3). When problems and trials arise in your business, confront them. Do not allow them to defeat or discourage you. Instead, draw closer to God, praying and seeking His help and allowing Him to make you stronger, not weaker. By looking at the situation as a growing experience, a time to gain wisdom and knowledge, you can face trials more positively and begin to develop a joyful attitude in the face of adversity.

You need to *do* something: you need to let the quality of perseverance develop within you. Persevering means far more than just putting up with trials and suffering, resigning yourself to their intrusion, and waiting for them to pass. Perseverance means that you press on and continue to endure, never giving in. It means that you exert the energy and effort to triumph over the hardships that come your way.

If you will look upon troubles as challenges and painful business problems as opportunities, you can begin to face them with a joyful spirit. And when you learn to persevere and rise above them, you will find yourself walking through them triumphantly in the joy of the Lord.

c. **Third, the results** of facing trials and suffering can be very positive (vv.3-4). When you persevere and rise above the trials of life . . .

- you become more mature, more perfect and complete, more developed in what is required to be successful in leadership, in business, and in your personal life.

- you overcome more personal weaknesses, flaws, and shortcomings than you can in any other way. The weaknesses that are holding you back from greater success in business or affecting your personal life negatively will be worked out or overcome in your life. And the qualities necessary to be successful and to rise above life's challenges will be nurtured and become more refined in you.

2. *Tackle every problem or difficult situation with the confidence that God can help.*

"But in all these things we overwhelmingly conquer through Him who loved us" (Ro.8:37, NASB '77).

"Now thanks *be* to God who always leads us in triumph in Christ, and through us diffuses the fragrance of His knowledge in every place" (2 Co.2:14, NKJV).

"I can do all things through Christ who strengthens me" (Ph.4:13, NKJV).

One thing is certain in business as well as in life: problems will arise. We will face trouble and challenging circumstances, sometimes even threatening crises. Just think of the serious things that could happen to your business or in your career:

- plummeting sales or loss of market share
- the loss of a major customer or contract
- a cash flow crisis
- an economic downturn—a recession or depression
- having to downsize or lay off loyal employees
- the loss of a key executive or employee
- betrayal by an associate or key employee
- a major lawsuit
- a strike or serious labor dispute
- an unwarranted investigation by a government agency

- a slanderous and damaging claim against you or your company
- new government regulations that heavily burden your business
- having to sell off assets to survive
- bankruptcy
- being terminated from your position

When one of these or any other devastating circumstance arises, it is easy to feel hopeless and defeated. You may be tempted to think you cannot overcome the problem, that failure is certain and unavoidable. When these negative thoughts begin to bombard you, you need to consciously resist them—push them out of your mind—and replace them with trust in God. This is exactly what Scripture says: trust His love and care for you. Place your confidence in God and stand on the promises of His Word. No matter what problems you are facing, you can conquer them through Christ (Ro.8:37). Now note the exact wording of Scripture: you can not only conquer them but also conquer them *overwhelmingly*, regardless of the circumstances and their severity.

Does this mean that everything will always turn out exactly as you would like? No. The reality of life is that things seldom do. For example, a devastating crisis or series of insurmountable circumstances may result in the closure of your business. Or you may have to make painful cuts in order to survive. Or you may be forced to file bankruptcy and reorganize. Or you may be terminated from your position for not meeting expectations. But, if the worst happens, it does not mean you *personally* are a failure. Do not allow a defeatist attitude overtake you. You must never lose confidence, for Christ promises to carry you *through* it all, strengthening and encouraging you along the way. No matter the severity of the situation, you cannot lose. Christ loves you and is going to take care of you. You can rest assured that Christ will deliver you through the severest circumstances. Adopt an attitude of confidence in Him and never give up. Through the strength that Christ gives, you *can* make it, you *can* start over again, you *can* succeed. No matter how devastating your situation is, you can do *all things* through Him (Ph.4:13).

Keep in mind that Christ does not do everything for us; neither do we do everything for ourselves. We and Christ *both* have a part in conquering the problems and trials that confront us. Our task is to get up and declare, "I can," and then face the difficult circumstances head-on. It is then that Christ steps in to give us whatever strength we need— *while we are tackling the problem.* He steps in when our strength is no longer sufficient, demonstrating His wonderful love and care for us. When you rise up to face your situation, you can be victorious even in the most difficult and devastating circumstances through the strength Christ gives.

Remember, God's Word plainly declares that He will always lead you triumphantly over or through all trials and problems (2 Co.2:14). The true follower of God will never know defeat—not permanently. Even if you fail for a period of time, God will eventually restore you and continue to use you. As long as you have breath, God is not finished with you. Your task is to call out for His help, to seek His will, and to have enough confidence in Him either to keep going or to start again. There is nothing, absolutely nothing, that can conquer and gain the final victory over you, not if you are truly His, not if you truly live to accomplish His purpose for your life. God will give you the strength to persevere through the most difficult days and darkest nights. He will lead you out of the crisis. He will give you wisdom and show you what to do to revive or restart your business or to recover from a devastating loss. Or, if you do not lose confidence in Him, He will lead you to start a new business or to find a new position. As you keep moving forward, praying and trusting Him to guide you step by step, He will help you conquer whatever you are facing. He will make you triumphant.

3. *Be courageous when facing fear and discouragement.*

> **"Haven't I commanded you: be strong and courageous? Do not be afraid or discouraged, for the LORD your God is with you wherever you go" (Jos.1:9, HCSB).**

To be successful in business, you have to be unwavering in overcoming fear and discouragement. As you have no doubt seen or experienced already in your company, things do not always go as planned or move in a positive direction. Setbacks arise. Crises occur. You may even find your company in survival mode at some point, where you or your executives are forced to take drastic measures to stay in business. You may have to make painful decisions that affect others, such as laying off employees or eliminating positions. In lean times, dire circumstances often call for dire measures. The owners of some businesses, especially small ones, might resort to using all their personal assets or even mortgaging their homes just to meet payroll.

On another note, people will sometimes disappoint or hurt you. Your business partner, top executive, or manager may break off from you to join a competitor or even start a competing business. Some employees, regardless how good you are to them, will leave without giving it a second thought for what they deem to be a better opportunity, or simply because they think they need a change. You can pour your heart and soul into training individuals for future advancement, and they might still turn elsewhere at the first opportunity. Some employees will steal from you. Long-time customers or clients whom you have faithfully served and even favored might take their patronage elsewhere over just a few dollars or a slight misunderstanding. The list could go on and on.

These are just a sampling of the challenges you might face as a business leader. Relentless pressures such as these can break down the strength and courage of even the strongest people.

Along with the endless challenges is the paralyzing fear of the unknown—fear that can strangle your confidence and peace if you let it. It may be fear of uncertain market conditions or a changing economy, fear of taking risks or repeating past mistakes, fear of insufficient profits to grow or income to survive, fear of possible bankruptcy or an unjust lawsuit. Any of these fears and many others can plunge you into sleeplessness and unmanageable stress.

God's encouraging words to Joshua are also meant for you as you go about your daily affairs and meet the demands of your business or job. Just as the LORD knew that Joshua would experience fear and discouragement as he led Israel, He knows the fears and disheartening factors that can hinder you as you lead your company, division, or department. Focusing on the truths found in this powerful verse will help you keep going when you feel like quitting.

a. **First, God has a destination for you,** just as He had a destination for Joshua and Israel—the promised land. Your destination does not necessarily revolve around market share or bottom lines. In fact, it is not so much a place or position or profit margin as it is a purpose. God has given you the ability and opportunity to own or be a leader in business in order to partner with Him to accomplish more important purposes. Your purpose, professionally, from God's perspective, is to . . .

- do honorable work in life that is meaningful and significant

- generate necessary income for you and your family

- provide jobs for other people to earn a living (if your leadership role involves hiring people)

- provide honorable work for other individuals that is meaningful, significant, and gives the opportunity for achievement in life

- create opportunities and a culture in which people can thrive, advance, and better themselves

- provide a beneficial service or product for the community, society in general, or a specific market

- help to change society for the better by setting up businesses, teaching a strong work ethic, training and empowering the jobless or downtrodden both here and abroad, and by stirring up passion within people to use their resources to be productive, to better themselves, and to help others

- contribute to meeting humanity's greatest need, the *spiritual* need, the need for the gospel and God's Word, by supporting your church and other missions, and ministries that are fulfilling the Great Commission

God encourages you to be *strong and courageous* in the task of leading your company (department, division) to fulfill its vital purposes. An array of challenges—financial, personnel, production, growth, and a host of others—will surface from day to day. These difficult and ongoing situations require skillful and deliberate handling, causing you to feel caught up in a never-ending cycle of trials. Throughout the days, months, and years of endless challenges, you have to stay the course in order to survive. But you cannot do it alone. It is only through God's enablement that you can be strong and courageous enough to make it through the most difficult struggles, never giving up, but always moving forward in pursuit of your God-given purpose and goals.

b. **Second, God encourages you** to be *strong and courageous* in overcoming fear and discouragement. Having to face challenge after challenge, week after week, month after month, and year after year, can cripple you with discouragement. God knows what you face, and He cares deeply for you. He wants you to call upon Him for help and to stand strong and courageous in overcoming whatever fear or discouragement may attack you. These enemies—fear and discouragement—can be conquered *only* as you trust Him and are strong and courageous. So, call upon Him and depend solely on His mighty hand, and you can overcome any fear.

c. **Third, God gives you the promise** of His continued, unbroken presence to encourage and assure you. As a believer, you never have to face your challenges alone. God is with you, and He will never leave nor forsake you. This is His promise to you just as it was to Joshua. God's presence is with you even in the most daunting circumstances. He lives within you through His Holy Spirit. Through His constant presence, you *can* stand strong and courageous against all challenges and trials. You *can* courageously face your deepest fears. No matter how many crushing problems, tough situations, or difficult people you encounter, no matter how many terrifying trials you face, God is right there with you! His *unfailing presence* will give you the strength and courage you need to face every intimidating foe, every seemingly unconquerable battle, and every debilitating fear.

> "... He Himself has said, '*I will never leave you, nor forsake you*'" (He.13:5b, NKJV).

> "**When you pass through the waters, I will be with you; and when you pass through the rivers, they will not sweep over you. When you walk through the fire, you will not be burned; the flames will not set you ablaze**" (Is.43:2, NIV '84).

4. *Fight discouragement and never give up—by looking to God daily.*

> "**Therefore we do not give up. Even though our outer person is being destroyed, our inner person [spirit] is being renewed day by day. For our momentary light affliction is producing for us an absolutely incomparable eternal weight of glory. So we do not focus on what is seen, but on what is unseen. For what is seen is temporary, but what is unseen is eternal**" (2 Co.4:16-18, HCSB).

When you face overwhelming pressure or problems that seem insurmountable, you may be tempted to quit, to turn over the crushing responsibility to someone else, to sell or close your business, or to resign from your position. When the urge to quit is strongest, do not give up. Fight against discouragement; do not allow your circumstances—as unbearable as they may seem—to defeat you. Never allow fear, embarrassment, exhaustion, other people, problems, conflicts, or severe opposition to get the best of you. Instead, find the resolve to get up and to press on each day. How? Where can you find the strength to keep on going and never give up? This Scripture tells us:

a. **First, renew your inner person**—your mind and spirit—by drawing near to God (v.16). You can be renewed every day when you call on God for strength to face your challenges, however formidable they may be. It is the presence and power of God within you that renews you. Seek His presence and power, His renewal day by day. *Daily* is the key. How do you seek His presence and power? By praying and reading the Bible. Ask Him specifically for whatever you need that day—strength, wisdom, peace, courage, comfort, confidence, clearness of mind, direction, patience, perseverance. Ask Him for everything you need, whatever it is. Find spiritual nourishment, hope, and power in His unfailing word. The *Psalms* are especially helpful when you are in the midst of deep trouble. When you seek the Lord, He will renew your mind and spirit. He will strengthen and give you what you need to face the day.

b. **Second, focus on what God is doing** in your life through your trouble (v.17). Your problem or affliction, no matter how heavy or burdensome, is light when compared to the glorious work God is accomplishing in you through the trial. In your darkest hour, He is working all things out for your good and conforming you to the image of His Son.

> **"And we know that God causes everything to work together for the good of those who love**

> **God and are called according to his purpose for them. For God knew his people in advance, and he chose them to become like his Son, so that his Son would be the firstborn among many brothers and sisters" (Ro.8:28-29, NLT).**

This great work, the work He is doing in you, "vastly outweighs" (2 Co.4:17, NLT) all the trouble you are facing. Picture a set of scales sitting before you. Now, balance your troubles on one end and the work God is doing in you—a work whose glory will continue throughout eternity—on the other end. Your trouble may be heavy and severe, so severe that you feel you cannot bear it, but when you place the eternal glory you are to receive on the scales, the trouble becomes light.

c. **Finally, focus on the future,** on what you cannot see, that is, the eternal (2 Co.4:18). When you are drowning in difficulties, all you can see are the problems, troubles, and challenges of the present. All of these trials are of *this* world. They are all temporary and, in time, will pass. But high above this fleeting world, God sits on His eternal throne. He is greater by far than all your troubles, more powerful than any circumstances that may rise up against you. Remember: He has put His powerful presence, His indwelling Spirit, *within* you. Do not focus on what you can see, on your overwhelming, seemingly insurmountable problem. Instead, focus on what you *cannot* see: the eternal, unlimited power and provision of God, along with His good plan for your life (Je.29:11). As you keep your eyes on Him—His faithfulness, His unfailing love, His strength, His constant presence—you will be inwardly renewed day by day. You will discover the sufficient strength that lies within you, the strength of the Lord Himself, and you will be able to keep pressing on, to keep moving forward, another day.

5. *Overcome unhealthy anxiety by following God's counsel: Pray about everything.*

> **"Do not be anxious about anything, but in everything, by prayer and petition, with thanksgiving, present your requests to God. And the peace of God, which transcends all understanding, will guard your hearts and your minds in Christ Jesus." (Ph.4:6-7, NIV '84)**

This counsel meets one of the most critical needs you face as a leader in business—the need to overcome *unhealthy anxiety*. As a leader, you are constantly having to meet schedules, deadlines, goals, and a host of other demands that cause unrelenting pressure. In addition, you may bear the enormous stress of seeking to please upper management or of keeping your business afloat and profitable.

A certain amount of anxiety is *healthy* in that it motivates you to get up and get to it—to work to meet your responsibilities and the demands placed upon you. But when you face demands beyond your control or a crisis due to someone's bad decision—maybe even yours—an unhealthy anxiety usually arises within you. Like the rest of us, you become overly distressed and begin to worry. If the crisis is serious enough, the stress or anxiety can overwhelm you and cause all kinds of problems:

- hasty or reckless actions.

- unwise or harmful decisions

- a fear to act

- hesitation

- a defeatist attitude

- discouragement

- withdrawal

- cowardice

- depression

- physical sickness or infirmity

- emotional or psychological problems

- lying, stealing, cheating

- distrust or unbelief

- anger or a reactionary spirit

The list could go on and on, but the point to see is the seriousness of anxiety. In the middle of such tense moments that can sweep over you and threaten your business or job, what can you do to control the stressful situation and assure the best outcome possible? God's Word gives you the answer: the remedy for anxiety (worry and stress) is prayer, learning to pray about everything (vv.6-7). As you walk through each day taking care of your responsibilities and facing the problems that arise, God wants you to present your needs to Him. No matter how small or insignificant a matter may seem, God cares. He is interested in the details of your life. He wants you to acknowledge Him in all that you do because He longs to help you and to give you guidance every step of the way (Pr.3:5-6).

Along with this invitation to present your needs or requests to Him, God gives you an amazing promise (v.7). If you talk or commune with Him throughout the day—praying and thanking Him for all He has done—He will give you peace, the very peace of God Himself. He will infuse you with a strong sense of His very own presence and a peace that is beyond human understanding!

But, never forget what God says in the above Scripture: you can experience God's peace only if you are walking in prayer and fellowship with Him. Only God can give you *lasting and permanent* peace as you face major problems in the workplace or anywhere else. The key words here are "lasting and permanent peace." Only God can reach your soul and make it alive. When you turn your life over to Him—genuinely begin to walk in prayer and thanksgiving—He infuses or instills within your soul a lasting and permanent peace. You receive a deep sense of assurance and security that He will guide and help you through anything, no matter how troubling or threatening.

Note again that this kind of peace, God's peace, transcends all human understanding (v.7). In fact, Scripture says that God's peace will *guard* your heart and mind. God's peace will stand against all the disturbing and stressful problems that arise. Therefore, if you truly have God's peace, it will calm your soul and help you more effectively deal with the worrisome problems that arise in your work. God's peace will flood your heart and mind. This is His wonderful promise to you, so learn to walk in a spirit of prayer. Pray about everything as you go through the day taking care of your business and your many responsibilities.

6. *Turn over the burdens of your business or position to God when they are too heavy for you to bear.*

> **"Cast your burden upon the LORD, and He will sustain you; He will never allow the righteous to be shaken" (Ps.55:22, NASB '77).**

> **"Give all your worries and cares to God, for he cares about you" (1 Pe.5:7, NLT).**

As you handle the day-to-day affairs of your job or business, serious problems will arise at times. When they do, you may be at a loss about what to do—especially when you see no solution for dealing with the troublesome situation. As a result, you might become extremely anxious or feel overwhelmed by the pressure.

At such times, you need to do exactly what the above verses say: "Cast your burden upon the LORD" and "Give all your worries and cares to God." You may be down, but you will not be defeated—not if you turn to the Lord. Sadly, our natural tendency as humans is to carry the full weight of our problems on our own shoulders. Far too often, we try to work out things on our own or else we seek help from every other source but God. However, God does not want you carrying the heavy load of your problems alone. He wants to strengthen you so that you can rise again and move forward (Pr.24:16). He invites you to throw off your troubles and allow Him to bear them for you. How? You need to take one definitive action: you have to trust God enough to commit your trouble to Him. First, stop, and take a step back. Then pray earnestly and repeatedly, asking God for the wisdom and discernment to handle your problem in a godly manner, with full integrity. When you fully trust God with your problem, your fears and anxiety will begin to vanish, and the peace of God will begin to reign in their place (Ph.4:6-7). You will learn to trust God more and more and to experience His sustaining and victorious power in your life (2 Co.4:13-14).

The Lord invites you to give your burdens to Him for a very significant reason: He cares about you (1 Pe.5:7). When the pressures, stress, and responsibilities of your work weigh heavily upon you, it is easy to think that God *does not* care about you. For example, if you lose a valuable contract or are facing serious financial problems, perhaps even bankruptcy, you might be tempted to think that the Lord does not love you, that He does not care about what is happening. Yet, it is during these trying times—when your worries and anxieties are the most paralyzing—that God's Word speaks to you and assures you: He *does* care about you and does not want you to be anxious (Ph.4:6). He knows every one of your problems, every detail of your troubling situation. He cares about you as you bear the heavy burdens of your business or position. In fact, He cares so deeply that He pleads with you to trust Him and to cast your burdens on Him. What an encouraging truth! He stands ready to receive your heavy load and to carry it for you. This exhortation could not be more clearly stated; indeed, it is a command: "Give all your worries and cares to God, for He cares about you." If you will give your cares to Him, God's mighty hand will...

- strengthen and secure you
- protect and provide for you
- give you wisdom to make decisions
- save and deliver you
- look after and care for you
- give you assurance, confidence, and peace

7. *Turn to Christ when you are weary and heavily burdened.*

> "Then Jesus said, 'Come to me, all of you who are weary and carry heavy burdens, and I will give you rest. Take my yoke upon you. Let me teach you, because I am humble and gentle at heart, and you will find rest for your souls. For my yoke is easy to bear, and the burden I give you is light' " (Mt.11:28-30, NLT).

When you are burdened by a difficult problem in your business or personal life, help is available to you. You can be set free from the heavy weight and the harmful stress. How? By accepting the two great invitations of God's Son, Jesus Christ:

a. **"Come to me,** all of you who [labor and] are weary and carry heavy burdens, and I will give you rest" (v.28). Most business leaders have no choice but to work hard, sometimes to the point of total exhaustion. Think of the times you have been utterly drained, feeling you could not go on. If you are a in a large company, long hours and hard work are typically expected if you hope to be promoted or, sometimes, even to keep your present position. If you are a small business owner, success usually depends upon you alone. You have to work long and hard just to survive. It is to you—all business owners and leaders— whom Christ extends His invitation. When you work hard and are weary, utterly exhausted and unable to go on, Christ invites you to come to Him. And if you come to accept His invitation, He promises to give you rest.

Note that Christ's invitation is extended not only to you who are weary but also to you who carry heavy burdens. Working long and hard does not always ensure success. As you well know, there are times when . . .

- the economy slows and business/sales decline
- costs increase or labor disputes arise
- downsizing occurs and jobs must be cut
- promotions are missed and employees become resentful
- immoral relationships begin and disturb the workplace
- spouses and children feel neglected due to the demands of your job or position

In addition to these, a host of other problems can surface in business management that weigh you down and place heavy burdens on your body, mind, and soul.

When you feel extreme pressure, as though you are about to be crushed or to explode, Christ invites you to come to Him. His invitation is open-ended, an *open door to come and to keep coming* to Him. Your coming is to be an ongoing relationship and dialogue with Him, seeking His help in all matters of business and life. As you walk through each day, every moment of weariness and every burden you carry should compel you to "come to Jesus." He longs for you to accept His invitation and to find *rest* for your soul. The rest that Jesus Christ gives is...

- the rest of *renewed strength and relief of pressure:* no matter how weary you may be, Christ promises to strengthen you within and to relieve whatever burdens you bear.
- the rest of *a clear conscience*: no matter what you may have done wrong—no matter how dreadful,

sordid, or shameful—when you turn away from wrongdoing and come to Christ, He will remove all guilt and give you a permanent, lasting sense of God's forgiveness and acceptance.

- the rest of *God's presence and guidance*: day by day, as you continue coming to Christ, He will deepen your sense of God's guidance through the trials, burdens, and difficult circumstances, trouble that arises both in your business and personal life.

- the rest of *renewed purpose and hope*: when your purpose or plans for life are threatened—whether in your business or family—Christ especially invites you to come to Him. Even if the worst happens, He will work all things out for good if you sincerely come to Him (Ro.8:28). He will give you a second chance, a new beginning, a fresh start. He will help renew your purpose and restore hope in your soul, inspiring you to begin all over again.

- the rest of *peace—peace of heart and mind*: this is a deep sense that God is with you, guiding you and taking care of you step by step as you face the many demands of the day. It is the assurance that God will help free you from worry, anxiety, confusion, doubt, and anything else that hinders you from performing effectively and making wise decisions.

Always keep in mind, however, that as God works in you to bring about His rest, doubts may begin to plague you. You may begin to feel guilty, to feel that your sins are too great to be forgiven, that God has deserted you and left you on your own. Nothing could be further from the truth! God's promises are sure, His love unconditional, His forgiveness complete. If you begin to doubt yourself or doubt God, call out to Him in prayer. Ask for His guidance and turn to His Word for further assurance.

b. **"Take my yoke** upon you and let me teach you" (v.29). The second great invitation of Christ also needs to be accepted to find rest for your soul. The *yoke* refers to an oxen's yoke. It represents the instruments or tools that help you as you labor and carry out your duties and affairs on earth. When you come to Christ, He gives you the greatest instruments He has—His very own Spirit and His Holy Word—to help you as you handle the demands of the day. His Word tells you how to live successfully and His Spirit empowers and guides you throughout each day.

Note that Christ's yoke is *easy to bear.* Obeying His Word or instructions and following His Spirit are not burdens that should weigh you down. To the contrary, when you truly follow God's instructions and the leading of His Spirit, whatever weight and weariness the world places on your shoulders will be eased and made lighter. You will find rest for your soul. This is the glorious promise of Christ if you come to Him!

8. *Resolve to press on through every challenge, no matter how difficult.*

> **"Therefore, since we have so great a cloud of witnesses surrounding us, let us also lay aside every encumbrance, and the sin which so easily entangles us, and let us run with endurance the race that is set before us," (He.12:1, NASB '77).**

The stress of your position as a business owner or leader can only be understood by others who have been in, or are in, similar leadership positions. Without question, yours is a strenuous race. It can be utterly exhausting and at times overwhelming. When particularly difficult times arise, you may feel that you cannot go on. Or that you cannot continue carrying such a heavy load.

During such times, when stress and pressure threaten to defeat you, you need to confront them with a spirit of endurance. The Greek word for *endurance* indicates fortitude, a state of persevering or remaining constant. *Endurance* is not passive; it is active. It is not the spirit that hesitates, withdraws, or just sits back and accepts whatever trials come. Rather, it is the spirit that stands up and faces the trials head-on, actively seeking to conquer and overcome them. When seemingly insurmountable difficulties challenge you, having a spirit of endurance will stir you to get up and vigorously tackle those trials. When you face the problems, the spirit of endurance will begin to propel you forward. You will be encouraged to conquer whatever confronts you. Always remember the teaching of James 1:2-4, that God allows you to face such formidable circumstances in order to make you stronger.

Indeed, all truly successful business leaders possess a common trait, a spirit of determination that endures and never quits. Every day when you arise, ask God for His help. Ask Him to fill you with a spirit of endurance, to let nothing stop or hinder you, not any...

- enticement or distraction
- discouragement or despair
- difficult encounter or confrontation
- overwhelming trial or problem

To succeed in business or any other area of life, you have to rise above and be stronger than whatever circumstances or problems you come up against. You do this by seeking God's help. He alone can give you the strength you need to endure—and ultimately conquer—every challenge.

> **"Dear brothers and sisters, when troubles of any kind come your way, consider it an opportunity for great joy. For you know that when your faith is tested, your endurance has a chance to grow. So let it grow, for when your endurance is fully developed, you will be perfect and complete, needing nothing" (Jas.1:2-4, NLT).**

9. *Overcome crushing problems by looking to the future.*

> "...looking to Jesus, the founder and perfecter of our faith, who for the joy that was set before him endured the cross, despising the shame, and is seated at the right hand of the throne of God" (Heb.12:2, ESV).

As a business owner or leader, you carry a heavy burden every day, a tremendous load of responsibility. After all, you are responsible for maintaining your business or for running your department or division. The responsibility to generate new business, meet expenses and payroll, and show a profit is a heavy load to carry even when sales are up, expenses are stable, and profits are growing. But when the economy is suffering, expenses increase, competition cuts into your business, or you are forced to lay off loyal employees, the burdens of leading your business can seem almost unbearable. Still, no matter what you face as a business owner or leader, there is always hope. You can find strength to press on through your most difficult days and darkest nights by doing what Jesus did: He focused on the joy that lay ahead, focused on the end results of His work. Simply put, He persevered—never quit, never gave up.

Indeed, the supreme example of perseverance through difficulties is the Lord Jesus Christ. Certainly, we can be encouraged by other business leaders who have trusted God and endured overwhelming challenges. They too are excellent examples for us, and we should look at their unstoppable spirit. But we should always be looking to our Lord, "*looking to Jesus* for strength to endure the most exhausting trials" (Heb.12:2, ESV).

The Greek word translated as *looking* means to fix your eyes on, to focus your attention and fasten your thoughts on. Thus, we are to focus our eyes and minds on Jesus Christ. Why? Because Jesus Christ Himself ran the race of life to the end. He persevered through the fiercest trials any person has ever endured.

When you face difficult times, if you will trust God and seek His help, He will be with you and carry you through the trial—no matter how troubling it may be. He will help you. Your duty, as difficult as it may be sometimes, is to persevere and stay focused; never quit and never give up. Take time to think of the joy that lies out in the future due to your perseverance, the joy . . .

- of solving and overcoming problems
- of being able to stay in business or keeping your job and providing for yourself and your dear family
- of continuing to provide a needed product or service that helps individuals as well as society
- of being successful—achieving your dream as a business owner or proving your value as an executive, manager, or supervisor
- of knowing you have done your best, gaining a sense of purpose, fulfillment, and satisfaction, a sense of being needed and helpful
- of experiencing God's presence and help—all in answer to your prayer and trust in Him

You can find the strength to endure overwhelming difficulties at work and in life. Just look to Jesus and follow His example: persevere, never quit, never give up. Keep your focus on the end results—the joy that comes from solving and overcoming whatever confronts you.

10. *Remember God's reward for those who overcome persecution.*

> "God blesses those who are persecuted for doing right, for the Kingdom of Heaven is theirs. 'God blesses you when people mock you and persecute you and lie about you and say all sorts of evil things against you because you are my followers. Be happy about it! Be very glad! For a great reward awaits you in heaven. And re-

> **member, the ancient prophets were persecuted
> in the same way' " (Mt.5:10-12, NLT).**

The list of challenges encountered by business owners and executives is endless. But business leaders who are genuine believers will face a unique set of challenges, problems not experienced by those who do not know Christ or by professing believers who compromise the principles of God's Word in their lives and business practices.

If you are faithful to Christ and His Word, you should expect to be persecuted. In every area of life, pressure to compromise the truths of God's Word abounds. In addition, many people are staunchly opposed to Jesus Christ Himself. This is true in public life, and it is no less true in the business world.

While much business is conducted honestly and ethically, some is not. Certain individuals whom you work for or do business with might press you to be dishonest in your dealings. For example, an individual may suggest that you do something unethical in order to make a deal or to show a larger profit. You could even be ordered to lie or to deceive a customer or client. Or, you might be told to be less than truthful toward a co-worker or employee in order to create a cause for dismissal. Another company could even suggest joining you in bid-rigging a contract or in shaving and undercutting the bids of other companies.

Equally common is the occurrence of immorality in the business world. You may be asked or expected to participate in, condone, or at least remain silent about immoral behavior within your company. Or you may be expected to participate in unscrupulous behavior that goes against God's Word and your biblical convictions.

As another example, government agencies or officials may demand you to adopt practices or policies that violate your biblical convictions. The above-mentioned possibilities are just a few ways you might face pressure to do something that is not right.

When you choose to stand up for what is right, you may very well be persecuted for it. What kind of persecution? Christ mentions three major kinds in this passage . . .

- being *mocked*: verbally abused, insulted, belittled, berated, scorned

- being *persecuted*: hurt, ostracized, attacked, treated hostilely, or in the most extreme cases, tortured or martyred, because of your faith or stand for righteousness.

- having *all sorts of evil things* spoken against you: slandered, cursed, and lied about

You may pay a price if you stand faithful to Christ and His Word. That price could be as low, comparatively speaking, as being mocked, insulted, made fun of, ignored, overlooked, or bypassed. Or, you might be excluded from certain meetings or functions, or from being involved in certain aspects of business.

On the other hand, the price you pay for doing right may be quite steep. You may lose customers or a lucrative contract. Some individual or company may refuse to do business with you or even boycott your company. You could also face heavy fines or even be forced out of business by the government.

If you are an executive or manager, raises or bonuses may be withheld from you. You might be passed over for a promotion or even demoted to a position with less responsibility and a lower salary. Or you could even be terminated, actually let go because of your stand for what is right and your refusal to do what is not right. If you do experience persecution, Christ commands you to respond in a strange way: you are to rejoice and be very glad (v.12). Why? Because the Lord, the Supreme Ruler of the universe, has promised to bless you, and the Kingdom of Heaven is yours, both now and eternally (vv.10, 11). Indeed, you have the assurance of salvation and of living eternally, and no one can take the assurance of God's spirit away from you!

You also have a great reward awaiting you in heaven (v.12). Remember, when you are persecuted, you are in an elite company: the prophets of the Old Testament, and, subsequently, all other believers who have suffered for Christ (v.12).

Scripture provides additional reasons why you should rejoice if you are persecuted:

- Because it is a special, sacred honor to suffer shame for Christ.

  "And they departed from the presence of the council, rejoicing that they were counted worthy to suffer shame for his name" (Acts 5:41, KJV).

- Because Christ Himself comforts you, both abundantly and personally."

  "For just as the sufferings of Christ are ours in abundance, so also our comfort is abundant through Christ" (2 Co.1:5, NASB '77).

- Because you become a greater witness for Christ. Your testimony of God's comfort will encourage and strengthen others who suffer.

  "[Who] comforts us in all our affliction, so that we may be able to comfort those who are in any kind of affliction, through the comfort we ourselves receive from God. . . . If we are afflicted, it is for your comfort and salvation. If we are comforted, it is for your comfort, which is experienced in your endurance of the same sufferings that we suffer" (2 Co.1:4, 6, HCSB).

- Because you are given a very special sense of the Lord's presence, a unique closeness to Him. God's Spirit of glory rests upon you.

  "If you are reviled for the name of Christ, you are blessed, because the Spirit of glory and of God rests upon you" (1 Pe.4:14, NASB '77).

Note one other important truth: when you take a stand for what is right, you are not to do so in anger. Nor should you be haughty or act as if you are spiritually superior to others. You should always do what is right with a humble and gentle spirit. When necessary, stand firmly, but at the same time, be kind, respectful, and gracious. This is the way to overcome persecution in the business world.

11. *Know that no trial or trouble can separate you from God's love.*

> "Who shall separate us from the love of Christ? *shall* tribulation, or distress, or persecution, or famine, or nakedness, or peril, or sword?...Nay, in all these things we are more than conquerors through him that loved us. For I am persuaded, that neither death, nor life, nor angels, nor principalities, nor powers, nor things present, nor things to come, nor height, nor depth, nor any other creature, shall be able to separate us from the love of God, which is in Christ Jesus our Lord" (Ro.8:35, 37-39, KJV).

When you are facing an overwhelming problem or devastating crisis in your personal life or business, you might be tempted to think God does not love you. You might feel He has turned His back on you or has forsaken you. But during such times, you need to remember this wonderful truth: there is nothing—no *circumstance*, no crisis, no crushing situation—that can cause Christ to turn away from you. No matter how terrible or severe the situation, it cannot separate you from the love of Christ. Even if you were to go bankrupt and lose everything, or be terminated from your job, or suffer a great personal loss, the unfailing love of the Lord will carry you through. Christ's love will sustain you through it all.

Always remember this critically important fact: difficult circumstances are not evidence that God does not love you. God did not put you in those circumstances. But God loves you no matter what circumstances you are in or how you arrived there. In fact, you are more than a conqueror through Christ who loves you (v.37, see also pt.2, p.179-180). And He will carry you through any and all situations, even the worst crisis you can imagine . . .

- bankruptcy
- loss of job
- betrayal
- terminal illness
- divorce
- loss of a loved one

One crisis after another can strike you in rapid succession (remember Job), but the Lord will never forsake you. He will strengthen and encourage you all along the way. No matter the severity of the situation, Christ loves you and is going to take care of you; therefore, you cannot lose. Christ will deliver you from the most extreme problems and the fiercest trials. Nothing in the universe can separate you from the love of God that is revealed in Christ Jesus our Lord. You can be fully persuaded of this encouraging fact.

If or when severe trouble strikes your business or employment, you need to trust the love of Christ. Just draw close to Him, seeking His presence, strength, and guidance. His love will assure and empower you to rise above whatever trial you are facing.

What You Need to Guard Against in Both Your Business and Personal Life

Contents

CHAPTER 8

WHAT YOU NEED TO GUARD AGAINST IN BOTH YOUR BUSINESS AND PERSONAL LIFE

1. *Guard against unwise partnerships.*

> "Do not be bound together with unbelievers; for what partnership have righteousness and lawlessness, or what fellowship has light with darkness? Or what harmony has Christ with Belial, or what has a believer in common with an unbeliever? Or what agreement has the temple of God with idols? For we are the temple of the living God; just as God said, 'I WILL DWELL IN THEM AND WALK AMONG THEM; AND I WILL BE THEIR GOD, AND THEY SHALL BE MY PEOPLE" (2 Co.6:14-16, NASB '77)

> "Can two walk together, unless they are agreed?" (Amos 3:3, NKJV).

One of the most crucial decisions you will ever make as a business owner is whether to enter into a partnership with other individuals or companies. Partnerships can have many positive benefits, and an effective partnership can propel you forward. At the same time, partnerships hold many potential pitfalls. God's Word offers two solid principles to guide you.

a. **Avoid partnerships with unbelievers** (2 Co.6:14). This passage is clear: you are not to enter a business partnership with unbelievers. In fact, God's Word strongly warns against it. Why? Because the two of you will not be able to agree on the most important issues, issues involving values, morals, and the guiding principles laid out by God's Word. It is simply unwise to collaborate with another party (individual or group) unless you know you will generally be in agreement on the important issues of life (Am.3:3).

Once you genuinely trust Christ as your Savior and Lord, you undergo a radical change and become fundamentally different from unbelievers, as different as light is from darkness (v.14). Your values change, and you begin to live by God's Word. Typically, people outside the Christian faith do not have the same values you have. They may not be as committed as you are to conducting business by the principles of God's Word. And an unbelieving partner may vehemently object to your living out your spiritual convictions through your business. In addition, the basis upon which you make decisions will likely differ profoundly. You will want to seek God's guidance through prayer and His Word as you make decisions, and the unbelieving partner probably will not, and may even object.

An unbeliever will have different business goals than you. Throughout this book, God's purposes for you, a Christian business leader, are emphasized. You cannot expect someone who does not know Christ to support all of these purposes. For example, will a woman or man who is not a believer be dedicated to taking God's Word and the gospel to the world? Will he or she be committed to fostering a Christ-like culture in the company?

A partnership with an unbeliever will usually produce one of two results: conflict or compromise. Things may go smoothly for a while, but eventually, some issue will arise that you cannot agree on. When it does, you and your partner will either experience serious conflict, or else one of you—usually the Christian—will compromise your principles for the sake of working together peacefully. Neither result is acceptable or pleasing to God; therefore, you should avoid ever entering a partnership with an unbeliever.

b. **Be sure you and your potential partner are in agreement** (Am.3:3). Even if a potential partner is a professing believer, the two of you still may not agree on business philosophies, principles, plans, and practices. For this reason, you need to have thorough and frank discussions concerning every matter of importance to you, whether large or small, *before* forming a partnership.

No two individuals will agree on *everything*, but it is critical that you and any potential partner agree on *most* things. It is even more critical that you agree on major issues relating to the business. Identify areas where you disagree *prior to* the partnership and try to find a workable solution for those matters in advance. While you can make concessions in a number of areas, you should never compromise scriptural principles or purposes. If irreconcilable differences arise on important matters in your discussions, be thankful that those differences came to light before the partnership became legal. And always walk away from forming a partnership with anyone who does not agree with you on the fundamental purpose of life and its values, morals, and beliefs. You should never compromise on what is right nor on what God is calling *you* to do.

As you carry on these preliminary discussions, you would be wise to keep a written record of everything. Draw up a legal agreement that will govern as many details and issues as possible. You should also cover how things will be handled if either of you wants out of the partnership at some point.

Unity is critical to the success of any venture. Jesus said that a house divided against itself cannot stand (Mk.3:25). But there must be agreement before there can be unity. When you and your partner do not agree, division is sure, and the partnership will ultimately fail, causing you much damage and pain. With that in mind, be certain that the two of you agree *prior to* forming a partnership. Protect yourself from suffering the pain of failure: guard against unwise partnerships.

2. *Guard against the damaging effects of anxiety and stress.*

> "Therefore I tell you, do not worry about your life, what you will eat or drink; or about your body, what you will wear. Is not life more important than food, and the body more important than clothes? . . . So do not worry, saying, 'What shall we eat?' or 'What shall we drink?' or 'What shall we wear?' For the pagans run after all these things, and your heavenly Father knows that you need them. But seek first his kingdom and his righteousness, and all these things will be given to you as well. Therefore do not worry about tomorrow, for tomorrow will worry about itself. Each day has enough trouble of its own." (Mt.6:25, 31-34, NIV '84)

Leading a business—no matter the type or size or your role in it—can fill you with apprehension. Indeed, constant worry (anxiety and stress) is so damaging that the Lord's counsel to guard against it is given three times in the above Scripture (vv.25, 31, 34).

Jesus is not suggesting that you escape worry by not preparing for life or that you ignore, flee, or pass off problems to others. Nor is He implying that you be lazy, shiftless, or uncaring about things that matter in life. God will not indulge irresponsibility or lack of initiative, effort, and planning. On the contrary, He expects you to be diligent in looking after your daily responsibilities (1 Co.4:2). In fact, you should work hard enough that you are able to help the needy when possible in addition to providing for yourself and your family (Ep.4:28b).

What Jesus is saying is this: you should not be preoccupied with wealth and the material possessions of life. Many people—especially those who have achieved a certain level of success—continue to focus their attention and energy on acquiring the necessities and luxuries of life. They grasp for and accumulate more and more. But you are called to live for a higher purpose. You are not to *seek first* the things of the world; instead, you are to *seek first* the kingdom of God and His righteousness. In return, God will see to it that you receive the necessities of life and whatever else (wealth and possessions) He wants you to have (v.33).

Jesus cautions you against being so wrapped up in securing things that you become anxious, troubled, or restless. Being fixated on worldly things keeps you from being at peace and genuinely enjoying life. Moreover, worry can cause serious health problems ranging from sleeplessness and headaches to depression, ulcers, high blood pressure, heart attacks, even cancer. And, just as detrimental, worry and stress can affect your relationships within the workplace as well as at home.

A person who puts wealth and possessions *first* never really comes to know God—not personally, not with the *full assurance* of living eternally with Him. This person never truly knows God's love and care, never experiences God's moment-by-moment presence, never learns that God looks after those who truly trust Him as they face the daily problems and trials of life.

Ultimately, Jesus is warning you not to become so entangled with the affairs of this earth that you forget eternity. You need to take care of your life and soul beyond this temporary, physical existence. Walking through life without God's presence means that at death you will walk into eternity without Him. Not knowing whether there is life after death would be especially troubling during the latter years of life or if suffering a terminal illness. Lacking that assurance of living forever with Christ—as opposed to the prospect of spending eternity in hell—would understandably bring enormous stress and anxiety to your soul. So, even if a person denies and argues against the fact of life after death, that denial does not erase the truth that we will all die and face God immediately. And at that moment, we will give an account to Him for how we have lived.

The Lord's counsel not to worry is for your good, lest you suffer the damaging consequences and health issues caused by anxiety and stress. But what exactly can you do to guard against it? The Lord has not left you hanging without an answer. He spells out the steps you need to take to overcome worry.

a. **Consider God's care for the world** and place your faith in Him. He has created the earth to produce and provide the basic necessities of life. The point is reassuring: if God has provided such a beautiful and productive earth for you to live in, how much more will He provide for you when you face devastating circumstances? Do not be a person of *little faith*, but rather trust in God. If you truly put Him first, He will take care of you (v.30).

b. **Seek the kingdom of God** and His righteousness first (v.33). As a business leader and a Christian, your first pursuit in life is not to be material things, as necessary as some of them are. Instead, you should seek first to live as a citizen of God's kingdom and encourage others to do the same. You should seek to live responsibly (righteously) day by day as you go about taking care of your business and other affairs.

Realistically, how can you keep from falling into despair if you face a financial crises or bankruptcy or the loss of your job and income? How can you keep from being gripped by anxiety and stress if you seemingly fail in the eyes of the world? If you genuinely put God first, you can rest assured of four wonderful promises:

- Your failure is temporary. God will help, strengthen, and even teach you through the trying times (Is.41:10; 43:1b-2)

- God will work all things out for good because you love Him and He loves you (Ro.8:28f).

- God will see to it that you always have the necessities of life (Mt.6:33; Ph.4:19).

- God has much better things in store for you, both in this life and in eternity. You have been faithful in your work, so God will reward you as a faithful servant, even if you have failed in the eyes of the world.

If you go through a failure (as all of us do at one point or another), you need to remember just one thing: be faithful. And continue to be faithful. By putting God first, He will lift you up now and eternally.

c. **Learn to live one day at a time (v.34).** When you face a devastating crisis, you should not be preoccupied with tomorrow and its affairs. Focus on today's responsibilities. Seek God's kingdom and His righteousness today, leaving tomorrow and its needs in God's hands. Note that Christ is not forbidding you to *take care of tomorrow*. Rather, He is striking at the tendency to worry and to ignore God and His righteousness. Consider these five attitudes toward the future:

- A *no-care, worldly attitude.* You seek to eat, drink, and be merry today while having little concern about the future. When you assume this attitude, earthly pleasure, power, and fame are your major concerns; therefore, your attitude is to get all you can now.

- A *fretful, anxious attitude.* You worry all the time, wondering if you will have enough to take care of yourself and your family tomorrow.

- A *fearful, panicky attitude.* In the face of trial or failure, you can barely function. Tragedy has hit; your job is threatened or gone, cutbacks must be made, serious adjustments are needed. Panic sets in, and your strength to act and continue on is greatly diminished.

- A *self-assured attitude.* You, like most business leaders, have a high level of confidence in yourself and your abilities. You feel you can take care of yourself in this world, and you do it. But there is one thing you fail to see, and it is fatal: the confidence you have in yourself will be shattered one day. One day you will face a devastating crisis that confronts us all: death. Death is beyond humanity's capacity to

control. At whatever point you face it, you will discover that no amount of self-confidence can bridge
the great gulf between mere mortals' help and God's
help, between this physical earth and super-natural
heaven, between our measurable time and eternity,
between the created and the Creator.

- *A calm, God-centered and trusting attitude.* You
go about living and working diligently and calmly,
trusting God's help and care in everything you do.
You do everything possible to provide the necessities of life for yourself and for others, working hard
to grow your business. But what sets you apart is
this: as you labor tirelessly, you seek God and His
righteousness first (Ep.4:28). As a result, you sense
God's presence with you and know He is there to
help as you face the worrisome, stressful crises of
life. This is Christ's promise to you, the business
leader who truly seeks God first. If you choose this
attitude, that of focusing your life and your business
on God and His principles, He will provide everything you need. In the most agonizing and traumat-
ic crises of life, you can know unexplainable peace.
You can rest in God's promise to care for you—the
promise of a God who cannot lie.

3. *Guard against being dishonest.*

> **"Better is a little with righteousness than
> great income with injustice" (Pr.16:8, NASB '77).**

> **"The wicked *man* does deceptive work, but
> he who sows righteousness *will have* a sure re-
> ward" (Pr.11:18, NKJV).**

One of the greatest temptations business leaders face is
that of using unethical or deceptive practices to increase
profits. Many people give in to the temptation because of
unbridled greed. Others are pressured by their superiors
or the owners themselves. For certain individuals, though,

the temptation to be dishonest arises out of the sheer need to survive.

a. **God's Word is clear: we should never act dishonestly** in our efforts to acquire wealth (Pr.16:8). Living righteously with little is far better than having riches gained dishonestly. You should keep this proverb in mind as you manage every operation of your business. Remember: God's Holy Word is your guide as to what is righteous and what is not—especially as you face adverse or difficult circumstances. Most small companies go through periods of hardship occasionally, times when the owners or leaders struggle to pay their employees or to meet other necessary expense—all while providing for their own families. In many cases, small business owners are compelled to make great personal sacrifices just to keep their businesses afloat. But it is always better to act righteously than dishonestly when we encounter financial difficulties. Indeed, we are to live righteously—to do what is right—in every area of our lives and businesses, obeying God's Word in all things.

When facing the need to cut costs and increase profits, resist the temptation to do so in a less than honorable way. Remember what God says in this verse: it is always better to do what is right and earn less than to do something wrong and increase revenues. Your end result or net worth might not grow, but God will bless in different ways, ways that He knows are best for you, your family, and your company.

Whether advancing yourself, increasing profits, or acquiring possessions, doing so *dishonestly* is wrong and it displeases the Lord. The primary quality God is looking for in you as a business owner or leader is *righteousness*. Rich or poor, much or little, does not matter without the key ingredient of righteousness.

When tempted to increase profits through dishonest means, stand strong. Refuse to compromise and do what is right instead. Stand firmly on Christ's promise given in Matthew 6:33:

> **"But seek first the kingdom of God and his righteousness, and all these things [material provisions] will be added to you" (Mt.6:33, ESV).**

b. **Honest and ethical business practices reap far more benefits** than do deceitful methods (Pr.11:18). But, tragically, an appalling number of people do business dishonestly by...

- not being completely truthful about a product or a service—concealing or misrepresenting certain information or details
- not fulfilling all the terms of an agreement
- using poor quality materials or craftsmanship
- not doing or delivering everything promised
- not completing a job promptly or when promised
- not paying their obligations on time
- producing a product or promoting a service that can harm people

The list could go on and on. Dishonest, unethical people either blatantly ignore or are oblivious to the law of sowing and reaping. Simply stated, they will reap exactly what is sown. These individuals disregard the fact that there is a just God in heaven who sees all and, in His timing, balances the scales. If you are deceitful in your business practices, you may profit in the short term, but eventually your evil ways will catch up with you. On the other hand, if you are honest and ethical in all your dealings, God promises you a sure reward.

Without question, the more righteousness you sow, the more benefits you will reap. You will gain the loyalty and respect of employees, customers, and suppliers alike. Your reputation among other leaders within the community will also be strengthened—a dynamic example for all to follow.

Too many leaders in the business world tarnish themselves and the companies they represent because of their unwise and unethical business practices. Sadly, many people who do not know Christ are more honest than some who claim to follow Him. As a business leader, the world is watching you, but even more so if you are a professing Christian. You therefore need to be diligent and determined to sow righteousness in your business practices. You need to make sure everyone associated with your company follows your godly example and lives up to the highest ethical standards in every aspect of their work. If you are deceptive in any way, your business or leadership position will eventually suffer. Of even greater concern, though, is the damage done to the cause of Christ when you are less than ethical. Strive to model Christ's leadership in all that you do and promote a business culture that brings honor and glory to His name.

4. *Guard against envying or coveting the success of those who are evil.*

> **"Do not envy a man of violence and do not choose any of his ways, for the devious person is an abomination to the LORD, but the upright are in his confidence. The LORD's curse is on the house of the wicked, but he blesses the dwelling of the righteous. Toward the scorners he is scornful, but to the humble he gives favor. The wise will inherit honor, but fools get disgrace"** (Pr.3:31-35, ESV).

Far too many in business have clawed their way to the top while trampling over others. They are, as this passage says, people *of violence*. Yet, most of them appear successful in the eyes of the world, indulging themselves in life's luxuries and pleasures. But, sadly, they have made their gains off the backs of others: their associates, employees, customers/clients, suppliers, and so on. In fact, they cheated, deceived, or mistreated these individuals as part of their scheme to acquire the trappings of earthly success.

Driven by an insatiable desire for worldly possessions, pleasure, power, and prestige, their behavior is most ungodly (1 Jn.2:15-16). Their methods are unethical and immoral, and their dealings with others are cruel.

God warns us: do not envy these people. Do not follow their ways. If envy flares up within you, smother the emotion immediately, or else it will tempt you to be as unethical as those you envy. To encourage you, God's Word highlights four contrasts between people who deal underhandedly and those who deal righteously. As you read through these examples, note especially the wonderful promises God gives when you put away or reject envy and do what is right (righteous) in all your dealings with others.

a. **The LORD detests the corrupt,** but He is with, close to, the upright (v.32). People who deal corruptly are an abomination to the LORD; He abhors their twisted, willful ways. Consequently, they will never know the delights of being God's friend. But if you strictly adhere to God's ways, you will experience the privilege of God's presence—His guidance, provision, and protection. You will have closeness or intimacy with Him.

b. **The LORD's curse is on the house (family) of the wicked,** but His blessing is on the home of the righteous (v.33). Imagine the horror of being under God's curse! Even worse, imagine the guilt of having that curse upon your entire household. Does this mean that God punishes innocent family members for another's wickedness? Absolutely not! Nevertheless, the trouble that the ruthless individual causes by his or her ways tragically affects the rest of the family. The entire family suffers the painful consequences, the resulting shame and resentment, and the withholding of God's blessing. Simply stated, when you are unethical in your dealings with others, it impacts not only your business but your family as well.

If you truly love your family, you will faithfully follow the LORD's commands in all your ways, including your business operations. By doing so, you will bring God's blessings upon your home.

c. **The LORD mocks the pride of the scornful,** but He gives favor, or grace, to the humble (v.34). Corrupt people are hardened toward sin and toward God. They scoff at God's commandments, shaking their fists at Him, daring God to act in judgment against them—and He will, according to His perfect schedule. A day of perfect justice is coming (He.9:27).

   In stark contrast, if you are humble—if you willingly submit to God and obey Him at work and wherever else you may be—you will receive God's blessing and favor.

d. **The corrupt are fools and will be put to shame,** but the righteous are wise and will receive honor (v.35). Honor is your reward if you are upright in all your dealings. You will be esteemed by others. If you treat people right—treat them well and fairly, as you should—they will think more highly of you and be more likely to do business with you again. But far more important, God will reward you one day for your faithfulness. Disgrace and reproach, however, will be the reward for the cruel and corrupt, the "legacy of fools" (NKJV).

   An intimate relationship with God, God's blessings on your home and family, God's favor on all you do, and an honorable reputation—these are the priceless rewards you forfeit if you choose ill-gotten, worldly success over obeying God's commandments in your business dealings.

As a Christian business owner or manager, perhaps one who struggles daily, it is easy to look at the prosperity of the wicked and be envious. God's people have always struggled with the inequalities of the world in this particular area. But, remember, unless they turn their lives around, those who walk the crooked path will lose far more than they gain through their devious business practices. God's reward in eternity and His blessings in this life far outweigh the enjoyment of worldly things acquired unscrupulously.

If you adhere to God's path, you *may* receive earthly wealth, possessions, and pleasures. On the other hand, you *may not* become wealthy or well-known. At times, you may even struggle to keep your business afloat. If so, you need to cling to this compelling and reassuring truth: what you will gain eventually by following God's principles now is far more valuable than everything this world has to offer.

> **"And the world is passing away along with its desires, but whoever does the will of God abides forever"** (1 Jn.2:17, ESV).

5. *Guard against oppressing those who are struggling.*

> **"The one who oppresses the poor person insults his Maker, but one who is kind to the needy honors Him"** (Pr.14:31, HCSB).

Throughout the course of doing business, you will deal with people who are struggling financially. This is especially true if you have a retail or service-oriented business and deal directly with the general public. But it is also true in many other types of businesses, both large and small. You may deal with companies that are struggling financially, failing to fulfill certain terms of their contracts with you, or with a vendor or supplier that has fallen on hard times and is not paying as agreed.

Scripture is clear about how you are to deal with those who are struggling: you are not to oppress them. Rather, you are to show kindness to them. The Hebrew word for *oppress* means to defraud, deceive, or mistreat, but it also means to deal harshly with or to take advantage of a person's circumstances. Oppressors cheat and take advantage of those who are struggling, making their circumstances much worse than they already are.

Consider some ways that businesses deal harshly with those who are genuinely struggling:

- by requiring or enforcing unusually harsh terms
- by charging an exorbitant interest rate, what Scripture refers to as *usury*

- by exploiting unfortunate circumstances for gain; for example, by inflating prices after a disaster such as a tornado, hurricane, earthquake, flood, or fire
- by failing to consider a person's circumstances
- by refusing to be patient and understanding during an economic downturn or recession
- by quickly repossessing an essential item (for instance, a car) and failing to give the individual a reasonable amount of time to work out the finances
- by turning accounts over to a collection agency before trying to work out a less demanding payment plan

Scripture issues a strong admonition to all who are tempted to oppress the needy: when you deal harshly or unfairly with them, you disrespect and insult God. How? God is their Creator. In fact, He is the Creator of every individual (Jb.31:15). Thus, you show your contempt for God when you oppress a fellow human being. No person has the right to oppress another person. God takes it as an open act of defiance when people abuse or take advantage of one another, especially those who are struggling. If you wrong someone who is struggling, you wrong God. But if you are kind and attempt to work things out, you honor God. You attribute to Him the position and glory He deserves because you are helping one of His dear people. Showing compassion, mercy, and kindness to those suffering adversity is the same as doing so for the Lord Jesus Christ Himself. Note the powerful words of our Savior:

> **"And the King will answer and say to them, 'Assuredly I say to you, inasmuch as you did *it* to one of the least of these My brethren, you did *it* to Me' " (Mt.25:40, NKJV).**

Furthermore, Scripture says bluntly that if you do not have compassion on the needy, God's love is not within you:

> **"If someone has enough money to live well
> and sees a brother or sister in need but shows
> no *compassion*—how can God's love be in that
> person?" (1 Jn.3:17, NLT).**

Unquestionably, there will be people in business who
deal unfairly with you. You will do business with individuals who take advantage of you, who purchase services or
products from you that they cannot pay for, or who spend
their money on unnecessary things or live extravagantly
while failing to pay you. Some businesses may even be unethical when dealing with you. For example, they may keep
their money a little longer to draw more interest instead of
paying you promptly. In such cases, you have every right to
pursue and collect payment by whatever means are necessary. Bear in mind that some who profess to struggle do
not. Others struggle because of their own poor choices or
bad decisions. Still others are simply dishonest or lazy. God
does not expect you to indulge the dishonest or lazy in society nor allow them to take advantage of you.

However, when you discern that an individual or company is doing its best to make things right with you while
genuinely struggling, the Lord wants you to honor Him by
treating that individual or company with compassion and
kindness. When you do, God promises to honor you. He
will bless you and reward you for extending His mercy to
others.

> **"He who is gracious to a poor man lends to the
> LORD, And He will repay him for his good deed"
> (Pr.19:17, NASB '77).**

6. *Guard against offensive and illegal behavior.*

> **"Don't give offense to [anyone] Jews or Gentiles or the church of God" (1 Co.10:32, NLT).**

> **"And this I pray, that your love may abound
> still more and more in knowledge and all discernment, that you may approve the things that**

are excellent, that you may be sincere and without offense till the day of Christ," (Phi.1:9-10, NKJV).

As business owners or leaders, we should avoid offending others as much as possible (1 Co.10:32). This does not mean that we should withhold or avoid the truth in order to keep from upsetting those who need correction, instruction, or information. It simply means that we are to be respectful when dealing with employees, customers, or others with whom we do business. We should always guard what we say and do around others, approving only the most excellent behavior to keep from offending them (Ph.1:9-10).

As you lead your business or department, you have a responsibility to ensure that your company has and follows specific policies governing employee behavior at work. Naturally, employee conduct should always be considerate and respectful, never offensive. Some disrespectful conduct is not only offensive, but also illegal. Therefore, it is imperative that you keep abreast of all laws and regulations within government (1 Pe.2:13-15). If you do not actively deal with violations, you may face lawsuits and penalties. To avoid legal action, you should work diligently to prevent offensive behavior and consistently correct employees who violate applicable policies. This is your duty. You are to doggedly protect your company, guarding against all offensive or illegal behavior.

a. Guard against prejudice and discrimination.

"The woman was surprised, for Jews refuse to have anything to do with Samaritans. She said to Jesus, 'You are a Jew, and I am a Samaritan woman. Why are you asking me for a drink?'" (Jn.4:9, NLT).

"For God shows no partiality" (Ro.2:11, ESV).

"Are they not the ones who blaspheme the honorable name by which you were called? If you really fulfill the royal law according to the

Scripture, 'You shall love your neighbor as yourself,' you are doing well. But if you show partiality, you are committing sin and are convicted by
the law as transgressors" (Jas.2:7-9, ESV).

By no means are you to tolerate any prejudice or discrimination in your business. The Lord commands you
to treat all people equally just as He does, regardless of
race, age, gender, religion, cultural background, or economic or social status (Ro.2:11; Ga.3:28). When Jesus
reached out to the Samaritan woman, He disregarded
racial and cultural barriers of His day (Jn.4:9). You are
to follow His example both in your personal life and in
your business.

God's Word speaks strongly against *partiality* or discrimination (Jas.2:7-9). Those who discriminate blaspheme the name of God—a startling statement! How
is this true? When we discriminate against a person or
group of people, we sin against the name or character
of God. God shows no favoritism to people. He sees every individual's heart, not his or her race, nationality,
gender, or financial status. He loves and judges all of
us equally. When we show partiality, we take a prideful
stand against the Spirit of God. We are actually cursing
or blaspheming the very nature of God's heart! In so doing, we commit a grievous sin against Him personally.
We become transgressors of God's law.

In the United States and a number of other countries,
it is illegal to discriminate based on race, ethnicity, gender, and other factors. For this and other reasons, you
need to take decisive action—both proactive and re-
active—against all prejudice and discrimination. You
need to have clear and firm anti-discrimination policies
in place and enforce them. God's Word teaches that you
should not allow discrimination in hiring, promoting,
or compensating workers. Applicants or employees
should not be judged or treated differently because
they may differ in some areas. Individuals should be
judged only by their character, training, abilities, expe-

riences, and performance on the job. As a leader, you are to show zero tolerance toward any prejudice being expressed. Hurtful joking, name-calling, racial or ethnic profiling, rude gesturing, and all other prejudicial behavior must be forbidden. Establish strict disciplinary measures for those who violate any of these policies, and enforce such measures without exception. Again, the compelling reason for taking such a strong stance should not be merely to avoid lawsuits or penalties but because of your duty to your employees and community as well as to the Lord.

b. **Guard against harassment.**

> **"You shall not oppress a hired servant *who is* poor and needy, whether *he is* one of your countrymen or one of your [foreigners] who is in your land in your towns" (Dt.24:14, NASB '77).**

> **"Thus has the LORD of hosts said, 'Dispense true justice, and practice kindness and compassion each to his brother; and do not oppress the widow or the orphan, the [foreigner] or the poor; and do not devise evil in your hearts against one another' (Zech.7:9-10, NASB '77).**

> **"Let all bitterness, wrath, anger, clamor, and evil speaking be put away from you, with all malice. And be kind to one another, tenderhearted, forgiving one another, just as God in Christ forgave you" (Eph.4:31-32, NKJV).**

Harassment is an area where clearly-stated policies and thorough training are critical. Unknown to many people, laws now exist governing harassment. Some actions that were not necessarily deemed offensive in years gone by are considered harassment in today's culture. Even within our own families, there are behaviors no longer considered acceptable. Shifts in cultural norms have brought great impact to the workplace and society in general.

For example, think of people you have heard about who were accused of harassment when they had no idea their behavior was improper or offensive. It is crucial for the well-being of your employees and the people around them that they be informed about company policies regarding behavior in the workplace. Make awareness of these policies a priority.

When hiring, be alert to any signs that a person might have behavioral issues. Check personal and business references carefully, and never hire any individual who has a record of bullying, threatening, belittling, or behaving hostilely toward other employees. Providing training for top management on down is beneficial, but it is no guarantee that harassment will never take place. Establishing proper protocols for dealing with harassment if it occurs is essential. Also keep in mind state and federal laws that need to be a part of your employee policy manuals.

Harassment can take many forms. It is generally defined as abusive or unwelcome behavior or comments based on:

- gender
- race
- religion
- nationality or ethnicity
- physical or mental condition or disability
- sex or sexual activity
- appearance
- age
- other factors

As a business owner or leader, you need to be sure you understand what constitutes harassment, lest you or one of your employees commit a violation. This is where good training comes in. But if an employee does file a harassment complaint, you have a responsibility to deal with it seriously and fairly, no matter how you feel about it personally.

What we refer to as harassment today falls under what God calls *oppression* in His Word (Dt.24:14; Zec.7:9-10). God hates oppression and is the champion of the oppressed. As an employer, you have a duty to God to guard against harassment. Do everything you can to create a safe work environment where harassing behavior of any kind is unacceptable.

c. **Guard against offensive or abusive speech.**

> **"But now you must also put away all the following: anger, wrath, malice, slander, and filthy language from your mouth" (Col.3:8, HCSB).**

God's Word commands us to *put away*—get rid of, renounce—all offensive or abusive speech. This instruction applies to each of us personally, but it also places a duty on you as a business owner or leader. You should not permit offensive behavior or abusive speech by anyone in your business. You have a *right* to govern the conduct of your employees while they are working. But even more important, you have a *responsibility* to protect your employees from abusive or offensive speech and to provide a pleasant, safe, and productive work environment.

To avoid any misunderstanding, you need to have policies in place regarding appropriate speech on the job. These policies need to be spelled out in the employee handbook and explained to every worker as a part of training. Be specific about what types of speech are unacceptable. Note three types of speech that God commands you to get rid of:

- angry, wrathful, malicious speech—abusive, full of rage
- slanderous speech—gossip, rumors, lies
- filthy speech—cursing, profanity, off-colored humor, dirty jokes, immoral suggestions or innuendos

As in other areas of behavior, disciplinary steps regarding speech need to be defined and strictly followed. No one should be exempt, including board members, executives, managers, and supervisors. And you, as the leader, should set the finest example for everyone else in your company.

7. Guard against showing favoritism or undue leniency toward any worker.

> "If a man pampers his servant [employee] from youth, he will bring grief in the end" (Pr.29:21, NIV '84).

It is only human nature to like some people better than others. This is true in every arena of life, including the workplace, and it will be true with you as a business leader. In fact, as you go about your work day by day, you may feel compassion for some employees due to the difficult circumstances of their lives. Or, you may choose to employ a friend, a relative, or the child of a friend or relative. You may even decide to give your own children jobs in your company.

These are just a few of the situations where you might lean toward being easier on certain employees than you are on others, or when you might be inclined to have lower expectations or requirements for a group of workers. But note the clear teaching of the above proverb: pampering employees will cause serious problems later. It will bring grief in the end. Therefore, you should always resist the urge to go easy on favored workers or to treat any employees differently than you do others.

Indeed, when an employee is favored or pampered in the workplace, it causes . . .

- strife and discord
- jealousy and resentment
- gossip and rumors
- murmuring and grumbling
- inefficiency and less production

- higher cost and less profit
- a diminished image of company or product excellence
- a diminished image of management

Showing partiality actually harms favored workers, hindering them from learning as strong a work ethic as they might have developed otherwise. It can keep them from reaching their full potential. Pampered employees may begin to expect more and more of things that are not rightly theirs: more authority, higher pay, more days off, longer vacations, and a host of other perks or favors. The Lord warns you as an employer and business leader: be wise, not foolish. It is most unwise to pamper workers, especially, as this proverb states, when they are young or first hired.

However, this counsel does not mean that you should not be gracious, considerate, and generous toward your employees. Scripture clearly instructs you to care for your employees (Ep.6:5-9). You are to value dedicated and productive workers who give their best effort and make sacrifices for the business. The Lord expects you to be fair and considerate of their needs. When the cost of living increases, you should increase their wages accordingly whenever possible. When an employee goes beyond and does more than what is required, you should show your appreciation and reward them appropriately. Furthermore, you should never try to take advantage of an employee by getting as much work as possible from the individual for as little money as possible.

Wise employers and employees show mutual respect and appreciation for one another. When each does his or her best for the other, the result will be a long, satisfying, and productive relationship.

At the same time, you should be equally firm and fair with all who work under you. You cannot allow emotional attachments to any employees that will cause you to be lenient toward them. All business owners and leaders need to understand that we harm ourselves, our companies, our employees, and ultimately our society when we fail to hold individuals to a high standard of performance. As the above Scripture plainly states, showing favoritism or undue leniency only brings grief in the end; therefore, you should never start it or allow it in the first place.

8. *Guard against employee theft.*

> "[Employees] must not . . . steal, but must show themselves to be entirely trustworthy and good" (Tit.2:9b, NLT).

> "He who has been stealing must steal no longer, but must work, doing something useful with his own hands, that he may have something to share with those in need" (Ep. 4:28, NIV '84).

The Greek word for steal in these verses conveys the theft of small, petty items. It could be taking something as simple as a pencil or tablet from the office, misusing a company vehicle, or padding an expense account. On the other hand, it could be something as complex as embezzling funds (for example, Ponzi schemes) or tampering with and falsifying financial records.

Some employees simply feel they are not getting what is due them, that you and the company owe them more than you pay them. Therefore, they feel justified in taking a little here and a little there, or even much here and much there. Other employees steal to increase their bank accounts, whether it is to cover the cost of living or to accumulate more possessions. Still other employees steal solely for the thrill of getting away with a crime. On rare occasions, you may employ a kleptomaniac—someone with a mental disorder that compels the individual to steal. If such a case occurs in your business, it is best to either recommend or bring in mental health professionals for guidance.

No matter what reasons your employees offer as justification for theft, God says they are not to steal—*not ever.* Your employees are to demonstrate that they are completely trustworthy; that is, loyal, faithful, and honest.

For your business or company to succeed, you must be able to depend on your employees at all times. They will more likely be loyal if you have a no-theft policy in your business or company's personnel documents, a policy that spells out the consequences of theft. Then, if an employee is found guilty of theft, your carrying out justice will be a strong deterrent to other employees, teaching them not to steal. By the same token, if you fail to follow through with the stated consequences, you set a precedent for leniency. You actually lay the groundwork for charges of favoritism or discrimination if you discover others stealing in the future and treat them differently.

Sadly, employee theft is such a big problem in business that significant markups often have to be added to products and services to make up for the loss. Of course, the higher costs are bad for everyone involved—you as the business owner or executive, your employees, and all consumers. It also affects your competitors and the economy as a whole. But it is especially bad for the poor who have to struggle for survival, for the very basic necessities of life. For these and many other reasons, you need to be alert and guard against employee theft.

9. *Guard against improper or suggestive clothing in the workplace.*

> "And I want women to be modest in their appearance. They should wear decent and appropriate clothing and not draw attention to themselves by the way they fix their hair or by wearing gold or pearls or expensive clothes" (1 Ti.2:9, NLT).

Common sayings such as "dress for success" and "the clothes make the man or woman" are not to be ignored. They point out a reality in business that needs to be talked about: the dress code—or lack thereof—in the workplace. Scientific studies have proven that a person's clothing affects not only that individual's behavior but also the behavior of people around them. An internet search of the subject produces an abundance of articles confirming that society recognizes this fact.

As a leader in your business, you need to remember that every employee is a representative of your company. Whether alone or among many in an office, out on a job site, away on a business trip, or out in public, your employees should exemplify the high standards you and your company wish to portray. God's Word offers you direction in setting clothing guidelines for your business. While the passage above is addressed to women, it applies to men as well, especially in today's society. It calls for a standard that you and your company would be wise to follow.

First, you should require your employees to dress *modestly*. The Greek word for modest means *orderly*. Your employees should dress according to what is *in order* for the workplace. Clothing should contribute to creating order on the job, not disorder. Modest also means *respectable and consistent with good behavior*. Clothing worn on the job should elicit respect from others; it should encourage them to act and to think respectably. It should communicate the individual's desire to be viewed as a person of good behavior—of upright morals and conduct. In no way should it distract fellow employees from doing their best on the job.

Second, your employees should dress *decently*. This word speaks of a reverence toward what is pure and right. It is the opposite of being bold, brazen, or shameless. Certainly, dressing decently rules out clothing that is revealing, suggestive, or outright seductive. Decent clothing...

- encourages professionalism and productivity, not fleshly or worldly behavior
- serves people, does not harm them through immoral thoughts and behavior
- does not distract others or attract them to yourself in an immoral or impure way
- promotes pure, respectful thoughts, not lustful thoughts

Third, you should insist that your employees dress *appropriately*. Simply stated, this means dressing with good sense, appropriately for the job they are doing. Obviously, the nature and requirements of the specific job determine this. What is in order in the office or in sales is different from what is in order on an assembly line. Some clothing is genuinely hazardous for certain jobs. But clothing that is offensive is always inappropriate.

Fashion and clothing styles will always be changing—largely by design. The fashion industry continually promotes different styles and trends to keep people buying new clothes. Regardless of what the world dictates, however, the three standards discussed should always be in fashion for your business. Spell out the dress code simply and clearly in your company policy. Be sure individuals at every level and in every position know what is, and is not acceptable: they are to dress *modestly, decently, and appropriately* at all times. Being proactive about this very relevant topic will help you and your employees avoid what could be embarrassing one-on-one discussions.

10. *Guard against immorality—both personally and within the workplace.*

> "It is God's will that you should be sanctified: that you should avoid sexual immorality" (1 Th.4:3, NIV '84).
>
> ". . . to preserve you from the evil woman, from the smooth tongue of the adulteress. Do not desire her beauty in your heart, and do not let her capture you with her eyelashes" (Pr.6:24–25, ESV).

At no time in human history has sexual immorality been as prevalent and as public as it is today. Not only are enticements for sexual sin present almost everywhere, but also opportunities to act upon them—including in the workplace and everyday business situations. Many who indulge in sexual sin are proud of their behavior, even boastful. They try to justify their lifestyle by insisting that their conduct is only natural and normal.

As a business owner or leader, you need to be prepared to deal with sexual temptation. In almost every occupation and business, men and women work together in various capacities. And it is by God's design that men and women are naturally attracted to one another. Thus, from time to time you will meet someone whom you find attractive or who finds you attractive. If you or the other person is married, you must do all you can to suppress the attraction. Suppression will require strong self-discipline. You must flee the temptation, give no place to such thoughts or fantasies, for all temptation begins in the mind.

But even if you and the other individual are not married, you need to bear in mind that being romantically involved with a coworker or business associate can cause complications on the job such as interrupted concentration and focus on one's work, less production, inter-office gossip and jealousy. The high incidence of this very problem has prompted many companies to adopt strict policies concerning coworkers' dating.

It is only natural that you form friendships with other coworkers in the course of your work. But it is important that you guard against sharing personal matters with any individual lest either of you develops feelings that go beyond friendship and what is appropriate in a working relationship.

As a business leader, you must also be aware that some will be attracted to you *because of* the position you hold or the financial success you have achieved. Our world is so corrupted by sin, that certain individuals might seek to further their careers by becoming romantically involved with you. It is sadly a scenario played out all too often in the work environment.

On this note, the job requirements of many business owners and executives include frequent travel. Being away from home and separated from your spouse—in a strange place where few people know you—presents unique opportunities and temptations that are unusually strong. Some business associates may even offer to provide you with inappropriate entertainment or a companion while you are in their cities.

You must always guard diligently against the sin of sexual immorality, protecting yourself and all you hold dear from its devastation. You need to recognize every temptation for the power it has to destroy you and everything you have worked for. One moral failure can cost you everything...

- your marriage
- your children
- your position
- your business
- your life

- your reputation
- your trustworthiness
- your wealth or finances
- your fellowship with God
- your health

What a high price sin demands! Even in a day when immorality is prevalent and, tragically, acceptable in society, those caught in adultery pay a costly public price. You may know someone personally—or have heard about certain celebrities, politicians, or other public figures—who are paying a steep price for this specific sin.

For these and so many more reasons, you should think twice if a person smiles at and flatters you, giving you attention that is inappropriate and sexually suggestive. The person's motive cannot be respectable, and if you give in, you are jeopardizing all that you hold dear. Sin will always cost you more than you want to pay. But, sadly, despite all the costs to you personally, you still do not pay the full penalty for your sin. Others—innocent victims—must pay as well. Consider...

- the major trauma to children whose lives and homes are suddenly shattered
- the devastation to an unsuspecting and crushed spouse

- the hurt and shame to parents and other family members

- the loss of friends who no longer trust or feel comfortable around you

- the sense of betrayal and loss of confidence felt by those who looked up to you or admired you

- the pain and broken heart of Christ

Indeed, sin demands an awful, inflated price for the brief pleasure it gives. In a manner of speaking, sin is purchased on credit; that is, you may receive the benefit of sin now, but you will most certainly pay for it later. A brief moment of extramarital sensual pleasure can require a lifetime of payments. This is the message Solomon is urgently trying to impress upon his son in Proverbs 6 as he pleads with him to avoid the painful consequences of immorality. His counsel to his son is applicable to all in the business world today: you must diligently guard against sexual sin.

Note that the instructions of this passage are from a father to his son. Because of this, the wording is gender-specific. However, the following principles and lessons are applicable to men and women alike.

a. **Guard your words and your ears (v.24).**

You need to be extremely careful in speaking to coworkers or associates, making every effort to avoid saying anything that could be interpreted as inappropriate or flirtatious. In addition, you need to weigh carefully flattering words spoken by those with less than pure motives. Do not allow yourself to be enticed or tricked by a colleague's suggestive or smooth remarks, remarks designed to lead you into sin. To keep from putting yourself in a compromising position, you have to guard your ears—everything that you listen to—as well as your mouth—every word that you say.

b. **Guard your eyes and your desires (v.25).**

You must not look at a woman or a man with lust in your heart (v.25a). You need to carefully guard your eyes at all times, for a lingering look can lead you to lust in your heart simply because of a person's attractiveness. And every act of sexual sin is the fruit or result of a *seed of lust* planted in the heart:

> **"But each person is tempted when he is drawn away and enticed by his own evil desires" (Jas.1:14, HCSB).**

> **"Do not covet your neighbor's house. Do not covet your neighbor's wife . . ." (Ex. 20:17, HCSB).**

Jesus took the above commandment from the book of *Exodus* a step further. He specifically taught that lust itself—the inner longing and desire to have illicit sex with another person—is sin:

> **"You have heard that it was said, 'You shall not commit adultery.' But I tell you that anyone who looks at a woman lustfully has already committed adultery with her in his heart" (Mt.5:27–28, NIV).**

More often than not, sexual sin begins with the eyes. The seed that grows into adultery is usually sown in your heart as a result of some*one* or some*thing* you have looked at. If you are genuinely committed to remaining pure, you will guard your eyes from looking at another person impurely. You will also shield yourself from a promiscuous person's glances (v.25b). A single glance can be as compelling as words. Knowing this, you have to ignore suggestive looks by immoral individuals who appeal to you and staunchly refuse to be drawn or influenced by their flirtatious ways.

> **"I made a covenant with my eyes not to look with lust at a young woman" (Jb.31:1, NLT).**

If you are a business owner, executive, or manager, you would be wise to do everything you can to protect yourself and your marriage from adultery. You need to exercise discretion, realizing that even the most innocent gestures can arouse desires within you or another individual, sinful desires that can lead to the destruction of your home or your business, profession, or job. Most importantly, you need to yield daily to the Holy Spirit, seeking His power to resist impure thoughts and temptation. Sexual temptation is powerfully enticing, and we need to be ever conscious of the weakness of our human nature and our need for God's strength. Practically speaking, the following actions will help safeguard your marriage:

- Focus on meeting your spouse's needs, keeping your spouse fully satisfied.

- Avoid entertainment (such as books, television programs, movies, pornography) that encourages, condones, or glorifies marital unfaithfulness.

- Avoid activities, settings, or circumstances that arouse sexual desires outside of marriage.

- Avoid fantasizing about other people.

- Be uncompromising and appropriate in all interactions with the opposite sex—on the job, on airplanes, in meetings, in restaurants, at business functions or parties, or anywhere else. Do not allow yourself to become too comfortable or too familiar with a coworker, employee, employer, client, or business associate.

- Be guarded in all physical contact with the opposite sex. For instance, hugging is a common form of greeting or welcome within many cultures. While most people intend it only in innocence, a hug can convey something more to some people. It can also stir inappropriate feelings in some people. Considering this, you should go out of your way to avoid even the appearance of anything improper or out of place. (Of note, an embracing hug can be avoided without offense by simply stepping sideways to avoid full contact and extending your arm only around the other person's shoulders.)

- Avoid excessive compliments to the opposite sex, compliments that could easily be misinterpreted.

- As much as possible, keep conversations with the opposite sex focused on business. Do not casually contact someone of the opposite sex through any means of communication, whether by letter, telephone call, email, text, or any other available media. Do not discuss personal matters, nor carry on deep, lengthy conversations.

- Shun close friendships with the opposite sex. Again, as much as possible, keep relationships focused on business. Of course, when you work frequently with another person, friendships will develop naturally. Always make your spouse a part of those friendships. Create opportunities to introduce your spouse to coworkers and associates of the opposite sex. Mention your spouse regularly in conversations. Always communicate your deep love and devotion to your spouse. Never say anything that could be construed as negative about him or her.

- Guard your eyes and your mind. Do not fix your gaze or thoughts upon another woman or man. Though enticing scenes and tantalizing opportunities may be within sight or reach, do not take a second look or touch or allow your mind to think a second thought. If you do, you leave the door open for Satan to draw you in.

- Dress modestly. Dress to draw attention to your face and to your inner spirit through smiling and being courteous, kind, and gracious. Think about it: Why would a woman or a man dress immodestly or seductively other than to attract the attention of the opposite sex?

- Be fully accountable to your spouse. Be completely open about your schedule, your activities, your friends, and your work. Allow your spouse full access to any personal accounts you may have, whether banking, telephone, mail, E-mail, internet, or any other social media. Husbands and wives should have no secrets from one another.

- Be sensitive to your spouse's cautions, instincts, and feelings.

- Avoid discussing your marital problems or dissatisfactions with others.

- Never allow yourself to be alone with a person of the opposite sex, if at all possible. If a one-on-one meeting is essential, avoid meeting behind closed doors or arrange to meet in a public setting, such as a restaurant. Include a third person in meetings with the other gender if at all possible. Likewise, never travel alone with a person of the opposite sex. You need to actively prevent any opportunity for indiscretion from arising.

When all is said and done, our human nature and fleshly desires are always subject to being enticed and seduced. Our ultimate protection against immorality is the Lord. If we find ourselves facing heavy temptation—fantasizing and focusing on immoral thoughts—we need to cry out to God for strength and deliverance. He will help us (1 Co.10:13). But we would be even wiser to plan ahead and do all we can to avoid compromising situations in the first place. We should always flee temptation.

"Flee sexual immorality" (1 Co.6:18, NKJV)

11. *Guard against the danger of overwork or burning out.*

"And it came about the next day that Moses sat to judge the people, and the people stood about Moses from the morning until the evening. Now when Moses' father-in-law saw all that he was doing for the people, he said, 'What is this thing that you are doing for the people? Why do you alone sit *as judge* and all the people stand about you from morning until the evening? . . . The thing that you are doing is not good. You will

> surely wear out, both yourself and these people who are with you, for the task is too heavy for you; you cannot do it alone. Now listen to me: I shall give you counsel, and God be with you. You be the people's representative before God, and you bring the disputes to God, then teach them the statutes and the laws, and make known to them the way in which they are to walk, and the work they are to do. . . . If you do this thing and God *so* commands you, then you will be able to endure, and all these people also will go to their place in peace.' So Moses listened to his father-in-law, and did all that he had said. And Moses chose able men out of all Israel, and made them heads over the people, leaders of thousands, of hundreds, of fifties and of tens. And they judged the people at all times; the difficult dispute they would bring to Moses, but every minor dispute they themselves would judge" (Ex.18:13-14,17-20, 23-26, NASB '77).

Overwork is a serious problem for many business owners and executives as well as managers and supervisors. Some go day and night and still have as much work waiting on them as they just finished. What is the answer? In this helpful passage, God's Word teaches us what to do when we are overworked.

Jethro, Moses' father-in-law, observed that Moses was overworked, utterly exhausted, and suffering personally. As a result, the people were not being served as carefully or efficiently as both sides desired. What happened next has proven to be an invaluable lesson for every generation since then. It serves as a strong example for business owners, executives, and leaders in any type or size of business. When you are overworked—or, preferably, before you get to that point—put the following seven principles into practice:

a. **First, evaluate** your organizational structure (vv.13-14). Moses' father-in-law suggested that Moses stop and look at his current workload and what was happening.

If you are overworked, take a step back and look at your current structure. Ask yourself the following questions:

* Why am I alone doing so much?

* Is my company well-served by my carrying such a heavy load?

* Are the needs of my customers/clients being effectively met with me personally trying to do so much?

* Can my customers/clients be equally or even better served by someone else?

* How is carrying such a heavy load affecting me personally? My family? My health? My church and/or community?

* How long can I continue like this?

b. **Second, determine** what you should be doing, what you do best, and what you alone can do (vv.19-20). Jethro pointed out Moses' most important responsibilities, what God had called him to do, what he alone could do. Similarly, you should look at everything you are doing and identify what you—the owner, executive, manager, or supervisor of your company—should be focusing on. What responsibilities are uniquely yours, and what can you do that no one else in your organization can do? Do these, and assign the other responsibilities to other people. For certain owners and executives, letting go is difficult. Nevertheless, if you are overworked and truly desire to live a balanced and fruitful life, you will have to assign responsibilities to others.

So, be honest and ask God to lead you to those specific individuals who can help you handle the workload of your business or responsibility. Then trust God and follow through.

c. **Third, structure** your workload into smaller units (v.25). Moses divided the total population of the people into smaller units, then broke down his overwhelming responsibilities into manageable categories. Likewise, you should evaluate everything you are doing and determine which responsibilities can be borne by others, along with the tasks that can be completed by others. Then, subdivide these responsibilities into the appropriate categories that other people can manage.

d. **Fourth, select** capable individuals and delegate appropriate portions of your workload to them (v.25). Moses did just that. He chose skillful, trustworthy people and assigned them portions of his responsibilities. He appointed them according to their respective abilities—leaders of thousands, of hundreds, of fifties, of tens. In like manner, to reduce your workload, select qualified people and let them do what they can do. Let them handle everything they can handle. When situations arise that they cannot handle, or when matters of crucial importance come up, they can bring these issues to your attention.

e. **Fifth, seek** God's guidance throughout this entire process, in every decision (v.23). Note that Jethro knew his idea should not be followed unless God approved it (v.23). In the same way, you should pray earnestly about every step of the process of reducing your workload, seeking the Lord's direction and wisdom all along the way:

- How should you restructure your business?

- What tasks would God have you do personally, and what responsibilities would He have you delegate to others?

- To whom should you assign the responsibilities you can delegate? Should you add to an existing employee's workload? Should you promote from within? Should you hire additional staff?

- How can you come up with the financial resources to hire additional employees or to promote from within?

- Who are the right people to hire? What should their qualifications be?

When you seek the Lord in every decision, He will help you and your plan will succeed. You will be able to reduce your load to a manageable level, one that allows you to achieve the critical balance with all your roles, responsibilities, and relationships. In addition, your company will be more effective in meeting the needs of your customers and clients.

f. **Sixth, follow through** with the plan God gives you (vv.24-26). This is a self-evident truth: you have to follow through with your plan, actually do it, if you honestly wish to reduce your workload. Many leaders are afraid to let go of their responsibilities, fearful that no one else will care about their work as much as they do. Obviously, selecting the right people for the appropriate responsibilities is crucial. But the reality is this: as difficult as it is to accept, some individuals will do a better job with certain tasks than you did. True, others will not do as well as you, but they will still do them adequately. Many will soar to new heights and reach their full potential when you give them the opportunity to do so. But you must be willing to let go and have faith in others whom you have judged to be capable, trustworthy, and honest.

g. **Seventh, listen** to those who tell you you are doing too much (v.24). This is one of life's basic principles that is difficult for many business leaders to accept, the very principle that stirred Moses to make a change: listen to the people who suggest that you are doing too much.

Men and women who rise to leadership in businesses are, almost without exception, highly driven. They are not afraid of working hard. They are committed to doing what has to be done and doing it with excellence. They are willing to put in the long hours and are happy to take on additional responsibilities when necessary.

They live with the constant awareness that they are setting an example for others. They are determined to be successful and to make their companies successful, no matter the cost to them personally. Because of their dedication, they might fail to realize that they are over-worked until it is too late, when they have reached a crisis point. Or, they simply will not admit that they are exhausted or are doing too much.

In most cases, people who care about them—husbands or wives, children, associates, friends, occasionally even loyal customers or clients—tell them that they need to slow down. When Moses' father-in-law spoke to him about his unreasonable workload, *Moses listened*, and so should we.

Wise, effective business leaders take care not just of their work responsibilities but also of their families, their employees, their customers/clients, and all the other valued people in their lives. And they also take care of themselves. As a leader in your company, one of the most important things you can do—if not *the* most important thing—is to take care of yourself.

God does not want you to shorten the years of your life by wearing yourself out. Nor does He want you to neglect your family or any other role, responsibility, or relationship. If someone speaks to you about your heavy workload, listen and evaluate, and if they are correct, do what you need to do to restore balance to your life. You will have a fuller, more fruitful life, and one that you can enjoy more with your loved ones as the years go by—recognizing that it is all a gift from the Lord.

12. *Guard against the dangers presented by modern technology.*

> **"Therefore, let us no longer criticize one another. Instead decide never to put a stumbling block or pitfall in your brother's way" (Ro.14:13, HCSB).**

Today's amazing technology is a gift from God. Over 2,500 years ago, God actually revealed that, as we approach the end of His plan for the world, knowledge would increase (Da.12:4). Although no one knows for certain, it seems that this period of history has begun. Indeed, modern technology—especially the computer—has changed, and is continuously changing, every aspect of the world in which we live.

As with every other amazing gift from God, technology is sometimes corrupted and used for evil, destructive purposes. Therefore, in the work environment, you as the leader have a duty to protect your employees from the dangers of modern technology. The above Scripture instructs you to never put a stumbling block or pitfall in any person's way. The term *stumbling block* refers to an obstacle placed in someone's path—a *pitfall,* a trap or snare, something that seduces or entices a person, causing the individual to fall or be entrapped.

In most cases, you provide your employees with computer and internet access—an absolute necessity for so many jobs. With this being true, you also have a responsibility to make sure that the temptations of the computer, as well as of the smartphone and other devices, do not destroy their productivity and, potentially, their careers and lives—at least not while they are on the job using *your* computers. You have a moral obligation to ensure that essential technology is not an obstacle to their well-being and success. Note two dangers in particular from which you need to protect your employees, serious dangers that you need to guard against in your life as well:

a. **First, you have to** be concerned about the danger of improper use of work time. Computers and other devices offer unlimited tempting distractions: games, books, videos, music, pictures, news, personal emails, countless applications, and on and on—every bit of information and diversion imaginable is available online. Most of these activities are not bad in and of themselves, but they are a constant presence, more or less lurking around, waiting to lure us away from what we *should* be doing.

For this reason, you need to have policies concerning internet usage, and you need to do everything you can to protect yourself and your employees from using work time for personal or non-work-related activities. You can provide accountability for your employees in a number of ways, including through software, office or workstation setup, production and outcome expectations, and direct supervision.

b. **Second, you need to** take specific steps to prohibit access to pornography on any work devices. Pornography is, without a doubt, indescribably destructive and dangerous to the human mind. And, sadly, with the advent of the internet, greedy and devious individuals have seized the unprecedented opportunity for mass distribution of obscene and often criminal material Who would have imagined that such filth would ever be so easily and freely available, even to children?

Statistics about internet pornography viewing are staggering. Pornography will corrupt your mind, overpower your morals, destroy your marriage, and rot your soul. It is addictive, just like drugs and alcohol. And it can destroy your life.

You should do everything in your power to safeguard your employees and keep them from poisoning themselves with pornography—especially through the technology *you* are providing. In addition to the measures mentioned above, you can have pornography-filtering software on all company computers and devices, accompanied by stiff penalties for any individual who disables or overrides such software. Whoever oversees your information technology needs to be sure that all pertinent settings on web browsers and filtration services are activated to forbid the accessing of pornographic materials. Restrictions should also control the involuntary inclusion of pornographic material in internet searches and through "pop ups" and other advertising.

Obviously, these dangers affect your business. Using work (or personal) computers or devices to play on the internet or to access social media is probably the most modern-day manner of loafing on the job. When employees use work time—time for which you or your company are paying—to engage in other non-work-related activities, productivity will suffer and you or your company will bear the financial loss.

Even more crucial, though, as a business leader in your community, you should be vitally concerned about the well-being of the people with whom you work. You should be concerned about their careers, their consciences, their relationships, their self-esteem, and their personal development. In fact, God expects you to help these individuals achieve success in every area of their lives, both professionally and personally. True, you are not responsible for what they do on their own time, but you can take measures to help them while they are on yours. You should be alert to the fact that you too are subject to these temptations. You can destroy your own career and productivity and your personal life if you fall into these dangerous snares. For these and so many other reasons we have all heard and read about, we need to take a strong stand against the dangers brought about by modern technology.

13. *Guard against vicious competitors and enemies—people or businesses that seek to harm you.*

"But I say to you who hear, love your enemies, do good to those who hate you, bless those who curse you, pray for those who mistreat you (Lu.6:27-28, NASB '77).

"Never take your own revenge, beloved, but leave room for the wrath *of God,* for it is written, 'VENGEANCE IS MINE, I WILL REPAY,' says the Lord. 'BUT IF YOUR ENEMY IS HUNGRY, FEED HIM, AND IF HE IS THIRSTY, GIVE HIM A DRINK; FOR IN SO DOING YOU WILL HEAP BURNING COALS ON HIS HEAD.' Do not be

> **overcome by evil, but overcome evil with good"**
> **(Ro.12:19-21, NASB '77).**

Operating a business in today's extremely competitive market is not for the faint of heart. In fact, it is often called a *cutthroat* environment. And unethical individuals will do everything they can to get ahead, including harming you and/or your business. Some competitors will try to win your customers or contracts, by slandering you or attacking your integrity. In some cases, they might even pay individuals to steal your secrets or to make false accusations against your business. Disgruntled customers might wage a personal war against you, doing all they can to get even for a perceived wrong they feel you committed against them. Despite your best efforts to satisfy them, you cannot please everyone. Some will not be content until they have done everything they can to hurt you or your business.

You could also develop enemies within your own company. Jealousy, greed, and ambition drive some people to extreme actions. A coworker might callously undermine you in an attempt to out-perform you, win a bonus, or take your position. A scorned employee—or former employee—may make false accusations or even file a lawsuit against you. If you are a top executive, a group of executives or managers under you may plot to have you forced out of your position.

If you operate your business by your biblical convictions, you might face persecution from people who disagree with you. You might find yourself on the receiving end of boycotts, protests, media campaigns, or lawsuits. You could also face retribution from government agencies and authorities.

How should you respond to those who try to harm you or your business? God's Word says the following:

a. **Love and pray** for your enemies: all who curse, hate, or mistreat you (Lk.6:27-28). No doubt, your raw emotions and human reasoning tell you to strike out and fight back. But revenge is not God's way. Instead of working against your enemies, Christ commands you to respond in four ways that will help both the offending party and your company:

- **"Love** your enemies" (v.27). The word used for *love* here is "agape." This is the love of the mind, reason, and choice. It is a sacrificial love, that is, a love that cares, gives, and works for another person's good no matter how the person may treat or react to you. In other words, you are to deliberately choose to love those who do evil against you and your business.

- **"Do good** to those who hate you" (v.27). *Doing good* goes beyond mere words or feelings. It means that you take action. You personally reach out to those who hate you and try to resolve the issue peacefully. Throughout the whole process, you are to seek ways to *do good* to or for them. Then, if you find a way, you go and do the good thing, the right thing—even as Christ Himself did.

- **"Bless** those who curse you" (v.28). When someone curses you, bless the curser. Do not react or curse back. Instead, speak quietly and calmly. Use kind, appeasing words. Do all you can to reconcile with the offender. Try to prevent and save the time, cost, and divisiveness of legal battles.

- **"Pray for** those who mistreat you" (v.28). People might mistreat, abuse, attack, or even persecute you. They might attempt to damage your reputation or that of your business in any way possible. What are you to do? Christ says, "Pray for them." Pray for God to forgive them. Pray for them to have a change of heart toward you. **Praying for your enemies will greatly benefit *you,*** and it will keep you from becoming bitter, hostile, and reactionary.

b. **Do not retaliate** or seek personal revenge against those who hurt or harm you (Mt.5:38-39; Ro.12:19-21). Christ is clear: you are not to retaliate against those who strike out against you (Mt.5:38-39). Instead, accept the wrong done and *turn the other cheek.* If at all possible, let it pass and accept it. Forgive and entrust the matter to God, expecting Him to work all things out for good as you go about your business and service for Him.

There is an exception to this: If someone is threatening your safety or the safety of those around you, then you certainly have a right to protect yourself and a responsibility to notify law enforcement officials. Christ does not expect you to subject yourself, your family, or your employees to danger. God has ordained civil authorities to protect society and to punish evildoers (Ro.13:1-4).

In addition, God does not expect us to indulge or give license to destructive evil, not against us personally nor against our businesses. To the contrary, the Lord instructs us to stand our ground against evil (Ep.6:13) and not to be overcome by evil (Ro.12:21). The Lord also commands us to look out for the interests of others (Ph.2:4). If those who maliciously seek to harm or destroy your business succeed in their efforts, you will not be the only person affected. Your family and the families of your employees, as well as those in other companies that depend on your business, will also be harmed. God surely does not intend for us to passively allow jobs, lives, and families to be financially ruined by your enemies' wicked attacks. Furthermore, if left unchallenged, the evildoers will be further emboldened to do the same to other competitors or innocent companies, harming more and more people in the process.

Ultimately, you should earnestly seek God's wisdom and guidance as to how He wants you to respond to your specific situation (Ps.32:8; Jas.1:5). He may lead you not to take action against your enemies. Or, He may lead you to take a stand against your attackers so that justice and righteousness can be established. If so, your motive is to protect yourself and others, not to retaliate or to get revenge. The difference between the two is a matter of the heart.

In conclusion, vengeance makes evil victorious (Ro.12:19c). If you retaliate or take vengeance against an enemy, then you allow evil to conquer you by becoming a participant. As you continue leading your business day by day, learn to conquer evil by doing good. Overcome lies and slander by making your business better than ever before. Focus on improving your weak areas. Take customer service to a new level. Seek new customers by marketing more aggressively. Consider offering deep discounts to first time customers, and reward loyal customers for referrals. Do more for your community, worthy charities, and the needy. And, as our Lord commands, do all the good you can for those who attempt to do harm to you. (See ch. 6, pp. 147-157 and ch. 7, pt.2, p.179, when dealing with legal suits and questions.)

> **"But I say to you, love your enemies and pray for those who persecute you" (Mt.5:44, NASB '77).**

14. *Guard against the worldly philosophy of self-sufficiency.*

> **"Common people are as worthless as a puff of wind, and the powerful are not what they appear to be. If you weigh them on the scales, together they are lighter than a breath of air. Don't make your living by extortion or put your hope in stealing. And if your wealth increases, don't make it the center of your life. God has spoken plainly, and I have heard it many times: Power, O God, belongs to you; unfailing love, O Lord, is yours. Surely you repay all people according to what they have done" (Ps.62:9-12, NLT).**

As a leader in the business world, you face the danger of believing you are self-sufficient and placing your security in money. The world's philosophy of self-sufficiency is rooted in materialism and secularism. This viewpoint places undue emphasis on gaining wealth, position, power, fame, and authority in order to *advance yourself,* enjoy the pleasures of life, and *protect yourself* in time of trouble. But Scripture is strong in speaking out against a spirit of self-sufficiency. You should reject this philosophy for two practical reasons:

First, trusting only in yourself and in your achievements is basing your life on a weak and deteriorating foundation. God is neither impressed nor influenced by your possessions or position. Whether common or powerful—that is, poor or rich, simple or noble, weak or mighty—we are all the same in God's sight: our lives are like a breath or vapor that quickly passes away (v.9). The sooner you and everyone else realizes this truth, the better prepared we will be to walk through life triumphantly by depending on God. But if you walk through life acting self-sufficient—cutting God out of your life—you will face the crises of life all alone, that is, without God's help. Imagine facing crises such as a failing business or bankruptcy, some serious workplace injury or death, an employees' strike or walkout, the loss of a business license or certification, some embezzlement or theft on a grand scale, the betrayal or ruined reputation by a disgruntled employee. The list of scenarios could go on and on. When facing times like these, you always need help beyond yourself, beyond what mere humans can provide. You need supernatural help—God's help (vv.11-12).

Second, trusting only in yourself and in your achievements can lead to serious failure (v.10). Scripture repeatedly warns us that the *love of money* is the root of all sorts of evil (Pr.28:20; 1 Ti.6:9-10). When you place your trust in money, making it the sole objective of your business or your life, you open yourself up to temptations that you might not otherwise encounter. This passage in Psalms mentions three sins in particular:

- oppression or extortion—acquiring money through fraud or deceit, by using or taking advantage of others
- stealing
- worshiping wealth—making money or possessions the most important thing in life

Opportunities to make or take money by dishonest means are seemingly endless and increasing every day. Overcharging, overbilling, embezzling, underpaying employees, filing false insurance claims, stealing competitors' ideas—these are just a few of the countless ways a person could acquire money deceitfully. For someone in a position of authority—a leader in the business arena—the opportunities are even greater. You are just such a person. People look up to you; they trust you; they believe in you. You could—if you were so inclined—take advantage of these trusting individuals as well as complete strangers and add to your personal wealth. You could build up your business and bolster your own image using stolen funds—if you were so inclined. How can you overcome the daily temptations and sins such as these? Where can you find the strength to reject the worldly philosophy of self-sufficiency? In God alone! Trust God! In Psalm 62 above, God speaks repeatedly of His ability and desire to help you when the world throws challenge after challenge against you:

- **First,** power—all power—belongs to God. He has the power to meet your needs. He can guide you through the worst situation imaginable (v.11b).

- **Second,** God is loving beyond our (humanity's) comprehension, and He wants to meet your needs (v.12a). His love is unfailing. You may fail the LORD, but He will never fail you, because He is true to His Word.

- **Third,** God is faithful to reward every person according to his or her work (v.12b). When you trust the LORD and obey His commands—live your life and conduct business in a way pleasing to Him—He will bless and help you. Remember; it is never wrong to do the right thing, and it is never right to do the wrong thing. And God sees it all. You can be certain that He will deal righteously with you as well as with those who wrong you. Therefore, wait quietly and rest in Him when trouble arises and your faith is challenged (Ps.62:1, 5).

> "I wait quietly before God, for my victory comes from him. . . . Let all that I am wait quietly before God, for my hope is in him" (Ps.62:1, 5 NLT).

15. *Guard against forgetting God when you become successful.*

> "When you eat and are full, and build beautiful houses to live in, and your herds and flocks grow large, and your silver and gold multiply, and everything else you have increases, be careful that your heart doesn't become proud and you forget the LORD your God. . . . You may say to yourself, 'My power and my own ability have gained this wealth for me,' but remember that the LORD your God gives you the power to gain wealth." (Dt. 8:12-14, 17-18a, HCSB).

One of the most critical pitfalls of success is forgetting God. When we have little and are just beginning our businesses or careers, we tend to follow the Lord more faithfully. We tend to pray more often, seeking God's help, guidance, and provision. We also tend to be more obedient to Him because we desperately need His help and favor.

However, when we become prosperous—when our businesses are established, or we advance in our careers—we face a dangerous temptation, that of forgetting God. We are prone to seek God less, to turn to other things instead of obeying His commands and communing with Him. Prayer becomes less important because our needs are less urgent. As we become increasingly comfortable, we are naturally inclined to think of God less and less. Eventually, our consciences can become insensitive, even callous, toward God.

As you become increasingly successful in business, you need to guard against the danger of becoming self-sufficient, complacent, indifferent, and unresponsive to God. Becoming *full* or satisfied, comfortable, and wealthy in the eyes of the world can lead to forgetting just how desperately you need the Lord. In the midst of your prosperity, you need to be on guard more than ever lest you ignore or forget God, for it is He alone who has given you life and the ability to become successful.

What can you do to keep from forgetting God once you become successful? Keep two vital thoughts foremost in your mind.

a. **First, never forget** that it was *God* who brought you through the lean times, the early years of your business or career when you had little and faced overwhelming struggles (vv.14-17). Remind yourself daily of all that the Lord has done for you.

- Above everything else, God has saved you (v.14). He gave His only begotten Son so that you could be delivered from the enslavement of sin and death and from the coming judgment (Jn.3:16-19). He has given you the hope of heaven and eternal life. You did not save yourself nor create this hope within your heart. It is *God* who saved you and gave you the hope of living forever with Him in the new heavens and earth (2 Pe.3:10-13).

- God has guided and protected you (v.15). Again, it is *God* who gave you life as well as the skills you have. It is God who led you to begin or to get into your business or to secure your position. It is God who has guided your steps to where you are now according to His will and purpose for your life. He brought you through all the difficulties of starting, building, leading, or learning a business. He steered you to the right lenders or investors to obtain financing, and He stirred them to place their confidence in you. He led you to clients or customers and to others who have helped you. He impressed others to give you a chance when you were only a startup business or were new in your leadership position without a solid record of accomplishment. He gave you wisdom to make sound decisions and protected you from making mistakes that could have ruined you. He sent you loyal, diligent employees, and He also helped you recover from those hired who were not so well chosen. He gave you insight into cutting costs. He infused you with courage to take risks, and He worked powerfully in your behalf to protect you from loss. He guarded you from those who would take advantage of you or cheat you.

- God has provided for all your needs (v.16). It is *God* who promises to supply the necessities of life—food, clothing, housing, transportation, and every other need—when our income is meager or even nothing at all. It is God who touched the hearts of family and friends to help you. He sent you customers, contracts, and jobs when you did not know how you were going to meet payroll or pay pending bills. It is God who kept you afloat until your business could grow and become established. It is He who provided the strength you needed to face problems and endure severe trials, humbling you along the way and, ultimately, making you prosperous.

b. **Second, never forget** that God is the source of your success (vv.17-18). You must never think—not even for a moment—that your success is due to your own knowledge and talents. How easily we forget that our lives, health, and strength—our very existence upon this earth—are due to God. Likewise, it is *God* who gives us the capability to work and produce. Your abilities and skills are due to God, not to you.

We need to vigorously guard our hearts from becoming proud and self-sufficient, from thinking that *we* have produced our prosperity, that *we* are the source of our success. We must not forget that everything we possess and everything we accomplish comes from God. God gives the ability to build and lead a business successfully. God gives the natural inclination, the aptitude, the desire, and the resourcefulness. God is the primary and ultimate source of everything you are and have: your capabilities, health, opportunities, and success.

Considering all this, there is no place for pride or self-sufficiency within our hearts. Such arrogance will lead us to forget God; therefore, we must vigorously guard against these two sins, grievous sins that will cause God to remove His hand of guidance and blessing from our lives, jobs, and businesses.

CHAPTER 9

What You Can Do to Help Build Healthy Relationships

Contents

CHAPTER 9

WHAT YOU CAN DO TO HELP BUILD HEALTHY RELATIONSHIPS

A. YOU AND ALL THOSE WITH WHOM YOU HAVE BUSINESS DEALINGS

1. *Be honest in all your business dealings.*

(See ch. 1, pt.4, p.15-16 and ch. 4, pt.7, pp. 94-98.)

2. *Communicate clearly, concisely and honestly—say exactly what you mean in all communications.*

> "Again, you have heard that it was said to our ancestors, You must not break your oath, but you must keep your oaths to the Lord. But I tell you, don't take an oath at all: either by heaven, because it is God's throne; or by the earth, because it is His footstool; or by Jerusalem, because it is the city of the great King. Neither should you swear by your head, because you cannot make a single hair white or black. But let your word 'yes' be 'yes,' and your 'no' be 'no.' Anything more than this is from the evil one" (Mt.5:33-37, HCSB).

"Say what you mean, and mean what you say." The Lord teaches two lessons in these verses that are essential to good communication:

a. **First, you are to be clear,** completely honest, and concise in all your communications, no matter what their method of delivery. Open, honest communication is one of the most important ingredients in any healthy relationship. With business relationships—whether with associates, employees, clients, investors, or anyone else—your communications should be clear and thorough, but also to the point.

Sadly, due to all the legal and technical jargon so prevalent in society, business communications today are anything but clear and concise. The key elements of contracts are lost amid excessive verbiage, technicalities, and a huge number of conditions and disclaimers. Wise business people and consumers carefully examine the *fine print*, because this is where unfavorable or unacceptable conditions are usually hidden. Many contracts are even intentionally designed to veil information that would raise concerns or questions or discourage their acceptance.

But this should not be. The Lord commands us to shun these practices and to make our agreements as simple and easy to understand as possible. Hence, you should be as thorough as necessary to prevent any misunderstandings, both in the present and in the future. Clear communication up front about conditions and terms will prevent threatening conflicts down the road. The Lord expects you . . .

- to refrain from including excessive or confusing language
- to never be vague, misleading, or deceptive
- to avoid technicalities
- to not hide or veil any provisions or conditions
- to not insert fine print in your contracts that mask questionable disclaimers or conditions
- to be truthful and clear in all your advertising, never misleading or deceptive
- to say yes when you mean yes and no when you mean no—nothing more and nothing less

Notice what Jesus says regarding any communication that is not transparent, sincere, and clear: it is from the evil one—Satan. He is the father of lies and deception (Jn.8:44). He is the inventor and master of half-truths, hidden meanings, fact-twisting, and veiled terms. He is the destroyer of all that is good, and he works tirelessly to sabotage your trustworthiness, your good name, and all relationships vital to your success. Knowing this, you need to guard against Satan's treacherous attempts to undermine all that you are trying to achieve. Never lie; never tell half-truths; never give in to the temptation to deceive.

b. **Second, you are to keep your word**—never break your promises, agreements, or contracts. Jesus' point is clear: you should mean what you say and follow through with it. Always keep your word. Your word should be the only oath and guarantee you need. You should not need to say more than "Yes, I will..." or "No, I will not...." Your word is as good as your character. If you are a person of integrity, your word is strong and not likely to be questioned. But if you are known to be dishonest, people will not trust or believe you.

People often long for the *good old days* when a person's word was his or her bond, and a handshake was as solid as a legally binding contract. While written agreements are a necessary part of doing business, especially today, your word should still be a sign of your ethics and bind you to what you promise.

You are to be faithful to your word in all matters regardless of their significance. When you promise to do something, you should do it, and do so in a timely manner. Whether it is a small obligation such as returning a phone call or keeping an appointment, or a large one such as honoring the terms of a multi-million-dollar contract, you should do what you promised to do. Nothing is more critical to your success in business or in life than being a woman or man of your word.

Be careful not to overcommit yourself or your business. While some in leadership overcommit out of inexperience or simply a lack of planning, others do it deceitfully with hidden motives, which naturally displeases the Lord. In whatever way you fail to keep your word, it reflects badly on you and your business.

Unfortunately, some businesses make and break promises every day. You should never make this a practice.

- If you have a "no questions asked" return policy, then you need to accept returns cheerfully, without any hint of irritation or suspicion.

- If you offer a warranty on your products or services, then you need to honor it without exception.

- If you promise not to sell your customers' information, then you need to reject every offer for your data, regardless how lucrative the offers might be.

- If you promise to perform a service by a certain date and time, then you need to perform it as promised.

- If you agree to fill an order by a specific date, then you need to do everything in your power to make it happen.

- If you advertise the use of a particular brand or quality of materials, then you need to use that brand or something superior, never inferior, less costly parts.

Despite your best intentions, circumstances will arise at times that keep you from doing what you promised. Knowing this, you should allow for that possibility *before* making commitments. You need to allow for unforeseen delays or costs. Give a window of time instead of an exact time. Make provision in your quote or estimate for cost increases. It is far better to give a higher estimate and come in under budget than it is to give a low estimate and end up charging more. And, no matter what line of work you are in, be sure your clients or customers understand whether you are giving them a *quote* or an *estimate*, an *exact* price or an *approximate* price. The distinction is key!

When unforeseen circumstances prevent you from doing what you promised, you should immediately inform your client or customer. And, if possible, you would be wise to offer a discount, extra product, or some additional service in return for your failure to fulfill your promise. This is what honest business people do. They will even take a financial loss if necessary in order to keep their word or make up for being unable to fulfill their promise. In your pursuit of excellence, keeping your word is one of the most important qualities you can possess.

3. *Be kind and respectful—controlled—in all your speech and behavior.*

> "Let your conversation be gracious [kind] and attractive so that you will have the right response for everyone" (Col.4:6, NLT).
>
> "A man of knowledge uses words with restraint, and a man of understanding is even-tempered" (Pr.17:27, NIV '84).
>
> "Words from a wise man's mouth are gracious [kind], but a fool is consumed by his own lips" (Ec.10:12, NIV '84).

Maintaining self-control, especially of your speech and emotions, is absolutely essential as you deal with people, problems, and pressure in your business. Angry, hurtful words and out-of-control tempers are among the most destructive forces in the world. If you are not able to control your words and your emotions, you will damage and eventually destroy your relationships with everyone around you: employees, associates, suppliers, vendors, customers, clients, even family and friends. None of us want this. Therefore, we need to work diligently to be kind and respectful in all our interactions with other people.

You will be tested in this area on a regular, if not daily, basis. In fact, few days will pass without your facing an unpleasant situation with someone. It could be a problem with an associate or employee, or a confrontation with an angry superior. It might be a difficult negotiation or a hard discussion with a supplier not fulfilling the terms of an agreement. It might be a rude or dissatisfied customer pushing you to violate a company policy—or worse yet, your conscience—just to please them.

No matter what the tone of the situation—subdued or volatile, friendly or hostile, orderly or chaotic—you should exercise discipline to keep your emotions in check. The Lord expects you to respond graciously, with kindness and courtesy in all things, at all times (Col.4:6). How? By *practicing* self-control daily, incident by incident, suppressing the urge to lash out or strike back, restraining your words and remaining even-tempered (Pr.17:27). Seek to remain calm; struggle against becoming agitated or upset. And surrender the need to have the last word—which goes a long way toward resolving a conflict and preserving a relationship.

Your business and personal relationships hinge largely on how you treat and speak to others. If you are wise, you will be gracious, pleasant, and encouraging (Ec.10:12). This does not mean that you are always to back down and give everyone else their way. Nor does it mean that you have to concede something when you are right. There are times when you need to be firm, and there are times when you have to hold your ground. But in all things, you are to be kind and respectful in your interactions with others. You are to speak the truth in love—be patient and kind, not intimidating or arrogant, not rude or demanding to have your way.

Gracious words have a dual impact. First, they usually have a pleasant and favorable effect *upon* others. The way to diffuse a tense situation is with a gentle answer. God clearly says this (Pr.15:1). Saying the right thing in the right way at the right time can be extremely effective in bringing about peace and preserving relationships (Pr.25:11). Second, gracious words draw out a pleasant and favorable response *from* others. When you treat others with kindness and respect, you will usually build yourself up in their sight. You will usually win their respect, loyalty, and good will (Pr.11:16; 22:11).

On the other hand, if you constantly react in an unkind or disrespectful way to employees, customers, and others, you will do irreversible damage to yourself and your business or career (v.12). Behaving ungraciously toward others will...

- ruin your reputation and diminish your dignity
- damage your effectiveness in your work
- destroy your relationships with others who are vital to your success
- wreck opportunities for future business

Being gracious toward others—treating them with kindness and respect—is a significant part of fulfilling Christ's great commandment to love others as yourself (Mk.12:31; Ga.5:14). By guarding your words and restraining your emotions, you will spare yourself a great deal of pain, heartache, and disappointment (Pr.21:23). And you will cultivate good, healthy relationships with those people who are essential to your wellbeing and success.

4. *Establish policies and procedures for resolving conflicts among your employees.*

"Casting the lot settles disputes and keeps strong opponents apart" (Pr.18:18, NIV '84).

Understanding the principle of this proverb requires understanding the custom of *casting lots* in Old Testament times. The lots themselves could be things like stones with symbols written on them or sticks with markings that were thrown into a small area and then the results interpreted. Casting lots was a common method of finding answers and making decisions to determine the will of God. People did not view casting lots as a method of chance, and God never condemned the practice. In fact, the people believed that God controlled the landing of the lots and through them ordained His sovereign will.

> **"The lot is cast into the lap, but its every decision is from the LORD" (Pr.16:33, NIV '84).**

> **"We may throw the dice, but the Lord determines how they fall" (Pr.16:33, NLT).**

Based on this confidence, casting lots was a method of resolving disputes as well. The lot prevented two powerful people from coming against each other in a lawsuit or altercation. The parties agreed to allow the lot—under the control of God—to rule in their dispute.

With this understanding, the principle becomes clear: you should establish clearly-defined policies and procedures for resolving conflicts within your company, and you should train your employees to follow them. As you draft policies and conduct training in conflict resolution, you would do well to keep Scriptural principles in mind and incorporate them as much as possible.

In order to avoid costly and harmful lawsuits, you would also be wise to include stipulations for resolving disputes—such as agreeing to private mediation as opposed to going to court—in your contracts with other companies. Establishing a process for dealing with conflicts before disturbances or differences arise will help you greatly as you oversee the business affairs of your company.

5. *Speak softly, not harshly, when dealing with confrontational people or heated situations.*

> **"A soft answer turns away wrath, but a harsh word stirs up anger" (Pr.15:1, NKJV).**

Much of the time, you can diffuse a conflict and its painful consequences by choosing to speak softly. There is a point in every escalating conflict at which the flames are either smothered or else further ignited. And the thing that fully ignites the fire or completely extinguishes it is often a single word. A harsh word can turn the conflict into a raging fire or a gentle word can turn down the heat. A single word, and how it is said, can make all the difference.

You should discipline yourself to deal with combative situations by speaking softly and speaking the truth in a firm, but gentle, way. And you should train your managers (and all employees) to do the same. Use your words to put out fires, not to fan the flames. A great deal is lost due to inflammatory words. Hurt feelings, damaged relationships, and lost productivity can do irreparable harm that could all be avoided if you, as the leader, will humble yourself enough to swallow your pride and speak gentle, gracious words in the heat of the moment.

6. *Do not speak rashly nor act in anger.*

> **"Short-tempered people do foolish things, and schemers are hated" (Pr.14:17, NLT).**
>
> **"People with understanding control their anger; a hot temper shows great foolishness" (Pr.14:29, NLT).**
>
> **"A hot-tempered man stirs up conflict, but a man slow to anger calms strife" (Pr.15:18, HCSB).**

Acting or speaking in anger never resolves conflict; it only incites more heated conflict. Therefore, one of the greatest virtues you need as a business leader is patience or self-control. You have to be patient in the face of conflict and not react in anger. To carry out your responsibilities most effectively, you need to master the impulse to act impetuously, not relying on your emotions in the heat of the moment but rather on facts and reason.

These Scriptures make three strong statements about the quick-tempered:

- They *do foolish things*—deal foolishly with situations and people—making damaging mistakes they later regret (14:17).

- They display their anger—*great foolishness*—before others (14:29). Lashing out in anger reveals that you have no self-restraint, that you disregard the feelings of others. You ignore the accepted standards of right and wrong and common courtesy.

• They *stir up conflict* (15:18). Their angry reactions sometimes create problems where none exist. At other times, they deliberately stir up trouble and provoke reactions where tension is already present.

When we flare up at the shortcomings of others or because a person does something that displeases us, we reveal a heart of sinful pride. It is sinful pride that causes us to feel superior, to feel that we have the right to react in anger. Always keep this truth in mind: our position does not entitle us to treat those who work under us disrespectfully. Remember also that the damage inflicted by harmful words cannot be undone. Hasty decisions cannot be reversed; piercing words spoken in anger cannot be taken back. Therefore, we need to learn to control our tempers, to master our emotional reactions and outbursts. We also need to make it our personal goal never to act or speak rashly or in anger. Instead, we should base our decisions and actions only on fact and reason.

7. *Do not jump to conclusions nor confront any in haste.*

> "Do not go out hastily to argue *your case;* Otherwise, what will you do in the end, when your neighbor puts you to shame?" (Pr.25:8, NASB '77)

> "The first to present his case seems right, till another comes forward and questions him." (Pr.18:17, NIV '84)

> "My dear brothers, take note of this: Everyone should be quick to listen, slow to speak and slow to become angry" (Jas. 1:19, NIV '84)

When in a meeting or engaged in personal conversation, your initial reaction to differences might be to argue or to pursue a confrontation. However, you should always be slow to make accusations or to express an opinion that might be combative or create conflict. This counsel is good advice with family as well as in business interactions and relationships. Often, the facts of a situation are not fully known or as clear as they appear. They may differ dramatically at times, when viewed from another perspective. For these reasons and more, you should hear both sides of a position before reaching any conclusions (Pr.18:17).

Remember, people who are closely involved in a matter are seldom able to be one-hundred-percent objective because of their own self-interests and opinions. They can therefore be very persuasive in convincing you to agree with them. With that in mind, it is wise to wait until all sides of a matter are known before forming an opinion.

If you are quick to make an accusation or to jump to a conclusion, you might be humiliated or disgraced. This could happen for any number of reasons. You might...

- be embarrassed by your own harsh words and angry behavior
- not have all the facts
- be completely mistaken
- have only suspicions, without any proof to support them

You can spare yourself from embarrassment and regret by waiting until your emotions have calmed down and until you have received complete information before taking action. In addition, delaying your response also gives you the opportunity to seek advice from others, if needed, as well as God's direction through prayer.

8. *Overlook minor offenses or mistakes.*

> **"A man's discretion makes him slow to anger,**
> **And it is his glory to overlook a transgression"**
> **(Pr.19:11, NASB '77)**

Confronting some issues creates greater problems than those caused by the issue itself. You can actually lose more by fighting some battles than you will gain if you win them. *Discretion*—insight and sharp, wise reasoning—will enable you to distinguish between offenses that you need to deal with and those that you should simply overlook. If you make an issue of every minor problem or mistake, you will quickly discourage your associates and employees. Rare is the person who does not become frustrated when micromanaged.

As a top leader in your company, you will discredit yourself and lose the respect of others if you choose to confront every minor misdeed. In contrast, if you are patient and kind in overlooking insignificant failures and mishaps, you will earn the respect and appreciation of your employees. Always pause to consider whether it is better to confront a matter or simply to let it go (v.11).

9. *Handle problems and differences with individuals privately as much as possible.*

> **"Argue your case with your neighbor himself, and do not reveal another's secret" (Pr.25:9, ESV).**

Within the work environment, you should always attempt to settle problems privately, if possible. Indeed, the very first step to take in settling a dispute or difference is to carefully think through the problem while seeking the Lord's direction. Then, *if wise*, go directly and privately to the person or persons involved. This is exactly what Jesus taught:

> **"If your brother sins against you, go and show him his fault, just between the two of you. If he listens to you, you have won your brother over" (Mt.18:15, NIV '84).**

Take into account, however, that it may not always be wise to meet with an individual privately. In dealing with conflicts, you need to protect yourself from false accusations and also protect your company from a potential lawsuit. Therefore, many situations will demand that you have a witness present to establish an irrefutable record of a meeting that could be contentious.

Some people are unapproachable and quick-tempered, making them incapable of working out personal differences. In such cases, personally confronting these employees may not be the best course of action. Some offenses, though, are harmful to others and actually violate laws. Such matters require reporting and cannot be dealt with privately. While you should train employees at every level how to resolve conflict, you should also specify clearly when and how personnel are to report various matters, especially those of a serious nature.

In all cases of conflict management, the steps to be taken should be clearly spelled out in your company's policies and procedures. These should be covered with each employee when first hired. Then, when conflict arises, it is wise to follow the instructions of Christ: immediately confront the issue before it has time to fester and cause serious problems. And, as stated above, be sure to keep a record of the conflict in the employee's file in order to legally protect yourself and your company.

10. *Seek reconciliation when others have broken a relationship.*

> "Therefore if you bring your gift to the altar, and there remember that your brother has something against you, leave your gift there before the altar, and go your way. First be reconciled to your brother, and then come and offer your gift" (Mt.5:23-24, NKJV).

> "If another believer sins against you, go privately and point out the offense. If the other person listens and confesses it, you have won that person back. But if you are unsuccessful, take one or two others with you and go back again, so that everything you say may be confirmed by two or three witnesses" (Mt.18:15-16, NLT).

So much of success in business hinges on relationships; therefore, you have to consciously work at preserving relationships with all who are vital to your business—associates, employees, customers/clients, suppliers, vendors, and so on. Yet, no matter how much attention you give some people, issues will still arise despite your best efforts to keep your relationships positive.

When a disagreement, misunderstanding, or conflict arises, you should spring into action in an effort to reconcile with the other person or company. As a follower of Christ, you have a responsibility to pursue reconciliation with others, regardless of who is at fault. Note that the above two Scriptures state this principle explicitly. When another person wrongs or holds something against you or your business, you are to go to them to seek reconciliation.

Either way, you are to take the first step. And you should do so as quickly as possible, before the situation worsens to the point where reconciliation is no longer possible. Failure to be reconciled could damage you and/or your company. The other party could spread rumors or negative publicity, lies or slander against you and your company or instigate a lawsuit (Mt.5:25, see also ch. 6, pt.2, pp.150-152).

But there is another reason why you should pursue reconciliation: a strained relationship with another individual affects your relationship with God. You cannot worship God when you are not right with someone else. In many cases, the disturbed relationship stays on your mind, dominates your thoughts, and interferes with your work. Whether executive or assembly line worker, a disturbed relationship always has an impact on our effectiveness and productivity. This is why Jesus instructs us to reconcile before doing anything else, even before offering our worship to God (Mt.5:23-24).

When you attempt reconciliation, follow the four helpful suggestions below:

First, before initiating the conversation, spend considerable time in prayer. Ask the Lord to give you a humble, peaceful spirit and to show you where you might be wrong. Pray that He will control your words and give you wisdom.

Pray for the other party as well, for the individual(s) personally and for the issue in conflict. Ask God to guide the conversation to a mutually-beneficial result that would bring the most glory to Him. Pray that, if an agreement cannot be reached, the relationship can still be salvaged. Be sure that your emotions are under control before moving forward.

Second, whenever possible, speak to the other party privately, just as Jesus instructed. A one-on-one conversation is the best first step toward reconciliation. However, in a business setting, it is not always possible (see pt.9, pp. 272-273). You would be wise to set up a time with the other party in advance, letting them know that the purpose of the meeting is to seek an amicable solution to the situation.

When you meet, display a humble, conciliatory spirit from the outset. Be sure your tone, demeanor, and body language do not project anything that can be construed negatively by the other party. Speak quietly and calmly, expressing your desire for understanding and for straightening out the matter so that reconciliation can take place (Pr.15:1). Finally, be willing to apologize for your role in the situation.

Third, if the other party is hostile or unwilling to work things out, propose bringing a mutually-agreed upon mediator or negotiator into the discussions. If hostility is involved, it may be wise to meet only when other appropriate parties are present so that an indisputable record can be established (Mt.18:16).

Fourth, be willing to work out a compromise and to make concessions whenever you can. Do not insist on getting the final word or on getting your way in every detail. Remember, you may stand to lose more by failing to reconcile than you would by making some concessions. Weigh your options carefully and objectively. Do not be guided by personal feelings, but by what is best for your business. If an agreement cannot be reached and reconciliation is not achieved, end the matter as kindly as possible. Communicate your willingness to discuss the matter further and to reach an amicable solution. Leave the door open for further conversation and future business dealings.

Christ teaches that your business stands only to benefit from repairing a vital relationship. But beyond the productive results for your business, a far greater objective might be achieved: *you and the person in conflict will be reconciled* (Mt.18:15). In addition, and more important than any amount of money, is the eternal soul of the other individual. If you can make a positive spiritual impact on that person, both of you will be eternally blessed and the cause of Christ will be greatly advanced.

B. You and Your Family

1. *Guard your marriage: Balance your business and marital responsibilities carefully.*

> "And further, submit to one another out of reverence for Christ. For wives, this means submit to your husbands as to the Lord. For a husband is the head of his wife as Christ is the head of the church. He is the Savior of his body, the church. As the church submits to Christ, so you wives should submit to your husbands in everything. For husbands, this means love your wives, just as Christ loved the church. He gave up his life for her to make her holy and clean, washed by the cleansing of God's word. He did this to present her to himself as a glorious church without a spot or wrinkle or any other blemish. Instead, she will be holy and without fault" (Ep.5:21-27, NLT).
>
> "So again I say, each man must love his wife as he loves himself, and the wife must respect her husband" (Ep.5:33, NLT).

Leading a business can be tremendously stressful and have a bearing on how you treat your spouse. Indeed, your stress can put intense pressure on your marriage. Therefore, it is essential to remember that your role as a husband or wife is totally different from your role as a business owner or leader. You need to consciously distinguish between the two roles in your thoughts, attitude, words, and actions.

In the above Scripture, God instructs us all—both husband and wife—to submit to one another. We are to submit to each other lovingly and willingly just as we do to Christ, out of respect and reverence for Him. Scripture then goes on to explain what each of our roles is.

a. **God instructs you—the wife—**to walk in a spirit of submission (vv.22-24). In your business role, you are required to take the lead. You make the rules and the decisions, set the direction and priorities, give instructions and orders—and others follow them. But this is not the wife's role in marriage. Your role is to lovingly and willingly place yourself under your husband's leadership. This is God's will, a commandment that simply expresses His order for the family (v.22).

When God speaks about the husband's being the head of his wife, He is not talking about ability or worth, competence or value, intelligence or advantage. God is talking about *function and order* within the organization of marriage. Every organization has to have a head for it to operate in an efficient and orderly manner, and God has ordained that the husband be the head of the marriage partnership.

As a female business leader, this may present some challenges for you, even if you genuinely want to submit to your husband's leadership in the home. You are used to being in charge and having others submit to you. Nevertheless, God says that in your home, you are to allow your husband to be in charge. Your transitioning between these two roles may require a conscious effort on your part.

You may, in fact, be a stronger and better leader than your husband. You may have started, and now lead, your own enterprise. You may be the CEO or a high-ranking executive of a large corporation. Still, God's order is that your husband be the head of the home. This certainly does not mean that you are to have no part in decisions or in matters affecting you or your family. Nothing could be further from the truth. It simply means that you are to submit to your husband's leadership role. In every marriage, the wife has abilities and strengths that the husband does not have, and vice versa. A wise husband recognizes this, and he and his wife work together to contribute their strengths to the family. Just as those who work with you respect, support, and encourage you as their leader, God wants you to respect, support, and encourage your husband as leader of your home.

Your husband *needs* to feel your respect. This is especially important if your husband's position in his occupation is not as high as yours, or if you earn more money than he does, or if your husband focuses on the needs of the home while you work. In your position of business leadership, you are admired and respected by many. Be sure you give your husband your deepest admiration and respect in his role as well. Acknowledge him as your protector, your chief advisor, your closest confidante. Give him assurance that you hold *him*—not some business associate, corporate titan, or anyone else in the business world—in the highest esteem.

Interestingly, when God's Word discusses the ideal wife, she is described as a virtuous businesswoman (See Pr.31). She is involved in real estate, agriculture, manufacturing, and selling merchandise (Pr.31:13, 16, 18-19, 24). But first, she makes sure that her husband trusts her wholeheartedly (v.11). As a businesswoman, this should be your primary goal. You need to be sure that your husband has complete confidence in you, that He knows your heart is completely devoted to him.

b. **God instructs you—the husband—**to go beyond submission and to love your wife with the very *love of God Himself* (vv.25-27). Grasp the full force of this statement: you are to love your wife with the very love of God Himself (agape love)! *Agape* love is a thoughtful and unselfish love, a giving and *sacrificial* love. It is the love of the mind and will as well as of the heart. True, it is a love of affection and feelings, but it is also a love of determination and commitment. It is a love that wills and commits itself to love a person forever. It is also love that works for the greater good of the wife—that is, what is best for *her*, not for *self*—regardless of what she says or does.

You need to make a conscious effort to love your wife with this kind of love, a sacrificial love. This means approaching things differently with her than you do with your employers or business associates. Your business role requires you to be strong and firm in managing others, but instead of managing your wife, you are to cherish her, be gentle and tender with her. It also means that you are to put your wife first. Meeting her needs should always come before the needs of your business. True, after a long, pressure-filled day at work, you usually want to come home and relax, to put your mind in neutral, so to speak. You have listened to problems and concerns all day long. But you should not allow fatigue or the pressures of your business to rob your wife of the loving husband she needs. She should always know that she is *first* in your heart, that when she needs you, your time and full attention are there for the asking.

c. **God instructs you—husband and wife—to love and respect each other (v.33).** A marriage is built on mutual love and respect. Note that God's Word stresses that the husband is to *love* his wife, and the wife is to *respect* her husband. In no way does this emphasis mean or imply that husbands can show disrespect to their wives or that wives are excused from loving their husbands. Rather, it points out the *primary needs* of the husband and the wife:

- The wife's primary need is for her husband to love her. He is to cherish her and give her alone his (spousal) affection and devotion.

- The husband's primary need is for his wife to respect him and be a loyal companion to him.

God designed men and women with different, yet essential, needs. And He ordained that these needs be met through marriage. Therefore, husbands and wives are to meet each other's needs. After your relationship with God, your most important relationship should be with your spouse.

As the owner or leader of a business, it is critical that you be wholeheartedly committed to your company. But, in doing so, you will need to consciously guard against being more committed or devoted to your business than you are to your marriage. You should never put your work ahead of your spouse. On the contrary, you need to let your spouse know regularly that he or she comes first in your heart and life. And you should faithfully demonstrate this through your attitude, words, and actions.

(For a general, more thorough discussion of what your relationship with your spouse should be, please see *What the Bible Says to the Believer: The Believer's Personal Handbook*, pp. 49-56.)

2. *Guard against provoking your children to resentment or rebellious behavior.*

> **"Fathers, do not provoke [exasperate] your children to anger..." (Ep.6:4a, NASB '77).**

As a parent, you are bound to upset and irritate your children occasionally. Your discipline and correction are seldom enjoyable experiences for them. The very nature of reproof or correction is that of disturbance and irritation. But your children's mild reactions to discipline are not what this instruction is referring to. The word *provoke* means to stir up, to incite or exasperate. In this instance, Scripture is instructing fathers (mothers as well) not to provoke their children to anger, to the point of utter exasperation and resentment.

If you are a business leader *and* a parent, there are some specific ways you can provoke anger, resentment, or rebellion in your children. Carefully consider these two examples:

a. **You can provoke your children** by making your business or job more important to you than they are. You can help prevent this by expressing your love and care for them daily. However, you should not merely *tell* your children that they are more important to you than your business but *show* them by your priorities and actions.

As an owner, executive, or manager, you usually face an overwhelming schedule. It is a constant struggle to do all that your business requires and still fulfill your other critical roles in life, especially your roles as a spouse and parent. Nevertheless, you should always keep this fact in mind: it is crucial that you be involved in your children's lives in every way possible. You need to be there when they need you, spend time with them, play with them, attend their activities whenever possible. You need to find the critical balance between leading a business and being the father or mother your children need and deserve—the kind of parent God wants you to be. Your individual situation will determine how you do this, but you should look for creative ways to devote time and attention to your family. Family members should never be made to feel that they are an inconvenience to you or that your work, recreation, or other interests are more important to you, higher priorities, than they are. (See pt. 3, beginning on next page on making significant schedule changes.)

b. **You can provoke your children** by taking the stress of work out on them. Even on the best days, you are still under tremendous pressure as a business leader. The burden to constantly meet expenses, to set and maintain goals, to attract new business, and to deal with employees and other business contacts never ceases. Unexpected challenges come up regularly and add to your heavy load. By the time you come home at the end of a grueling day, or even a good day, you are usually exhausted physically and mentally. Your patience might be totally spent and your nerves on edge.

But there is one fact you should always keep in mind: it is at the end of your work day that your most important job begins: that of being a mother or father, a wife or husband. The most important people in your life are not those whom you are with from 9 to 5 (possibly longer). They are the people waiting for you at home. Your spouse and children are the ones who matter most. Therefore, you should learn to leave your troubles at the office or at your place of business. You should certainly not take them out on your family. From a practical standpoint, some individuals sort out or work through their frustrations and problems as they travel home. Then as they approach home, they learn to lay aside whatever issue or decision remains until morning or, at least, until everyone goes to bed. Ask God to help you lay aside all that needs to be done and to put on a calm, quiet spirit—a spirit that is tender, kind, patient, gentle, and loving (Col.3:12-14).

Regardless of what is going on in your business, do everything in your power to be upbeat when you walk through the door of your home. Give your family your very best. Your happy and loving spirit will usually be contagious and go a long way toward preventing resentful and rebellious children.

(For a general, more thorough discussion of what your relationship with your children should be, please see *What the Bible Says to the Believer: The Believer's Personal Handbook*, pp. 56-61.)

3. *Make significant changes when your family feels neglected.*

> **"Enjoy life with the woman [or man] whom you love all the days of your fleeting life which He has given to you under the sun; for this is your reward in life, and in your toil in which you have labored under the sun" (Ec.9:9, NASB '77).**
>
> **". . . bring them up in the discipline and instruction of the Lord" (Ep.6:4b, NASB '77).**
>
> **"These commandments that I give you today are to be upon your hearts. Impress them on**

your children. Talk about them when you sit at home and when you walk along the road, when you lie down and when you get up" (Dt.6:6-7, NIV '84).

One of the biggest challenges we face as business leaders is striking the proper balance between fulfilling the demands of work and spending adequate time with family. Making time for our spouses and children while keeping up with our work is indeed a challenge, and one that must be balanced well to keep from toppling. Allowing our work to take away time that we should be spending with family is a form of neglect—neglect that could provoke them to resentment or bad behavior. While our families need to understand that heavy responsibilities demand much of our time, they also need to know that we love them very much. One way of showing love is by carving out or reserving family time and making it a priority. If we are neglecting our families, we have only one way to resolve the situation: alter our schedules accordingly so we can spend more time with them.

You and other Christian business leaders serve a vital purpose for God and society. You provide needed services or products, create employment for people to support themselves and their families, help the needy and disadvantaged, support your communities, and provide resources for ministries to take God's Word to the world. Indeed, these are exceptionally important causes.

But none of them—neither individually nor collectively—is any more important than responsibility to family. In fact, after your commitment to the Lord, your first responsibility is to husband or wife, and then to children. Enjoying life with your spouse, whom the Lord has given you, is to be one of your chief priorities and responsibilities. It is also your reward from God for your labor (Ec.9:9). Why would you want to neglect this great gift?

The gift of marriage also provides you with the wonderful opportunity to make a difference in this world through your children. You can change the future through nurturing your children, by disciplining and instructing them in the

Lord (Ep.6:4b). Why would you want to pass up this precious opportunity? Why would you want to throw it away?

Never forget, parenting is far more than just teaching facts and principles, far more than just passing along information. It is experiencing truth personally and living it out before your children. It is applying God's commandments to your own heart and experiencing the truths within your own life. Your children then see the truth of God's commandments lived before their very eyes, and they absorb the truth automatically. It becomes a part of their lives. This is exactly what God's Word means when it speaks of talking about the commandments when you sit at home, when you walk along the road throughout the day, when you lay down, and when you get up. You are to live by God's commandments, experience them, obey them, and set the dynamic example before your children (Dt.6:6-7). The point is, you are to immerse your children in your life and to immerse yourself in theirs. You are to be a vital part of their lives.

Being influentially involved in your children's lives requires doing whatever is necessary to spend adequate time with your family. Control your schedule rather than letting it control you. You may find...

- that you can delegate more of your responsibilities
- that you can trust other people and train them adequately to do some of what you are doing
- that you can hire someone else—an assistant or an executive or manager—to assume some of your duties
- that you should turn down some business opportunities or expand your personnel and operation

Scripture gives you the keys to wise time management. The first key is understanding the Lord's will (Ep.5:16-17, see also ch. 3, pt.4, pp. 53-55). It is *not* God's will for you to spend every waking moment working. It is *not* God's will for you to neglect your spouse and children. It *is* God's will for you to enjoy life with your spouse and to sacrifice to meet his or her needs. It *is* God's will for you to be there for your children, to nurture, discipline, and instruct them.

The second key to time management is numbering your days—realizing the brevity of life and how precious time is (Ps.90:12). Once time and the opportunities it brings are gone, you cannot reclaim them. If you do not spend adequate time with your spouse and meet his or her needs, somebody else probably will. Then it will be too late. You *cannot* go back and do things differently.

Your time with your children is frighteningly limited, especially the early years of their lives when their trusting hearts are most pliable and teachable. Your window of opportunity is short, and these years go by at a lightening pace. Once they are gone, you *cannot* go back and salvage them. You have only *one* chance, *one* opportunity to be what God commands you to be to your spouse and children.

Indeed, if you are wise, and if you truly love your family, you *will* listen when they tell you that they need you to spend more time with them. You *will* take them seriously and discuss the problem with them when they say they feel neglected. And, if needed, you *will* make significant changes to your schedule in order to spend adequate time with them.

CHAPTER **10**

What Your Responsibilities Are to the Local Community and to the World

Contents

CHAPTER 10

WHAT YOUR RESPONSIBILITIES ARE TO THE LOCAL COMMUNITY AND TO THE WORLD

1. Promote a strong work ethic.

> "Work with your own hands, as we command-ed you, so that you may walk properly in the presence of outsiders and not be dependent on anyone" (1 Th.4:11b–12, HCSB).

> "For even when we were with you, we gave you this rule: 'If a man will not work, he shall not eat.' We hear that some among you are idle. They are not busy; they are busybodies. Such people we command and urge in the Lord Jesus Christ to settle down and earn the bread they eat. And as for you, brothers, never tire of doing what is right" (2 Th.3:10-13, NIV '84).

Obviously, you must work hard in order to succeed. However, the people working with you must also be dil-igent if your company or division is going to be success-ful. But the sad truth is, within our society, some people are lazy. They do not want to work. They have no drive to achieve, and they want to do as little as possible for as much money as possible.

However, God's Word is clear: Work! If people are able to work, they should be working (1 Th.4:11b). And if they will not work, then they should not eat; that is, their idle-ness should not be condoned nor encouraged by support from government or social programs (2 Th.3:10). Note that this command deals only with those who choose to be idle and refuse to work. It is not dealing with those who are unable to find employment or are unable to work due to disability. If people are able to work, they are supposed to work. If they refuse, they are not to be fed; they are not to be allowed to sponge off the government, church, commu-nity, society, or family. There is no excuse for a person's not working if they are able to work—not in God's sight. Even if they cannot find a paying job, they should be working to secure more education and/or to retrain themselves. They should be working around their house and throughout their community, city, or village—volunteering to help the needy or to make their community a safer, cleaner, and more attractive and appealing place to live. Think how different neglected communities, villages, and inner cities would be if only a few people within each would take the lead and truly obey this commandment of God: *Work with your hands.* If the unemployed were put to work through public work programs and community services, just imagine how much stronger our society would be.

The phrase "work with your own hands" speaks of working to support yourself as opposed to sponging off others (1 Th.4:11b). There may be times when potential workers need help, but these occasions should not be permanent, not if the workers are able to provide for themselves or their families. God says that all able-bodied people are to be responsible: all are to work and not become dependent on others to take care of them. Yes, seeking and accepting temporary help is sometimes necessary. But permanent assistance for those who can provide for themselves is not God's way.

God says we all should work in order to live properly before others (1 Th.4:12). Few in this world respect those who exploit or sponge off others, refusing to work or to educate or train themselves for gainful employment. This is the reason we, as true followers of Christ, should set a dynamic example in our work. We demonstrate how God wants us to live, and we bear a far stronger example for society and for Christ. And hopefully, through our diligent labor, we influence and win the respect of outsiders (unbelievers).

With this truth in mind, you, the leader of a business, have to guard against being idle on the job, wasting time, or handling personal matters on company time. Also guard against sponging off your business—the business you own or manage or oversee—by squandering resources or money that could be used to boost the company, improve a product or service, or help employees. As business leaders within the community and nation, you are the people who provide most of the jobs for the population. For that reason, you have a unique opportunity to take the lead in challenging others by setting a dynamic example in being responsible and working hard.

You also have the opportunity to stand against idleness and the public support of those who are unwilling to work. Your position as a business leader may open doors for you to influence society, both locally and nationally. You should seize every opportunity to promote a strong work ethic and what God says about those in society who will not work and sponge off those who do. In addition, you should take the lead in stirring up and joining hands with government and community leaders in . . .

- organizing public works projects for the legitimately unemployed
- challenging the idle and spongers of society to get up and go to work
- standing against the ongoing public support of those who refuse to work

As an employer, you seek to hire individuals with a strong work ethic. But no matter how diligent you may be in the hiring process, you will inevitably employ some who are not productive. Some people are simply lazy slackers who do not want to work and cannot be helped. You are under no obligation—to God, to any individual, or to society—to carry anyone who will not work. In fact, as a faithful steward (manager) of what has been committed to you, you have an obligation to employ only those who are industrious and productive.

Others, however, have not been taught to work and have not learned a strong work ethic. The Lord will bless you if you if attempt to train and help these individuals. Those who *will* listen, learn, and improve will make you and your business prosperous. And by caring enough about the people you hire to train them, you will help them to prosper. You will fulfill one of the purposes to which God has called you as a business owner or executive: to help people support themselves and find fulfillment, meaning, and significance in life through productive labor. By promoting and teaching a strong work ethic, you will help your company, your employees, and society as a whole.

2. *Promote a positive perspective and philosophy toward work.*

> "The LORD God took the man and put him in the garden of Eden to work it and keep it." (Gen. 2:15, ESV).

Many people in our society have a flawed perspective toward work. As a result, they hate their jobs and dread going back to work after a weekend, holiday, or vacation. Countless individuals throw their money away on gambling and get-rich-quick schemes, all with the hope of striking it rich and never having to work again. Others simply refuse to work, choosing instead to sponge off those who do.

Rather than despising work, though, we need to see it for what it is: work is a blessing—a gift from God (Ec.5:19). Many people misunderstand Scripture, thinking that work is a curse inflicted upon humanity after Adam's and Eve's sin. Nothing could be further from the truth. When God created Adam, He placed him in the Garden of Eden and gave him a job: Adam was to tend to the earth, to look after and take care of it (Ge.2:15).

In spite of the difficulties and frustrations of laboring in an imperfect world with imperfect people, work is still a blessing. You need to recognize its purpose and many benefits and then help your employees do the same. Their having a proper perspective toward work and their jobs will make them, you, and your business more successful. Therefore, you should promote the following truths about work whenever you have the opportunity.

a. **Work provides for life's necessities and some of its desires.**

> **"For even when we were with you, we gave you this rule: 'If a man will not work, he shall not eat'" (2 Th.3:10, NIV '84).**

> **"Whoever works his land will have plenty of bread, but he who follows worthless pursuits lacks sense" (Pr.12:11, ESV).**

If you think about it, the things we truly need to survive are few. Jesus identified food, water, and clothing as the necessities of life (Mt.6:25-32). We might appropriately add shelter to His list. In today's modern world, we consider many other things to be necessary also, but, in reality, we can survive with the items listed above, and multitudes across the globe do just that every day.

Through our labor, critical needs are met. And this is exactly what God intended: we are to work in order to have the things we need. In fact, Scripture even states that if people are not willing to work, they should not eat (2 Th.3:10).

By working, we secure not only the things we need but also many things we desire, things that are not necessities. As Scripture notes, the diligent are often blessed with *plenty*—an abundance far more than they need—which enables them to acquire some of the comforts and luxuries of life (Pr.12:11). While God's Word warns us repeatedly about being covetous and materialistic, it also states that God richly supplies us with all things to enjoy (1 Ti.6:17; Ec.5:19). These things, things we do not need, but nevertheless enjoy, are attainable for us through the blessing of work.

b. **Work provides a constructive or productive use of time.**

> **"We hear that some among you are idle. They are not busy; they are busybodies. Such people we command and urge in the Lord Jesus Christ**

> **to settle down and earn the bread they eat"**
> **(2 Th.3:11-12, NIV '84).**

The human mind is *always* active, never still. It is thinking either positive or negative thoughts, building either responsible or irresponsible behavior. As is commonly said, an idle mind is the devil's playground. This is why so many of the idle—regardless of their age—get into trouble.

The fact is, people need something to do, something to occupy their minds and their time. Those who do not work often fill their time with activities that are harmful to themselves, to others, or to society. Or they waste their time on activities that are not productive, having their needs met by sponging off those who do work. As Paul wrote in this passage, this was the case in the early church, and it is also true in our society today. The answer to this serious problem is simple: *work.* God's Word gives a straightforward command: idle people are to get busy by working and using their time productively. They are to stop occupying their time with things that are unproductive or destructive. Note that God is not talking about individuals who are unable to work due to disability or the unavailability of jobs. He is addressing those who could be working but choose not to.

c. **Work enables us to build wealth honestly and respectably.**

> **"Idle hands make one poor, but diligent hands bring riches" (Pr.10:4, HCSB).**

> **"Wealth *obtained* by fraud dwindles, But the one who gathers by labor increases *it*" (Pr.13:11, NASB '77).**

People obviously need money to pay for the necessities of life. Sadly, though, many do not want to work for it, so they do whatever they have to to get it. Those who will not work usually get their money dishonestly or dishonorably—whether by sponging off the government (welfare) or other people, begging, stealing, selling drugs, prostitution, or any number of other shameful and contemptible methods.

In contrast, there are individuals who work hard to *earn* money honestly and respectably, so they can acquire the things they need and want. It is work that empowers us to build wealth, to save, to invest, to prepare for the coming time when we might not be able to work. By building up wealth, we are able to leave something behind for loved ones, for other worthwhile causes, and most important, for the spread of the gospel throughout the world.

d. **Work enables us to help others—those who cannot work.**

> **"And I have been a constant example of how you can help those in need by working hard. You should remember the words of the Lord Jesus: 'It is more blessed to give than to receive' " (Acts 20:35, NLT).**

> **"Let him who stole steal no longer, but rather let him labor, working with *his* hands what is good, that he may have something to give him who has need" (Ep. 4:28, NKJV).**

One of the greatest blessings of working—and one of the greatest joys in life—is being able to share what we have with those in need. All who obey the command to help the needy know firsthand what Jesus meant when He said, "It is more blessed to give than to receive" (Ac.20:35). Keep in mind that the needy referred to in Scripture are those who *cannot* work due to circumstances beyond their control, as opposed to those who *will not* work.

God's Word is clear: we are to work enough so we can help meet the needs of those who cannot work. This obligation extends, first, to our family (1 Ti.5:4, 16), then to other believers (Ga.6:10), then to society as a whole.

Many people within industrialized nations are guilty of selfishness despite having a tenderness and concern for the needy in the world. But minimal giving and fleeting moments of concern are not enough to fulfill God's requirement that we share and meet the needs of our fellow human beings throughout the world. Every day that we awaken and get out of bed, the world is reeling under the weight of *masses...*

- who are hungry and literally starving to death
- who are without safe drinking water
- who are without adequate clothing
- who are diseased and without medical care
- who have no roof or shelter over their heads
- who have no one to protect or teach them
- who have never heard of God's love and salvation through His Son, Jesus Christ

What is the answer? How are we to help meet the desperate needs of the world: the physical, spiritual, temporal, and eternal needs? Through diligent work—working to have enough to help others. This is the will of God: working to have enough to give away. Work is to be honest and, yes, it is to meet our family's needs. However, working just for ourselves and our family is selfish if we have more than we need. And selfishness corrupts. It leaves our hearts empty and our work aimless. But working to help others in the name of Christ—this is the will of God. This is the only way the needs of the world can be met. Work is to be for the Lord's purpose, the cause that provides the means to reach out and help people (1 Jn.3:17).

You should practice this truth and model it for all who work with you. And you should encourage your associates and employees to give to help others as well. Get your business personally involved in meeting needs within your community. Initiate projects such as holding food drives for the needy, purchasing school supplies for underprivileged students, collecting clothing and blankets for the homeless, and so on. The list of opportunities in nearly every community is endless. As a business, adopt schools, work with civic organizations who assist the needy, hold fundraisers for worthy causes and foundations. Lead your employees to join you and your company in giving so that you can do more to help the needy. Make it your cause, your purpose as a team, your reason for getting up and going to work and doing your best every day. Believe, practice, and teach your employees the heart-gripping truth of Proverbs 19:17:

> **"Whoever is generous to the poor lends to the Lord, and he will repay him for his deed" (Pr. 19:17, ESV).**

e. **Work gives us a sense of purpose, satisfaction, and fulfillment in life.**

> **"Then I realized that it is good and proper for a man to eat and drink, and to find satisfaction in his toilsome labor under the sun during the few days of life God has given him—for this is his lot. Moreover, when God gives any man wealth and possessions, and enables him to enjoy them, to accept his lot and be happy in his work—this is a gift of God" (Ec.5:18-19, NIV '84).**

> **"A man can do nothing better than to eat and drink and find satisfaction in his work. This too, I see, is from the hand of God, for without him, who can eat or find enjoyment?" (Ec.2:24-25, NIV '84).**

God created us to have a strong sense of purpose and of self-worth. As human beings, we are mental and emotional creatures. We need strong purpose in life, to feel that we are worthwhile, that what we do is significant and counts for something. We also need a strong self-image, to feel that we are important and acceptable, that we matter to other people. Both purpose and self-image come, to a great degree, from the work that we do. If our work is significant, then we have a reason for getting up in the morning and for living. This is the way God made us. This is the reason God charged the first human being to work and to look after the Garden of Eden and the world. We need to think, plan, discover, and work; because, ultimately, we will all find satisfaction in work and in doing something worthwhile. This capacity for work and satisfaction in work are gifts from the hand of God. (Ec.2:24; 5:18). So are the ability and strength to work.

But work alone does not bring complete satisfaction. Apart from the Lord, there is no permanent enjoyment in life, no lasting sense of fulfillment (Ec.2:25). This is the driving theme of *Ecclesiastes* (1:1–2:26). Even though Solomon was highly successful—extraordinarily accomplished, powerful, and wealthy—he testified that he hated his life and that he hated his work (2:17-18). Why? Because he had forsaken his relationship with God. He left God out of His life. When he was first starting out in his career, Solomon sought the Lord's help and was dedicated to Him. But as he became more and more successful, he drifted further and further away from God. As a result, his life, work, and success were meaningless, futile, and empty. All of his education, all of his hard work, all of his accomplishments, all of his wealth and possessions, all of his pleasures, all of his power—all of it meant absolutely nothing without God at its center.

What a lesson for every aspiring and accomplished business leader! It is a lesson we should never forget. And it is a lesson we should teach to our associates and employees whenever we have the opportunity. Work gives us the satisfaction of helping others and of committing to a cause greater than ourselves, helping to make the world a better place. And when we know the Lord and labor as though we are doing so for Him, we have a sense of fulfillment when the work day is done. With God at the center of our lives and our work, we will find true purpose and meaning, satisfaction and fulfillment.

3. *Set an example in the workplace: Live out the teachings of God our Savior.*

> "[Christian employees are] . . . to show that they can be fully trusted, so that in every way they will make the teaching about God our Savior attractive" (Tit.2:10b, NIV '84).

What a descriptive way to state this instruction! As a Christian, you are to show that you can be fully trusted so that the teachings of Christ will become attractive to your clients, patients, customers, suppliers, and fellow workers. This means that you are to live for Christ and follow His instructions in the workplace as well as everywhere else:

- You are to be an example in following workplace policies and instructions, in building up and promoting the company, and in serving the public by providing the very best products or services possible.
- You are to set an example in being trustworthy and hard working.
- You are to be totally honest—never lying, cheating, or stealing.
- You are to be kind, helpful, caring, and encouraging.
- You are to be positive and joyful—rejoicing in the privilege of having a job, earning a living, and contributing to society.
- You are also to rejoice daily in the redemption God our Savior has provided—as long as it is not prohibited in the workplace. If prohibited, rejoice and praise the Lord silently within your own heart.

God's instruction to you as a Christian business owner or leader is unmistakable: you are to be trustworthy and dependable in the workplace. If you are, then some who see you and observe your behavior will be attracted to the Christ-like qualities within you, the teachings of God, your Savior. You will set an example for other workers, and your life will be a strong and effective witness for the Lord.

4. *Stand against the unfair treatment and oppression of laborers throughout society.*

> "Again, I observed all the oppression that takes place under the sun. I saw the tears of the oppressed, with no one to comfort them. The oppressors have great power, and their victims are helpless" (Ec.4:1, NLT).

> "The people of the land have practiced oppression and committed robbery, and they have wronged the poor and needy and have oppressed the sojourner without justice. And I searched for a man among them who should build up the wall and stand in the gap before Me for the land, that I should not destroy it; but I found no one" (Ezk.22:29-30, NASB '77).

Throughout the world, people are hurting and suffering under the weight of oppression, injustice, inequality, and abuse. Many laborers—trapped by their circumstances and a lack of opportunity—have no choice but to work for greedy, unprincipled employers. These employers take advantage of their workers by paying unfair wages, making unreasonable demands, and ignoring unsafe working conditions. So, when we see businesses or employers oppressing the less fortunate or less powerful in life—we should be deeply troubled. We need to be alert to the circumstances under which many people live and work: the sweat shops, the labor camps, the factories that enslave adults and even children for the purpose of the almighty dollar. We should be both alarmed and disturbed by the scant wages and appalling working conditions imposed upon some people in our communities and throughout the nations of the world.

Business leaders have varying degrees of influence within their communities or areas of service. Some have minimal influence, and others have national or international influence. No matter what the size and scope of your business and influence, you should not close your eyes to the unfair practices and wretched conditions to which so many people around the world are subjected—even here at home. Instead, you need to make sure that you are providing safe and adequate working conditions as well as fair wages for your employees, and then stand together with others in defense of workers who are mistreated.

God longs and looks for people of influence who will stand in the gap by insisting on righteousness and fairness (Ezk.22:30). He is continually searching for leaders in the business world who will not only do what is right in their own businesses, but also stand boldly against the mistreatment of laborers throughout society.

The world desperately needs leaders in business who have character, integrity, and compassion, leaders who will courageously speak up for righteousness. Righteousness—simply doing what is right—builds the foundation of a strong society, and God longs for business leaders who will seek to expand a righteous society to the ends of the earth. One way you—as an individual business owner or manager—can do this is to deal with your own employees fairly in all areas, and then take a stand against the unfair treatment and oppression of laborers around the world.

5. *Respect the government and its authority.*

> "Submit yourselves for the Lord's sake to every authority instituted among men: whether to the king, as the supreme authority, or to governors, who are sent by him to punish those who do wrong and to commend those who do right. For it is God's will that by doing good you should silence the ignorant talk of foolish men. Live as free men, but do not use your freedom as a cover-up for evil; live as servants of God. Show proper respect to everyone: Love the brotherhood of believers, fear God, honor the king" (1 Pe.2:13-17, NIV '84).
>
> "Remind the people to be subject to rulers and authorities, to be obedient, to be ready to do whatever is good, to slander no one, to be peaceable and considerate, and to show true humility toward all men" (Tit.3:1-2, NIV '84).

As a leader in business, what should your attitude be toward the government and its authority? In no uncertain terms, God says that you are to respect or submit to those in power; you are to obey the laws of the nation in which you live and work. God's instruction is especially compelling because the believers of that day were being severely persecuted by the government. Most, if not all, had been forced to flee their homes. They had to leave everything behind: property, clothing, furnishings, businesses, and jobs. Respecting government authority is sometimes difficult, especially if the government is taxing you beyond reason, hampering your business through endless regulations, or persecuting you because of your faith in God and obedience to His Word. Nevertheless, the word *submit* (respect) is an imperative; it is a strong command. God expects you—both in your personal life and in your business or job—to respect the laws at every level of government.

Note some of the key points in these passages of Scripture:

a. **You are to respect civil authority,** because authority has been *ordained* by God (Ro.13:1; 1 Pe.2:13-15; Tit.3:1). It is God's will that government exists and that leaders have the authority to rule within the government. Obviously, at each level of government, many officials are faithful to what is right and do an excellent job; some are uncaring or corrupt and do an awful job.

Generally, you can do little about how the authorities in government conduct their affairs. However, you can do a great deal about your behavior as a business owner or leader in relation to these authorities, and God is very clear about what your behavior is to be. You are to obey all civil authority.

God has ordained that it is the responsibility of civil government to establish laws and regulations for the well-being of society. As you are well aware, many of these laws apply directly to businesses and have a significant impact on the way your company operates. Some laws are designed to protect your business or company;

whereas others protect your community, employees, consumers, or the environment. You are to follow the laws and regulations the authorities establish, whether dealing with employment practices and policies, environmental issues, safety practices, tax requirements, discrimination and equality issues, or any other matter they decree. Unquestionably, without the government and its laws, society would be in utter chaos; lawlessness and violence would be out of control. There would be no civilized society or community.

As stated, some of the government's regulations are helpful, but, practically speaking, others may hinder or restrict you in the operation of your business. Certain laws may even be unfair and cost you a significant amount of money. Nevertheless, God's commandment stands. We are to comply with the government's laws and regulations, not merely out of fear of penalties or fines or even imprisonment, but out of obedience to Christ (Lk.20:25). As followers of Christ, we are not to be lawless citizens but law-abiding citizens.

However, when the opportunity arises, you should point out exactly how unfair, unnecessary regulations affect your business negatively, how they drive down profits, increase prices, and prevent you from hiring more employees.

On a local level, you can address many of these issues personally. On the state or national level, being a part of a trade association or coalition of businesses often affords you the benefit of being represented before government bodies and officials on such matters. The more you and others stand up against unfair and costly regulations, the stronger society will become. After all, it is through businesses that the products and services flow out to help meet needs. And it is businesses that provide meaningful work for people and keep money flowing to sustain life, bringing a sense of satisfaction and fullness to the human soul.

Remember, those who have not had the day-to-day experience of running a business—no matter their level of education—live in a theoretical world of business. And the theoretical world is very different from the reality of a company's daily operations. A regulation may look good on paper, but its application can be very costly, leading to stymied growth or massive unemployment and bankruptcies. So, if you believe certain laws or regulations imposed on you (your company) are unfair or unnecessary, speak up and add your voice to those who are opposing such unjust laws. Speak up clearly and passionately, but do so to the right person, through the right channels, in the right venue, and in the right spirit—remembering always that before other people, you are a representative of Christ.

At this point, a question naturally arises. Is there ever a time when you are *not* to submit to civil authorities, when God does *not* require you to obey a law or regulation? Scripture allows just one exception to obeying government and those in authority: when the mandate of the government goes against what God teaches in His Word. When the government orders us to disobey God, "we must obey God rather than men" (Acts 5:27-29). You should always do what is right, moral, and just. You will serve the highest good of the government and society by insisting upon the execution of *true justice* and *righteousness* within society. By resisting unjust and immoral laws, you strengthen society and work for greater justice by bringing about change within the state or nation. However, the justice and morality you pursue must be that of God's Holy Word and not of your own making.

If you are the owner or a board member of a business, you are the one who has to determine if a law or regulation is unjust. Because you operate your business in a secular society, you may need to seek both spiritual and legal counsel as to what issues are under the government's authority and what issues are under God's (Lk.20:25).

If you are an executive or manager in a business owned by others, then your decision or opinion regarding the law or regulation may be different from that of the owner or board of directors. It is ultimately their decision whether or not to follow a law that is unjust. If they order you to comply with a law or regulation that your conscience tells you is wrong, you may be forced to choose between following their instructions or resigning your position.

In either case, if God leads you to take a stand, you should stand, regardless of the cost. As stated above, if human law stands against God's law, you are to obey God rather than the human law. But you should never disobey a law and claim it is unjust when in fact it is not. You have no right to disobey merely because you do not like a law or because it is not beneficial to you or your business. The point is this: once you receive Christ, you are God's servant, not the servant of your own ideas, purposes, or desires. You have no right to break the laws of government unless they directly oppose or violate God's perfect law of love, for love demands *true justice* and the *equal and moral treatment of every citizen*.

b. **You are to respect all citizens (1 Pe.2:17).** Keep in mind that at the time Peter wrote his first epistle, the early church and its believers were surrounded by the most corrupt people imaginable. Believers found themselves among heathen worshipers, people who wallowed around in a cesspool of lawlessness, immorality, injustice, and drunkenness. Yet, Peter instructs readers to respect *all citizens*, the bad as well as the good. Of course, this does not mean to respect them because of their bad behavior, but rather...

- because they are God's creation, equal in His sight and greatly loved by Him

- because their souls are of more value than all the wealth in the world

No person is to be looked down upon or disrespected, no matter who he or she may be: poor or rich, corrupt or honest, bad or good, evil or righteous, destructive or constructive.

Just as Christ showed compassion and reached out to help everyone, so should we. No person is to be counted beyond reach or help. God's charge is clear: respect all citizens.

In whatever capacity you serve as a business leader, use your visibility and position as influences for good. You have the opportunity to be a shining example before believers and unbelievers alike. Knowing that, be a role model for order and discipline, righteousness and justice, respect and honor. Be careful to set the right example before other leaders in your company, your employees, and the community at large by respecting, honoring, and submitting to civil authorities. Even if you disagree with or must take a stand against an unjust law, always do so with an attitude of respect. In fact, your respect, or lack thereof, for the institution of government and its officials demonstrates a lot about your character as a leader. It either strengthens or weakens others' respect for you.

6. *Pay taxes—all you owe—honestly.*

> "'Now tell us what you think about this: Is it right to pay taxes to Caesar or not?' But Jesus knew their evil motives. 'You hypocrites!' he said. 'Why are you trying to trap me? Here, show me the coin used for the tax.' When they handed him a Roman coin, he asked, 'Whose picture and title are stamped on it?' 'Caesar's,' they replied. 'Well, then,' he said, 'give to Caesar what belongs to Caesar, and give to God what belongs to God'" (Mt.22:17-21, NLT).

> "Therefore, it is necessary to submit to the authorities, not only because of possible punishment but also because of conscience. This is also why you pay taxes, for the authorities are God's servants, who give their full time to governing. Give everyone what you owe him: If you owe taxes, pay taxes; if revenue, then revenue; if respect, then respect; if honor, then honor" (Ro.13:5-7, NIV '84).

The government of the nation in which we live and do business provides certain services for us. Therefore, we owe payment, or taxes, to that government for the services we receive. Personal feeling and opinions aside, it is as simple as that.

Never forget: the institution of government was established by God Himself. For this reason, He commands us to submit to government authority and rule.

When civil authorities establish a system of taxation, we are to pay what is required. The Scripture above gives us two compelling reasons for paying our fair share (Ro.13:5-6a):

- to avoid facing punishment by the government
- to avoid feelings of guilt, that is, for conscience' sake

If we fail to pay the taxes we or our businesses owe, we resist God's will and, consequently, violate our consciences. And bear this fact in mind: it is the conscience that determines our state of being. A restful conscience brings peace; a disturbed conscience brings restlessness and pain. As a person of integrity, not paying taxes will disturb your conscience and force you to live under the restless fear of being caught and punished. For this reason, God's Word exhorts us to maintain a clean conscience, to do nothing that violates our consciences:

"So I strive always to keep my conscience clear before God and man" (Ac.24:16, NIV '84).

Another very practical reason we should pay taxes is this: government is ordained to provide public services or benefits *through taxes.* These services obviously must be funded. As part of the ordained government, civil authorities are God's servants. They carry out their assignments, and so they need to be paid (v.6b). As officials appointed by God, they are to minister to the citizens by providing the following essential benefits:

- The government provides justice and protection for its citizens. It establishes laws that keep the strong from dominating the weak, that keep life from becoming the law of the jungle. The government also provides services such as roads, public transportation, electricity, garbage disposal, and other public works that help to bind a nation together and to make life more efficient and comfortable.

- The government keeps the world from diving into chaos. Whatever peace is known within a country, it is known through the government that exists. It is not perfect peace, but usually within its boundaries there is a semblance of peace. Therefore, we are to work for worldwide peace through the framework of government.

Every citizen is obligated to pay taxes for the benefits he or she receives from the state or federal government. These benefits come through the cooperative effort of people within a state. None of us could receive these benefits acting as individuals. Even the wealthiest among us could not supply all the services for themselves that the government provides through the joint cooperation of us all. We enjoy these benefits and privileges because the government has brought them about and made them available to us. For this reason, we are obligated to the state to pay our fair share of taxes.

The Lord Jesus Christ sanctioned the paying of taxes, both in His teaching and in His actions. When asked if it is right to pay taxes, Jesus plainly taught that all of us—whether as individuals or as representatives of companies—are to pay our fair share of taxes (Mt.22:17-21). Scripture records that Jesus paid His taxes, demonstrating good citizenship and setting an example for us to follow (Mt.17:24-27). Consequently, not to pay what we legitimately owe is to live in disobedience to Christ. And disobedience results in our . . .

- forfeiting God's blessing
- being exposed as dishonest—as lawbreakers

- losing our Christian testimony
- bringing shame to Christ's name

The loss of God's blessing upon our lives—both personally and professionally—is a staggering price to pay just to have or to keep more money in the bank. As Jesus taught, we are to support the government and pay our fair share for the benefits we receive.

As a good steward of both your personal finances and your company's, you should certainly take advantage of every opportunity the government affords you to reduce your taxes. There is nothing wrong with claiming every deduction and taking every credit available. At the same time, we always need to be impeccably honest in doing so, for the very reasons God's Word gives us in this passage. Furthermore, it is critical that we base our actions solely on what God tells us to do, not on our personal views about the fairness of the taxes or the character of the individuals or government collecting the taxes. It is God, not the government, to whom we must ultimately answer!

7. *Be wise in using the world's resources—protecting, not destroying, the earth.*

> **"Then God blessed them, and God said to them, 'Be fruitful and multiply; fill the earth and subdue it; have dominion over the fish of the sea, over the birds of the air, and over every living thing that moves on the earth'" (Ge.1:28, NKJV).**
>
> **"The Lord God . . . put him in the Garden of Eden to . . . take care of it" (Ge.2:15, NIV '84).**

God has committed the management of the earth and all its resources into our hands. We have a heavy responsibility to use the world's resources wisely in our businesses. Thus, we should always strive to protect the earth and to conserve and replenish the earth's assets for future generations, never harming or destroying it.

When God created Adam, the first human being, He gave him two clear assignment that subsequently apply to every human being, two tasks that express our primary responsibility while on this earth. First, God commanded humans to *subdue* the earth (Ge.1:28). This means...

- to rule and master the earth
- to look after and take care of the earth
- to investigate, research, and discover the earth's resources
- to develop and use the resources of the earth
- to be wise in managing the earth with all its provisions

The earth is under our care. God has given us the earth as a gift, an inheritance, a trust. It is our estate, our home and property—and our responsibility. We have a duty and obligation to look after it.

As we manage the earth, we must acknowledge that God's earthly provision meets all of humanity's needs. This means that, in one way or another, your business uses what God has provided to meet a particular need or desire. You offer a product or service that makes people's lives better or easier. Everything you use in your business begins with something God made, some element of the earth. Even if you utilize human ability to perform a service, materials made from the earth's elements make it possible for you to do so. Human beings cannot create; we can only discover or invent. Consequently, everything we have—every product, every source of power, every convenience, every ingredient, every material, every tool or complex machine, every mode of transportation, every medication, every modern gadget—is the result of human beings' having used the knowledge God has given to subdue the earth.

Second, God also commands us to *fill* the earth, to *replenish* it, to assure that the earth continues to be filled with the things needed for our existence (Ge.2:15). God commanded the first human—and subsequently us—to *work* the earth and to *take care of* it. God has made us personally responsible for His creation, the earth and its resources.

With this in mind, you are to take this responsibility seriously and do everything you can to make the best use of the world's resources in your business. This includes conserving energy as well as conserving, recycling, and properly disposing of materials. You should constantly be evaluating your processes, doing studies, and challenging your employees to find new ways to conserve. And when new technologies are discovered that significantly preserve earthly resources, you should update to the latest conservation methods as soon as financially possible to save power and materials. You should not be set in your ways but always open to learning new skills and processes. Doing so will save you time and ultimately money as well as making you a better steward of the earth's resources.

Simply stated, you are a steward of the environment and your business's impact upon it. The environment matters to God; therefore, it ought to matter to you. You should do everything possible not to pollute the air or water, nor to contaminate or destroy the earth or heavens above. You have a responsibility to do your part, to keep the byproducts of your business from damaging God's creation.

Another element of protecting the earth is preserving its beauty. You should strive to make your properties attractive and to maintain them meticulously. When you develop land for business, keep as much of its natural beauty as possible. Also try to replace the resources you have taken from the land in worthwhile ways, for instance, with beautiful gardens, parks, or natural areas.

While some people go overboard in their philosophies and activism for saving the environment, others lean too far in the other direction. Sadly, they care little about their God-given responsibility to take care of His creation. Being a good steward of the earth and its resources may add to your business expenses, but know that God will bless you when you honor Him by doing your part to care for the wonderful world He has given us.

CHAPTER 11

What Your Attitude Toward Money Should Be

Contents

CHAPTER 11

WHAT YOUR ATTITUDE
TOWARD MONEY SHOULD BE

1. *Fight against making money your master.*

> "No one can serve two masters, for either he
> will hate the one and love the other, or he will
> be devoted to the one and despise the other. You
> cannot serve God and money" (Mt.6:24, ESV).

As a business leader, you have a key decision to make.
You must decide whether God or money will be your Lord.
Christ is blunt: you cannot serve both.

Your role as a business leader requires you to take the
matter of making money seriously. Obviously, a business
will not survive, nor will leaders keep their positions, when
no effort is being made to be profitable. However, as you are
pursuing money (or its equivalent) that is so essential in life,
you need to guard against allowing money to control you.

As Christ says, a person cannot be devoted to both God
and money. If you are devoted to—focused solely upon—
money, you will not be faithful in your walk with God. If
money is your master, then God is not, and you will lean
toward putting your desire for money before the welfare
of your company, job, employees, and society in general.
Consider what could occur if money is your master:

a. **You might be tempted** to do whatever it takes to make
the most money, regardless of what God says is right.

b. **You might be tempted** to cut corners in order to increase profits, or sacrifice quality, and, perhaps even
the safety or welfare of employees and consumers.

c. **You might be tempted** to pay your employees as little as possible instead of paying them adequately and
fairly.

d. You might be tempted to be greedy, hoarding your money or spending it on extravagant and unnecessary things, instead of being generous and giving to help meet the needs throughout society.

Remember two strong warnings from Scripture. First, the desire or longing to be rich—the love of money—is a destructive trap (1 Ti.6:9). Second, the love of money is a root of all kinds of evil (1 Ti.6:10). When money is your master—whether you hoard it or enjoy a luxurious lifestyle—you walk on a treacherous path. At the end of that road lies crushing sorrow and destruction.

For this reason, as a business owner or leader, you should continually examine yourself. You should keep a close guard on your heart lest money and possessions become a consuming passion (Pr.4:23). Staying close to God and working as He instructs in His Holy Word is crucial. If you are devoted to God, He will be the master of your money. And if you are fully dedicated to serving Him through your business or career, then you will avoid the dangerous pitfalls greed can create, for, as Jesus said, "you cannot serve God and money." Loving God and serving Him wholeheartedly will keep you from becoming enslaved to money and possessions or the pursuit of them. In the process, you will fulfill your great purpose of providing an essential product or service to your community or society in general. At the same time, you will be a dynamic example of reliance on the Lord and of keeping money in the proper perspective.

2. Avoid becoming materialistic, seeking only the treasures of this earth.

" 'Do not lay up for yourselves treasures on earth, where moth and rust destroy and where thieves break in and steal, but lay up for yourselves treasures in heaven, where neither moth nor rust destroys and where thieves do not break in and steal. For where your treasure is, there your heart will be also.' 'The eye is the

lamp of the body. So, if your eye is healthy, your whole body will be full of light, but if your eye is bad, your whole body will be full of darkness. If then the light in you is darkness, how great is the darkness!'" (Mt.6:19-23, ESV).

Your work as a business owner or leader revolves around things that are a part of *this* world. You manufacture products or provide services that contribute to the betterment of people's lives and businesses in this world. In return for your investment and tireless efforts, you are rewarded with this world's currency. With currency, you purchase things that are a part of this world. In the current passage, our Lord speaks directly to what your priorities should be as you work and live day by day in this world.

a. **First, there is the subject of earthly riches.** The concern of Christ is for your heart. He does not want the things of *this* world—money and possessions—to capture your heart. The reason is simple: nothing on this earth is permanent. Rather, it is aging, decaying, and wasting away. Moreover, money and possessions can be stolen or lost in an instant. Through financial difficulty, economic collapse, an accident, illness, or a myriad of other avenues, what you have accumulated can suddenly disappear.

   Now, this does not mean that you are not to have money and possessions, that you cannot enjoy the hard-earned fruits of your labor. Scripture clearly states that God gives us all things, and He gives them for our enjoyment (1 Ti.6:17).

   What Christ is saying is this: you can possess earthly treasures, but your treasures are not to possess you. You are not to focus your life *only* on earthly things, not to set your eyes and mind *solely* on such passing treasures. As a believer, you have a greater purpose in life, that of living as a testimony for Jesus Christ and helping to meet the needs of the poor, helpless, and disadvantaged of the earth. Furthermore, you cannot take a single thing with you when you pass from this world into the next. Note the following Scriptures:

> **"For we brought nothing into this world, and it is certain we can carry nothing out" (1 Ti.6:7, KJV).**

> **"For one can see that wise men die; foolish and stupid men also pass away. Then they leave their wealth to others" (Ps.49:10, HCSB).**

b. **In sharp contrast to earthly riches, Christ also discusses heavenly riches.** There are things in heaven that genuine believers desire. Christ calls these heavenly treasures. These riches include the spiritual blessings that we can receive in this life, blessings such as . . .

- becoming a true child of God
- receiving the forgiveness of sins
- gaining wisdom
- receiving a lasting purpose, meaning, or significance in life
- knowing that you will be God's heir to an enormous, eternal inheritance
- being blessed and comforted by the Holy Spirit of God Himself
- receiving daily guidance and direction

Christ encourages you to build up heavenly riches because they cannot be destroyed. There is an incorruptible inheritance, one that will never perish or fade away, waiting in heaven for you (1 Pe.1:4)! You should lay claim to and set your heart on this heavenly, eternal inheritance. In addition, heavenly riches are secure. Thieves cannot break through into heaven; they cannot penetrate the spiritual dimension. No person or thing can take away your heavenly riches. The love of God assures this (Ro.8:32-39).

How can you invest your life in heavenly treasure when your business and work revolve around earthly things? Note what Jesus said: your heart will be where your treasure is (v.21). For your heart to be right, your treasure must be right. And for your treasure to be right, your perspective and focus must be right (vv.22-23). You need to value the kingdom of God and the things of heaven more than you value earthly things. Simply realize that you, as a believer, are called to a higher level of living, to a greater purpose than laboring merely for the temporary, material things of this world. You are called to live and work for that which is eternal, the spiritual treasure that will abide forever. You have the opportunity to invest yourself and your income in those things that will reap eternal dividends. If you are a business owner, this marvelous opportunity is multiplied: not only can you invest your own life in the eternal, but you can also create a business that exists to help people in this life and in the life to come.

If a mighty army of businesses across the earth existed both to supply earthly needs—products, services, jobs, income—and to build up God's kingdom, people's lives would be radically improved. As you labor for this exalted purpose, our Lord promises to bless you in *this* life. If you will focus your life and work on heavenly treasure, God will meet your earthly needs:

> **"But seek first his kingdom and his righteousness, and all these things will be given to you as well" (Mt.6:33, NIV '84).**

3. *Resist greed and covetousness.*

> **"He then told them, 'Watch out and be on guard against all greed because one's life is not in the abundance of his possessions.' Then He told them a parable: 'A rich man's land was very productive. He thought to himself, "What should I do, since I don't have anywhere to store my crops? I will do this," he said. "I'll tear down my barns and build bigger ones and store all my grain and my goods there. Then I'll say to myself,**

'You have many goods stored up for many years. Take it easy; eat, drink, and enjoy yourself.' " 'But God said to him, "You fool! This very night your life is demanded of you. And the things you have prepared—whose will they be?" That's how it is with the one who stores up treasure for himself and is not rich toward God' " (Lk.12:15-21, HCSB).

As a business man or woman with a certain level of authority, you have a heavy responsibility to those who work under you. Your actions and attitudes affect everyone around you—either for good or bad. Both personally and professionally, you are to labor for a higher purpose than just earning money for yourself, accumulating possessions, or growing your business for selfish purposes. God calls you to reject the selfish, greedy, materialistic philosophy of this world. You are to live and work by a nobler philosophy, one that serves others, not yourself.

Sadly, our materialistic world falsely associates success with money and possessions. In fact, a person's worth is often measured by his or her houses, vehicles, investments, and other holdings. And tragically, many individuals equate fulfillment in life with the *things* their work or profession affords them.

Jesus condemned this worldly philosophy with a brief but sobering statement: *There is so much more to life than the abundance of possessions* (v.15)! Living is about far more than accumulating temporal worldly things. To reinforce this, Jesus issued a strong charge, a double warning to which we should give our utmost attention: "Watch out . . . be on guard." The Greek word for *be on guard* means to guard yourself from a *deadly* enemy.

a. **This enemy is *greed* or *covetousness*.** It is one of the most common sins in our world and also one of the most dangerous. It is desiring more and more and being dissatisfied with what we have, no matter how much we acquire. Greed is:

- a selfish burning desire deep within that seeks happiness in things, material possessions, as well as through authority and power.

- a deep desire that craves the power that comes with having the possessions, the big salary, the prestigious title even more so than the possessions themselves or the satisfaction of having served people and done our job well.

- an intense appetite or passion for the pleasure that success can bring, surpassing the pleasure of having built or run a business well, of providing a quality product or service for society.

We need to be aware that true happiness and comfort do not depend upon what we have. Many people who own little of this world's goods are happy and comfortable with healthy souls and bodies. As stated above, life is about more than possessions, titles, and salaries; more than position, power, and authority.

b. **Note how Jesus gets across the fact of our greed.** He shares a parable about a businessman who was *aggressively self-centered*. In just three short verses, the rich man describes his thoughts by using the personal pronouns "I" and "my" five times. This man's attention is solely upon himself:

- The man is tremendously blessed but has never thanked God for his blessing.

- The man calls the fruits of the ground and the possessions he owns, my crops and my grain and my goods (vv.17-18).

- The man speaks of his life as his own. There is no indication he has given his life to God.

- The man becomes puffed up, prideful with what he has done. He thinks only of bigger and better, focusing on I and me, and my and mine.

c. **In your position or role of authority,** you, too, need to guard carefully against what was this man's big character flaw: self-indulgence and extravagant living. His sole purpose was to be at ease, to have plenty to eat and drink, and to enjoy life as he wished. Several facts need to be noted:

- He thought only of self, of living at ease and in comfort extravagantly, of having enough to last him the rest of his life. He gave no thought to helping others. He forgot that he lived in a needy world that was lost and dying.

- He put off living and enjoying life until he built and filled his barns. Obviously, he was a *workaholic* who was consumed with the passion to get what he wanted. (How many of us are just like him when we want something!)

- Lastly, and most shockingly, he only *thought* these things. He never experienced them; they were only notions or wishes in his mind. *He died unexpectedly, leaving everything he had worked for behind, with nothing of eternal value!* He was rich in this life, but poor toward God—bankrupt in eternity (vv.20-21).

As a responsible business person in a position of power and/or authority, you have a nobler purpose for living and working. And as a Christian, you have a higher calling. You are to live . . .

- to provide for your needs and the needs of your family

- to generate jobs for others to earn a living for themselves and their families

- to provide purpose, significance, and a path to achievement in life by providing meaningful work and jobs for others (Ge.1:28; 2:15)

- to provide a beneficial—never harmful—service or product for society in general.

- to be able to help the poor and disadvantaged, those who are unable to work (Ep.4:28)
- to meet humanity's need for food (hunger), housing (homelessness), health (sickness and disease), and education(ignorance)
- to provide for civilization's greatest need of all—the need for the gospel and God's Word

Never lose sight of the fact that your abilities and opportunities are gifts from God! It is He who gives you whatever capabilities, skills, and strengths you have to produce wealth and succeed (Dt.8:18). While He blesses us all with many things to enjoy as fruits of our labor, He also warns us about the dangers of greed. He commands us to get our thoughts off ourselves and to use our wealth for good works, to be generous and ever eager to give instead of accumulating more and more for ourselves. By obeying this command, we are becoming rich toward God and laying up treasure for ourselves in eternity (1 Ti.6:6-10, 17-19).

Like the man in Jesus' parable, we are all going to die. If we live and labor only for ourselves and the things of this world, everything we have worked for will be left behind. But if we live and labor for a higher purpose, we will have an eternal reward.

4. *Do not hoard wealth.*

> **"Now listen, you rich people, weep and wail because of the misery that is coming upon you. Your wealth has rotted, and moths have eaten your clothes. Your gold and silver are corroded. Their corrosion will testify against you and eat your flesh like fire. You have hoarded wealth in the last days" (Jas.5:1–3, NIV '84).**

Without question, many business owners and executives, as well as some managers are rich, especially when compared to most people in this world. Technically, any are rich who have more than what they need to live and to provide for their families. These verses and this point, however, are speaking specifically to those who have abundant wealth. This wealth may be in cash, in property, in material possessions, or a variety of other assets.

However your wealth is packaged, God says if you are rich, you will face a fierce temptation, one so ferocious that it can consume you. What is this powerful force that draws you? It is the temptation to bank and hoard your money instead of using it to meet the desperate needs of the world.

The Bible never condemns the wealthy. It only condemns the rich who store up their wealth instead of using it to feed the hungry, clothe the naked, shelter the cold and homeless, nurse the sick, teach the uneducated, and sound the glorious news of God's salvation around the world. Within this world—a world reeling under the weight of so many desperate needs—how can anyone keep from making a commitment to help and minister to people? How can anyone not give sacrificially to help the needy? God knows that people have no acceptable excuse. Therefore, He issues a strong warning to all who are rich in this world: you must not hoard wealth. If you are hoarding wealth, you ought to weep and groan in deep anguish. Why? Three reasons are given.

a. **Hoarding wealth will bring misery upon you (v.1).** You will suffer the serious consequences of its vice-like grip on your life, such as...

- a restless, insecure heart that lacks permanent peace

- an empty soul—lacking a meaningful and lasting purpose

- a selfish, covetous, and greedy spirit

- a mind consumed by the desire for more and more—a craving that cannot be fulfilled

- a life enslaved by worldly passions

- a heart filled with sinful pride

- an unbalanced life—a life preoccupied with making money, sometimes to the neglect of family, friends, and other areas of responsibility

- a sense of insecurity, a nagging fear of losing what you have

- a misplaced trust that dooms you to this world's corruption and empty promises

- a sense of never being complete—never feeling truly fulfilled or satisfied permanently

- a life with very few genuine friends, friends not interested in your money

- a spirit that lacks assurance of being acceptable to God

- a spirit of anxiety about your investments and their unpredictability

- a life of self-dependence—a life that never knows God's love, care, provision, protection, and forgiveness through the trials and crises of life

- a life of alienation from God—cutting yourself off from God's wonderful blessings and assurance of living forever

Riches that are hoarded will fail you; they will not satisfy, and they will doom you. Hoarded wealth will bring all kinds of trouble and misery. Therefore, you should heed this summons of God.

b. **Hoarded wealth is wealth that will not last (vv.2-3a).** To illustrate the point, God's Word gives three examples based on what was valuable in that day and time: food, lavish clothing, and gold and silver. Naturally, the principles apply to whatever items people value in their culture. Interestingly, in our modern world, we hoard in much the same way. Most of us have more food than we need or will use and end up throwing things away that have rotted. Most of us have more clothing than we need or ever wear and yet we buy more rather than repairing or protecting what we already own. We stockpile money or gold or silver in banks and stocks. We purchase houses and cars and boats and all sorts of material things in excess. And they sit unused.

The point is this: if wealth—money, possessions, or anything else—is hoarded instead of used, it is wasted. It does nothing but occupy space, and eventually it will deteriorate, rot, or otherwise lose its value. It is never used for the good that it could do. The person who owns it contributes little, if anything, of significance to his or her generation . . . at least not anything of lasting value.

What a tragedy! To have nothing to leave the world but material things. Wealth that sits unused is worthless to its owner.

> **"The increase of his house shall depart, and his goods shall flow away in the day of his [God's] wrath" (Jb.20:28, KJV).**

c. **Hoarding wealth will condemn you (v.3b-3d).** It will condemn you in three ways. First, your hoarded wealth will stand as a witness against you (v.3b). When? Both now and in the coming day of God's judgment. When you hoard money and live extravagantly, others witness your greed; they see how insensitive and self-absorbed you are. Take, for example, people who dedicate their lives to help meet the desperate needs of this world. When they see you and other greedy people living a selfish life, they wish that you and all who cling to their wealth would wake up and realize that you have a responsibility to help the needy.

Then there are all the needy individuals who see all the hoarders of the world living a selfish life. They see and know that some of the rich care and help, but others do not. As history bears witness, it is often the extreme gulf between the rich and the middle class or poor that fuels the cry for a more equitable pay scale and distribution of wealth within society. And it is the cry for *just treatment* that leads to dissension, riots, and revolution within both businesses and nations. Selfishness by so many of the rich leads to tragic consequences. Even more tragic, far too many of the rich are oblivious to or completely ignore this fact. They do not care enough to change or to fulfill their duty to the world and to God.

The point is this: if you hoard wealth, it stands as a witness against you while you are on earth. But the witness that you need to fear the most is the witness that will be borne against you in the terrible day of eternal judgment. You will have to give an account to God for what you do with all that God has given you—a terrifying thought!

Second, hoarding wealth will condemn you by eating away at you like a fire (v.3c). For example, if you stockpile money, the passion to store up more and more money will burn within you. The more you hoard, the more you will desire to hoard. The craving for more will burn within you, and the passion for more and more will consume you. You will never be truly fulfilled or satisfied in life, not in a lasting sense. The unquenchable passion for wealth will destroy you not only now but also for all eternity if you do not surrender your life to Jesus Christ. It will eat away at you until it finally and utterly destroys you.

> **"But people who long to be rich fall into temptation and are trapped by many foolish and harmful desires that plunge them into ruin and destruction. For the love of money is the root of all kinds of evil. And some people, craving money, have wandered from the true faith and pierced themselves with many sorrows."** (1 Ti.6:9–10, NLT).

Third, your hoarded wealth will be stored up against you in the last days (v.3d). This refers to the days of coming judgment. Your *hoarding* is a picture of your working day by day to heap up treasures on earth; however, *at the same time*, you are heaping up wrath against yourself in the terrible day of God's judgment.

Treasures of wealth heaped up on earth become treasures of wrath heaped up at the final judgment—all of which will fall upon the person who hoards. Why? Because while the rich person clings to his/her wealth, a world of needy people die from hunger, cold, and disease—many without ever having heard the wonderful news that God loves them and has sent His Son, Jesus Christ, into the world to save them (Jn.3:16–17).

God's Word is clear: you must not hoard wealth. Do not come to the end of your life and be faced with this stark reality: despite all your riches, you are utterly poor because the only thing you have is money (Mt.6:19-20). When you come face to face with the Lord, be sure to have this testimony to share with Him. "Lord, all that you entrusted into my hands, I gave and willed to ministries that help the needy and carry your holy Word to the world."

> **"Do not lay up for yourselves treasures on earth, where moth and rust destroy and where thieves break in and steal, but lay up for yourselves treasures in heaven, where neither moth nor rust destroys and where thieves do not break in and steal" (Mt.6:19-20, ESV).**

5. *Heed God's charge to the rich: Do not be arrogant, nor place your trust in wealth.*

> **"Command those who are rich in this present world not to be arrogant nor to put their hope in wealth, which is so uncertain, but to put their hope in God, who richly provides us with everything for our enjoyment. Command them to do good, to be rich in good deeds, and to be generous and willing to share. In this way they will lay up treasure for themselves as a firm foundation for the coming age, so that they may take hold of the life that is truly life" (1 Ti.6:17-19, NIV '84).**

As a business owner, executive, or manager, you may earn more money than the average person in society. And depending on the nature of your business, the size and success of your company, and your level of responsibility, you could eventually become quite wealthy. But even if you are not moderately wealthy, you will still be rich compared to many people in your community and around the world.

If you are a person whom God has blessed with money and possessions, He has a specific message for you—a strong charge. In fact, in the original language of Scripture, the charge has the force of a military command. At the same time, it has the tenderness of an appeal. God is appealing to you, like a commander in the armed forces, in love and tenderness, but He expects you to do exactly what He says. He spells out five firm instructions that you are to follow:

a. **You are not to** be high-minded, proud, or arrogant (v.17a). The world honors money. Practically everyone in the world wants more money, and the majority strive to make more money. Indeed, the pursuit of wealth is so interwoven into the fabric of society that it is certainly one of the most sought-after objectives for a large percentage of the world's population. Because so many want to be like the rich, they put the rich on a pedestal. Thus, it is extremely difficult for the wealthy to keep a proper perspective of themselves.

   As a business owner or executive, if you are rich, you face the danger of thinking too highly of yourself. The danger is that you will become high-minded, prideful, and arrogant, perhaps considering yourself better than others. Then you may begin to look down on others and downplay their value, both as individuals and employees. As a wealthy person, you need to guard against feeling that you are more important than other people. Riches and possessions do not make you a *quality individual*. They do not make you *better*, or *of higher quality*, than anyone else. As Jesus taught, your life is not measured by the abundance of your possessions (Lk.12:15). Your true worth has nothing to do with *how much* of this world's money or things you have.

   Again, God's charge to you is forceful: "[The] rich in this present world [are] not to be arrogant." Yet because of the world's prevailing attitude toward riches, the temptation to be prideful will always be there confronting the rich. But God's instruction in the above Scripture is clear: do not be high-minded, proud, or arrogant (v.17).

b. **You are not to** trust in the uncertainty of riches (v.17b). Ask yourself this question: *Is there anything in life more uncertain than riches?* The world's economy is never fixed or static. Rather it fluctuates constantly, going through slight shifts here and major upheavals there. One crisis follows another in world affairs, with the markets responding and reacting to each crisis. Even if you are able to keep your wealth in this life, a disease or an accident could happen overnight, then your wealth would do you no good whatsoever. The value and benefits of riches may be here today, but they can easily be erased tomorrow. In light of this, placing your ultimate trust in something so uncertain as wealth is foolish. This is one reason God's charge is so strong. Wealth is one of the most uncertain things in life, a very shaky foundation upon which to place your hope and trust.

> "If I have put my trust in gold or said to pure gold, 'You are my security,' if I have rejoiced over my great wealth, the fortune my hands had gained, . . . Then these also would be sins to be judged, for I would have been unfaithful to God on high" (Jb.31:24-25, 28, NIV '84).

c. **You are to** place your hope in God (v.17c). Fix your heart and life upon Him instead of upon your wealth. God is! He exists! He is living, and He is the only One who possesses every good and perfect gift. Therefore, He alone can give you . . .

- the good and perfect gifts necessary for this life
- the good and perfect gifts necessary for the next life

> "Every good and perfect gift is from above, coming down from the Father of the heavenly lights, who does not change like shifting shadows" (Jas.1:17, NIV '84).

In fact, every *good gift* that you receive now—the ability and strength to work, to earn a living, and to secure riches—has come from God. You must not miss this fact; it bears repeating: every good gift that you now have has come from God. Therefore, if you want more and more of the good things of this life, you must put your hope in God.

d. **You should do** good—be helpful and generous to those in need (v.18). If you are rich, be wise and help meet the desperate needs of the world. Too many wealthy people cover their ears when they hear God's command regarding this. They turn their attention elsewhere because they do not want to think about giving away large sums of money. They reject the fact that God expects them to give—to give to the point of sacrifice just as God did when He gave His only Son. But think honestly and realistically, not allowing yourself to be deceived:

- First, literally millions of people are hurting and dying from hunger, disease, and lack of fresh water, every day. Millions of others are suffering from ignorance, sin, loneliness, and emptiness. When God looks down upon earth and sees those who are hurting, dying, uneducated, or spiritually dead, and then He sees us—the wealthy of the world—what do you think God expects us to do? Does God not expect us to meet the needs of the poor and disadvantaged of the world when He Himself sacrificially met our needs?

- Second, why do you think you and others have wealth? To hoard it? To bank it or bury it or store it up and then let it sit around and never be used? You and I know better—every one of us knows better.

As a business owner or executive, God expects you to do good and to be rich in good deeds. He expects you to distribute and to be generous and sacrificial in helping the needy, the poor, the uneducated, and the lost and dying of this world.

e. **You are to** lay up wealth for the world to come (vv.18-19). How does a rich person do this?

- By distributing and giving generously and sacrificially while here on earth (v.18)

- "By giving it away"[2]—willing one's estate to ministries that help the needy and take the Word of God and the gospel to lost and dying world.

- By using "wealth to do good [and being] . . . ready to share . . . [remembering] that a Christian is essentially a man [or woman] who is a member of a fellowship"[3]

- "By works of charity"[4]

Again, think of all the desperate needs in the world as well as in your own community or city. Any example or need could be used, but consider a person who is hungry and has no way to get food. If you and the other business owners and executives of the world do not reach out to save the starving person, you are willfully disobeying God's direct command to you. In other words, you are not laying up treasure for the coming age—eternity (v.19a). While you may be rich in this life, you will be poor in eternity. By refusing to obey God's command to help the needy, you are forfeiting the eternal rewards you can receive for obeying the Lord.

> **"But store up for yourselves treasures in heaven, where moth and rust do not destroy, and where thieves do not break in and steal" (Mt.6:20, NIV '84).**

> **"If someone has enough money to live well and sees a brother or sister in need but shows no compassion—how can God's love be in that person?" (1 Jn.3:17, NLT).**

---

2 A.T. Robertson. *Word Pictures in the New Testament*, Vol.4 (Nashville, TN: Broadman Press, 1930), p.596.

3 Barclay. *The Letters to the Philippians, Colossians, and Thessalonians*, p.159.

4 Matthew Henry. *Commentary on the Whole Bible* (Old Tappan, NJ: Fleming H. Revell Co.), Vol.5, p.83.

Furthermore, by not giving to those in need, you are failing to grasp the essence of eternal life, "the life that is truly life" (v.19b). The essence of eternal life is *giving*. You have eternal life because God *gave* His only Son for you (Jn.3:16; 2 Co.9:15). Christ became a man and *gave* His life for you—became poor that you might be made rich (2 Co.8:9). When you or any of us selfishly hoard what God has given us—whether material or spiritual riches—and refuse to share with those in need, we fail to take hold of what eternal life is truly about.

God's charge to you is militarily strong: you are to be rich in good works, ready to give, willing to share, so you can lay up treasure for yourself as a firm foundation for the age to come—eternity (vv.18-19).

6. *Recognize that godly contentment surpasses all that the world has to offer.*

> **"But godliness with contentment is great gain. For we brought nothing into the world, and we can take nothing out of it. But if we have food and clothing, we will be content with that. People who want to get rich fall into temptation and a trap and into many foolish and harmful desires that plunge men into ruin and destruction. For the love of money is a root of all kinds of evil. Some people, eager for money, have wandered from the faith and pierced themselves with many griefs" (1 Ti.6:6-10, NIV '84; cp. Mt.6:33).**

Contentment, in simple terms, is a state of happiness and satisfaction. But contentment without godliness is not enough to fully satisfy the human soul. Neither is godliness without contentment. So, what is the above Scripture saying? It is a combination of godliness plus contentment that will help you lead a fulfilled life and have that deep sense of satisfaction you crave. Sadly, though, when we look around the workplace or anywhere else in society, godly contentment is not what we usually see.

What we see too often are people who are unhappy, unfulfilled, and without lasting purpose or meaning in life. Where they work, the positions or titles they hold, and the money they make seem to have little effect on their being content. Why? People are discontent because they are chasing after things that are fleeting, that pass away, that can be lost or stolen or destroyed in a moment, things such as . . .

- money and possessions
- worldly success and approval
- positions and power

Any true believer who slips back and lives a carnal, fleshly life loses the deep-seated contentment God had given him or her. It is only when you live as God tells you to live and find your sufficiency in Him, rather than in the world, that you gain a deep sense of contentment. This godly contentment brings true satisfaction, fulfillment, and completion—a sense that you lack absolutely nothing. Only living as God says can do this for the human soul. Therefore, Scripture declares that godliness along with contentment is great gain (vv.6-8).

The secret to contentment is not money (vv.9-10). This seems strange, for the rich usually cling to their wealth, and those without usually seek more of it. But if you think getting rich will make you content, you are sorely deceived. Just read or listen to the news on a daily basis to discover how miserable so many of the rich are! God is clear about the matter: money and wealth do not bring contentment, not contentment that lasts. In fact, even desiring to get rich can place you in serious danger:

a. **Craving riches** brings the danger of temptation and enslavement (v.9a). How can craving money tempt and enslave? The answer is, money and the things it buys cannot fully satisfy. No matter how much you have, it will never be enough. As a result, you will be tempted to live selfishly and to hoard what you have. You will be tempted to keep on buying, tempted to indulge the flesh and to live more extravagantly, tempted to control people through the power of your wealth.

Because of the bombardment of temptations, you will seldom have peace. You will have fallen into the trap of living a life of selfishness and sin, and you will never be content. Knowing this, as you succeed in your business or position and your income increases, you need to carefully guard against falling into this trap.

Thirsting for money creates the danger of foolish and harmful desires (v.9b). While some people have a strange affection for money itself, most want money for the *things* it buys. Even those who have an abundance of money must constantly battle the desire to buy or to do whatever they want, simply because their money allows them to do so. Foolish or harmful desires might include . . .

- craving closets full of clothing when so many have little or no protection from the cold or heat
- desiring only the finest foods and other delicacies of life when so many are hungry and starving
- acquiring multiple homes, properties, and vehicles when so many have no shelter at all and no means of transportation, not even to work

If you have the money, you can fulfill your desires by purchasing and possessing almost anything you want. Obviously, not every purchase or possession involves sinful desires or foolish behavior. But if your desires or possessions consume your thoughts to the point that they interfere with your work, your responsibilities, or your relationships, they are harmful and wrong. What good does it do you to gain the whole world if you lose your soul—all that is truly meaningful in life—in the process? (Mt.16:26).

What do you gain by hoarding money beyond what you will ever need or use? What value is wealth that sits—whether in banks or investment firms or under a mattress—and is never used to help or benefit anyone else?

How foolish and harmful is it to feed your desires for more and more money and for the luxuries of this world when millions are going to bed hungry, cold, and sick? Untold numbers are perishing daily from lack of food, clothing, shelter, and disease. Even a lack of education—not knowing how to survive or how to make a living—costs people their lives. And, most tragic of all, many of these people are dying without Christ, without any hope of living eternally with Him. You, as a Christian leader in the business world, need to keep this fact in mind: hoarding wealth is both foolish and destructive, especially in light of people's tremendous needs and the desperation of those who do not know Jesus as Lord.

b. **Craving money** can drown or plunge you into ruin and destruction (v.9c). The word *plunge* is a descriptive picture of the longing for wealth being "a personal monster, which plunges its victims into an ocean of complete destruction."[5] The word conveys the idea that the person who falls into the foolish and hurtful lusts of this world will be utterly destroyed and ruined, both in body and soul. And the destruction and ruin will be for eternity.[6]

c. **Seeking to get rich** can lead you into all sorts of evil. Note Scripture's distinction: it is the *love of money*, not money itself, that is at the root of all kinds of evil (v.10). Note the reasons: the *love of money*...

- causes you to covet, and covetousness is idolatry (v.10a)

- causes you to wander away from the faith (v.10b). If you love money, you will be gripped by the ungodly passions of this world.

---

5 Donald Guthrie. *The Pastoral Epistles* (Grand Rapids, MI: Wm. B. Eerdmans Publishing Co., 1990), p.113.

6 Robertson. *Word Pictures in the New Testament*, Vol.4, p.593.

- causes you to pierce yourself with many sorrows (v.10c). The things, possessions, and thrills of this world cannot satisfy or fulfill your life, nor can they bring lasting contentment to your soul. The love of money only consumes and eats away at you. It pierces your heart and fills the void with grief—the grief of emptiness and worry, anxiety and insecurity. Money cannot buy true love, health, or deliverance from death. Of even greater significance, money cannot buy God. And no amount of it can buy you the assurance and confidence of living forever.

William Barclay makes another noteworthy point:

> *Money in itself is neither good nor bad; it is simply dangerous in that the love of it may become bad. With money a man can do much good; and with money he can do much evil. With money a man can selfishly serve his own desires; and with money he can generously answer to the cry of his neighbour's need. With money a man can buy his way to the forbidden things and facilitate the path of wrong-doing; and with money he can make it easier for someone else to live as God meant him to live. Money is not an evil, but it is a great responsibility.*[7]

In conclusion, we have within us a *natural, inner craving* for the necessities of life. Once we have the necessities, though, our sin nature still craves more. The necessities do not satisfy our inner cravings and emptiness, the void, hunger, and thirst for something more. Therefore, we seek to satisfy our cravings by getting more of this world's possessions and pleasures. We seek more comfort, enjoyment, wealth, power, and everything else we think will satisfy our inner cravings.

But what we sometimes overlook is this: the craving within our hearts—the void, the hunger, the thirst—is not for more money, material possessions, recognition, position,

---

7 Barclay. *The Letters to Timothy, Titus, and Philemon,* Published as a volume in the Daily Study Bible Series. (Philadelphia, PA: Westminster John Knox Press, 1953), p.152.

or power. It is not for more honor or more thrilling experiences. The craving is actually for *spiritual satisfaction*, the *filling up* of another part of our being. Our craving is for contentment—true and lasting godly contentment. This comes from having both our physical and spiritual needs met. One without the other leaves us feeling empty and incomplete (Col.2:8-9). True satisfaction and lasting fulfillment come only from godly contentment, from living precisely as God's Word says to live and finding our sufficiency in Him and Him alone.

> **"Seek the Kingdom of God above all else, and live righteously, and he will give you everything you need" (Mt.6:33, NLT).**

> **"Blessed are those who hunger and thirst for righteousness, for they shall be satisfied"(Mt.5:6, NASB '77).**

7. *Be faithful in your daily responsibilities: God will then trust you with things of greater importance.*

> **"One who is faithful in a very little is also faithful in much, and one who is dishonest in a very little is also dishonest in much. If then you have not been faithful in the unrighteous wealth, who will entrust to you the true riches? And if you have not been faithful in that which is another's, who will give you that which is your own?" (Luke 16:10-12, ESV).**

This passage contains an eye-opening truth: how you handle your money and business is a test to see if God can trust you with that which is of eternal importance. Note that the words *very little* do not refer to a small amount of money, nor does the word *much* speak of a large amount (v.10). *Very little* refers to *wealth* or money of any amount; in contrast, *much* actually refers to *true riches* (v.11). What a striking statement by the Lord: true riches are something totally separate from money or worldly wealth!

a. **Money and possessions are the least things** God has entrusted to you (v.10). They are nothing compared to the daily experience of true love, joy, peace, and the absolute assurance and confidence of living forever with God throughout eternity. They are nothing compared to sensing God's care, presence, and guidance day by day. They are nothing compared to knowing God personally and to being made an heir of God and a joint heir with Christ. They are nothing compared to the lasting sense of purpose, meaning, and fulfillment that God gives to all who truly follow Him.

b. **Unfaithfulness in the care** or use of your business, job, money, and possessions disqualifies you from being trusted with true, heavenly riches. Do not be deceived by thinking that what you have is your own to do with as you wish, because it is not. Your life, business, and possessions belong to God. God has entrusted you with these things only for as long as you are on this earth. You are merely a steward or manager of all you are and have. You cannot take any of these things with you when you die and leave this earth. Your life—your time, abilities, opportunities, responsibilities—and your possessions have been given to you by God only temporarily, given as a trust for you to look after. If you handle or care for your life and possessions poorly, you show that you are not qualified to be trusted with responsibilities of eternal importance, both in this life and in the new heavens and earth.

c. **Unfaithfulness disqualifies you** from all that God wants to give you (v.12). The reference to *another's* refers to God. Your life and worldly possessions are His; He has entrusted them to you. If you are not faithful in caring for or using them, how can you expect God to give you the blessings He wants to bestow upon you, blessings such as . . .

  • *additional* abilities and insights that will enable you to be more efficient and thereby increase your business, which in turn will help you do more to improve people's quality of life and help society as a whole

- a *larger* business or *additional* businesses, or a *more* influential position and *greater* responsibilities
- *additional* opportunities to make a difference in people's lives, both now and for eternity
- *greater* opportunities in your work and in spiritual service

If you are not faithful with your money, business, and possessions, you disqualify yourself from the *greater* works that God wants to use you to do. Consequently, when you stand before Christ to give an account for your life and work, you will suffer the loss of the rewards you could have received. You will suffer the loss of the rewards the Lord so deeply desired to give you, if you had only proven yourself to be trustworthy.

> **"His work will be shown; for what it is, because the Day will bring it to light. It will be revealed with fire; and the fire will test the quality of each man's work. If what he has built survives, he will receive his reward. If it is burned up, he will suffer loss; he himself will be saved, but only as one escaping through the flames"** (1 Co.3:13-15, NIV '84).

> **"Your wickedness has deprived you of these wonderful blessings. Your sin has robbed you of all these good things"** (Je.5:25, NLT).

CHAPTER **12**

What God Expects of You Personally

Contents

CHAPTER 12

WHAT GOD EXPECTS OF YOU PERSONALLY

1. *Be certain you are saved—set free from the bondage of sin, death, and eternal condemnation.*

> "Once you were dead because of your disobedience and your many sins. You used to live in sin, just like the rest of the world, obeying the devil—the commander of the powers in the unseen world. He is the spirit at work in the hearts of those who refuse to obey God. All of us used to live that way, following the passionate desires and inclinations of our sinful nature. By our very nature we were subject to God's anger, just like everyone else. But God is so rich in mercy, and he loved us so much, that even though we were dead because of our sins, he gave us life when he raised Christ from the dead. (It is only by God's grace that you have been saved!)" (Ep.2:1-5, NLT).

Suppose your business were on the brink of a devastating dissolution. Suppose you have leveraged and mortgaged every asset you have, and that you owe an overwhelming amount of debt you can never repay. Despite your best efforts to revive the business, there is nothing further you can do. You are broke. You have no other choice but to file for bankruptcy, lose everything you have spent your life working for, and deal with the consequences.

Then, suppose your primary creditor—the wealthy individual or institution to whom you owe the largest amount of money—does an unbelievable thing. Your creditor offers you a gift beyond your wildest dreams: he offers to forgive all that you owe him and to pay all your other personal debts, giving you a chance at a new life and a fresh start. The only condition? You have to humbly receive the unimaginably gracious gift being offered to you.

Sounds ludicrous, right? Yet every one of us, whether or not we acknowledge it, are spiritually bankrupt and indebted to our Creator. We have sinned and come short of His glory and perfection (Ro.3:23). Because of our horrible imperfection and sin, we owe an unpayable debt to God. No matter how much good we do, despite our best efforts, we can never repay that debt. To state it bluntly, we are ruined, both now and for eternity.

But God Himself paid our debt through His Son, Jesus Christ:

> "... but God shows his love for us in that while we were still sinners, Christ died for us" (Ro.5:8, ESV).

The only condition to having our debt paid? We have to receive, or accept, the incredible gift that God is offering.

What does it even mean for you to receive Christ? When God looks down on you, what does He see? If you have not received Christ as Lord of your life, what does that absence mean to your present life? What does it mean for your future? What will it mean if you *do* receive Christ?

a. **If you have not received Christ,** you are living life totally separated from God, living as though you are *dead* toward God. Note the words in Ephesians 2:1, "you were dead" (v.1). How can you be living and yet be dead? To answer this question, you need to understand that death, in biblical terms, means *separation*. It never means extinction, annihilation, non-existence, or inactivity. Death simply means that a person is either separated from his or her body or from God or from both. Holy Scripture speaks of three deaths:

   • *Physical death*: the separation of your spirit from your body. This is what commonly comes to mind when speaking of death. It is when life departs from your body on this earth and you are buried.

   > "Just as man is destined to die once, and after that to face judgment" (He.9:27, NIV '84).

- *Spiritual death*: the separation of your spirit from God while you are still living on earth. This is the *natural state* of people who have not received Christ. People can even be religious and still be *spiritually separated* from God; they are dead toward God.

  "But she who lives in pleasure is dead while she lives" (1 Ti.5:6, NKJV).

- *Eternal death*: the separation of a person from God's presence forever. This is the second death, the conscious, eternal separation from God that continues beyond the death of the body.

  "The Lord Jesus [will be] revealed from heaven in blazing fire with his powerful angels. He will punish those who do not know God and do not obey the gospel of our Lord Jesus. They will be punished with everlasting destruction and shut out from the presence of the Lord and from the majesty of his power" (2 Th.1:7-9, NIV '84).

  "But the cowardly, the unbelieving, the vile, the murderers, the sexually immoral, those who practice magic arts, the idolaters and all liars— their place will be in the fiery lake of burning sulfur. This is the second death" (Re.21:8, NIV '84).

b. **If you have not received Christ,** you are living in disobedience and sin (Ep.2:1-3). Note that it is disobedience and sin that separates you from God. To disobey means to turn aside or wander away from God and His Holy Word.

   To sin means to miss the mark. It is what is meant by coming *short of the glory of God, short of His perfection and righteousness* (Ro.3:23). God is perfect, but you are imperfect. You sin; you miss the mark. You may be respectable, but you are imperfect. You are never all that you should be.

   If you have not received Christ, you are living just like the disobedient of the world (v.3). You are following the desires and passions of your flesh, gratifying the long-ings and cravings of your sinful nature. Therefore, you are destined to face the wrath of God, doomed to eternal separation from Him.

c. **When you receive Christ,** you are redeemed and for-given of your sins through the death of Jesus Christ. To redeem means to deliver, buy back, or set free by pay-ing a ransom. For example, a prisoner of war or a kid-nap victim is ransomed or redeemed—saved from the threat of death. In every case, the person is powerless to free himself. He cannot make the payment demand-ed to liberate himself from his bondage or fate. Some-one else has to pay the ransom to redeem him.

It is Jesus Christ who has paid the ransom to liber-ate you, to set you free from the bondage of sin, death, and hell. When He died on the cross, He exchanged His life for your life. He died for you. He actually took the penalty of your sins and bore the punishment Himself. Consequently, you have been set free: your sins are re-moved—washed away, erased—forgiven forever.

d. **When you receive Christ,** you are saved from sin and death and given life through Jesus Christ. There is no question, if you have truly trusted Christ as your Savior and Lord, God will give you a full and satisfying life, both now and for all eternity. This is His wonderful promise. In light of this, you should always remember *how* God saved you: through the death of His only Son.

> **"But God demonstrates His own love toward us, in that while we were still sinners, Christ died for us" (Ro.5:8, NKJV).**

> **"For God so loved the world, that He gave His only begotten Son, that whoever believes in Him shall not perish, but have eternal life" (Jn.3:16, NASB '77).**

You receive Christ by believing in Him, simply plac-ing your faith in Him. But be absolutely sure that your faith in Christ is genuine, the right kind of faith. The right kind of faith is known as saving faith. How can you know whether or not you have saving faith? One way to measure is to know what saving faith *is not*:

- Saving faith *is not* just believing the fact that Jesus Christ is the Savior of the world.

- Saving faith *is not* just believing history, that Jesus Christ lived on earth as the Savior just as George Washington lived on earth as the first President of the United States.

- Saving faith *is not* just believing the words and claims of Jesus Christ in the same way that a person would believe the words of George Washington.

- Saving faith *is not* head knowledge, not just a mental conviction or intellectual commitment to Christ.

The right kind of faith, saving faith, is two things. First, saving faith is *believing in* Jesus Christ, believing in who and what He is, that He truly is the Son of God, the Savior and Lord of life. It is believing that Christ died in your place—for your sins—on the cross, and rose again (1 Co.15:3-4). It is fully trusting Him and His sacrificial death as payment for your sins. You need to confess or acknowledge Jesus Christ as your Savior and Lord.

> **"That if you confess with your mouth, 'Jesus is Lord,' and believe in your heart that God raised him from the dead, you will be saved." (Ro.10:9, NIV '84; see Ac.16:31).**

Second, saving faith is the surrender of your life to Jesus Christ. It is the surrender to live for Christ—to *obey Him* and to *live righteously* as you walk through life day by day. Anything less is not true saving faith. True saving faith is *obedience* to God's Holy Word.

> **"And having been perfected, He became the author [source] of eternal salvation to all who obey Him" (He.5:9, NKJV).**

If you are a *professing believer*, that is, you profess to be a Christian, be sure that your belief in Christ is genuine and wholehearted. Be sure that you have a *true saving faith,* faith that *obeys* God. If you do not know Christ personally, in a way that leads you to obey Him, you will come up short.

If you sense that you do not have a true saving faith, just call upon the name of the Lord to save you, and He will! He cares for you this much. No matter what you have done or how unworthy you feel, if you ask God to forgive your sins and to save you from eternal death, He will. And the life that He gives you will be both abundant and eternal.

> **"For 'whoever calls on the name of the Lord shall be saved'" (Ro.10:13, NKJV).**

(For a general, more thorough discussion of what your relationship with Jesus Christ should be, please see *What the Bible Says to the Believer: The Believer's Personal Handbook,* pp. 1-25.)

2. *Worship God daily: Set aside a quiet time for Bible reading and prayer.*

> **"Draw near to God [in worship] and He will draw near to you" (Jas.4:8a, NASB '77).**
>
> **"In the morning, O Lord, you hear my voice; in the morning, I lay my requests before you and wait in expectation" (Ps.5:3, NIV '84; see Ps.55:17).**
>
> **"I rise before dawn and cry for help; I have put my hope in your word" (Ps.119:147, NIV '84; see Ps.130:5-6).**
>
> **"And in the early morning, while it was still dark, He arose, and went out and departed to a lonely place, and was praying there" (Mk.1:35, NASB '77).**

Daily worship—Bible reading and prayer—is essential for every Christian business leader. You need God's help to deal with the heavy responsibilities of your position and the personal crises that come up in all our lives. You need God's strength to face the constant challenges that develop. You need His wisdom to make the right decisions, critical decisions that affect not only you but also your employees, their families, and all others impacted by your business or area of responsibility. You need His grace to deal with difficult people and situations in a way that is productive for you and pleasing to Him. You need . . .

- hope
- guidance
- confidence
- patience
- perseverance
- peace
- rest
- self-control
- strength
- power

. . . and so much more. And all of this, everything you need, is available from your Heavenly Father. Always remember this astounding fact: God—the only living and true God, the Creator and sovereign majesty of the universe—wants a close personal relationship with you. He wants to spend a lifetime with you, and He also wants to spend *every day* with you throughout eternity. Amazing! He wants to walk with you as you go through your stressful schedule each day. He wants to be your business partner, your confidante, your source—the first one you go to for everything you need. Therefore, while you complete your walk here on earth, God wants you to set aside a special time every day just for you and Him, a special time for worship, a time when you...

- listen to Him by reading His Word
- praise Him for who He is
- thank Him for the great salvation He has provided and offered to you and the entire universe (Ro.8:18-21; 2 Pe.3:10-13)

- ask Him to help and guide you and to meet whatever needs you may have

God wants to share all the promises of His Holy Word with you and to give you instructions about how to succeed in life and in business. He desires to give you everything you need to get through the day. He wants to help you to be effective and productive, to triumph over every trial, to make every critical decision, and to deal with every situation you face.

For these and many other reasons, your daily worship time needs to be when your mind is most alert, a time of day when you can focus without the distractions and pressures of daily affairs. For many people, this time is in the morning, when they are fresh and rested. For others, it is in the evening, after the duties of the day are done. You need to find the time that works best for you and make it a priority in your life. Set a daily appointment with God and do everything in your power not to miss it. Here are several practical suggestions that may help:

a. **Read God's Word.** Before you begin to read, ask God to show you. . .

- what He is saying in His Word

- what lesson He wants you to learn

- what He wants to say through you to others

b. **Begin reading** and read to the end of the paragraph, story, or subject. Then, read it again, over and over, until God's Spirit shows you the lesson He wants you to learn from that particular passage of Scripture.

c. **Once you see** the lesson God wants you to learn, briefly write it and the date down in a notebook. By writing it down, you will build up a collection of all the lessons God teaches you from that time forward. You will then have them for review and also for a precious reminder of how God is working in your life.

d. **After reading** God's Word, pray. And pray as the Lord taught you to pray:

> **"In this manner, therefore, pray: Our Father in heaven, hallowed be Your name. Your kingdom come. Your will be done on earth as *it is* in heaven. Give us this day our daily bread. And forgive us our debts, as we forgive our debtors. And do not lead us into temptation [rescue us from, or "don't let us yield to," NLT] but deliver us from the evil one. For Yours is the kingdom and the power and the glory forever. Amen" (Mt.6:9-13, NKJV).**

Pray *through* the points of the prayer. The *Lord's Prayer* is not to be recited just by memory or as a form prayer, as it so often is. The *Lord's Prayer* is a model prayer that is to be *prayed through*. It is "in this manner," *in this way*, that you are to pray. Christ was giving words, phrases, thoughts that are to be the points of your prayer. You are to develop the points as you pray by making each part personal, specifying your personal needs and requests. For example:

- *"Our Father"*: Thank You for being my Father, for adopting me as a son (or daughter) of yours. . . .

- *"Who is in heaven"*: Thank You for heaven, the hope and promise of being there with You eternally. . . .

- *"Hallowed be your name"*: You are holy—the very embodiment of perfection—righteous, pure, just. . . .

- *"Your kingdom come"*: Help me to do all I can to bring your kingdom to earth. Today, as I face this problem or decision (about an employee, financial shortfall, contract, major purchase, or whatever), help me. . . .

Pray through every point of the *Lord's Prayer* in this manner. Christ taught us—you and all other believers—to do this.

God does not want you bearing the heavy burdens of leading your business alone. He does not want you making decisions without the wisdom He alone can give. Nor does He want you dealing with adversity and pressure all alone. He loves you, and He cares about every detail of your life and business—every need you have. He wants to be a part of it. He wants to give you everything you need to be successful. Knowing this, you need to learn to connect and commune with God. Share everything with Him. Learn to pray as Christ taught us to pray; pray through the points of the *Lord's Prayer*. If you are not already doing this, make a commitment this day to pray as Christ taught His followers (disciples) to pray.

e. **Be faithful** to your daily worship time. Slipping away from or missing prayer and Bible reading will affect everything in your life—your family, your performance in your business, your strength to deal with challenges and adversity, your ability to make wise decisions, your relationships with associates, employees, suppliers, vendors, and customers. God's presence and help is your most *vital business resource*. If you fail to have your daily worship time, take the following steps.

First, if you missed because of a legitimate emergency, some unanticipated crisis, rest assured that God understands. As you are able, offer up brief prayers throughout the day. In fact, you—all of us—should always pray throughout the day, asking God briefly for help in every specific situation that arises. Remember, you do not have to stop, get on your knees, bow your head, or pray aloud. Simply and sincerely call out to God in your mind and spirit. He knows when you are talking to Him. Ask Him for what you need when you need it. Thank God for His love and understanding, and continually ask for His help as you deal with the pressures and decisions of the day.

Second, if you missed for an unacceptable reason (laziness, lack of priority, lack of discipline, living in sin, . . .), ask God to forgive you. He loves you, and He will cleanse you of your sin and failure (1 Jn.1:9).

Third, if you missed or have become inconsistent in your daily worship time, do not become discouraged or defeated. It is easy to fail in your devotional life when you have more to do than you can accomplish in a day, or when you are exhausted. Do not allow feelings of guilt, shame, or unworthiness to overtake you. These are tools Satan uses to discourage and defeat you. Instead, get up and begin again. Remember, your Father loves you, and He longs for your fellowship and worship (1 Jn.1:3).

Fourth, restart your daily worship time on the very day of your failure, if possible, and if not, then on the very next day. Never think that your worship time is unimportant or that something else is more important. Nothing is further from the truth. Your worship time with the Sovereign Lord—the Lord God of the universe—is far more important than any other appointment or meeting on your schedule. It is the key to gaining everything you need to live and to fulfill the demands of your business or position. It is the secret to your living triumphantly. When you acknowledge and honor God, He will acknowledge and honor you. He will hear and answer your prayers.

3. *Worship with other believers regularly.*

> **"So He came to Nazareth, where He had been brought up. And as His custom was, He went into the synagogue on the Sabbath day, and stood up to read" (Lk.4:16, NKJV).**

> **"They worshiped together at the Temple each day, met in homes for the Lord's Supper, and shared their meals with great joy and generosity" (Ac.2:46, NLT).**

> **"And let us not neglect our meeting together, as some people do, but encourage one another, especially now that the day of his return is drawing near" (He.10:25, NLT).**

> **"Praise the Lord! Sing to the Lord a new song, *And* His praise in the assembly of saints" (Ps.149:1, NKJV).**

Along with your daily, private worship time, you need to gather with other believers regularly to worship God. Our Lord set an example for us in this area: it was His custom to worship at the synagogue on the Sabbath (Lk.4:16).

As a Christian business leader, you need the presence, fellowship, strength, encouragement, and care of other believers. Every week, you need to briefly set aside the burdens and pressures you face and focus wholly on the Lord. You need to pause from your busy life and honor God by worshiping Him in His house. And you need a day of rest and worship every week, a day to be refreshed physically and spiritually. None of us should ever deliberately neglect meeting together, not even for a brief time (He.10:25). We are to assemble regularly...

- for worship
- for prayer
- for the study of God's Word
- for ministry and witnessing

As difficult as it may be at times, you should guard diligently against allowing your many business responsibilities to keep you from going to church. In one of Jesus' parables, He told of a man who invited his friends to attend a large banquet at his house. He proceeded to single out one person who had previously accepted the invitation, but, at the last minute, did not attend. He was simply too involved in business (Lk.14:16-18).

Every week, God extends an invitation to you to come into His house, to feast on His Word, and to fellowship with His people. You should not allow your business or career to consume your life to the point that you neglect gathering with God's people for worship. God, not your work, is to be the center of your life, the one around whom all else revolves.

Granted, there will be times when things come up unexpectedly, things that demand your immediate attention
whereby you are not able to go to church (Lk.14:5). But these
times should be the exception, not the rule, for your life.

It may be necessary for your business to operate on Sunday. If this is the case, then you should still work out a way
to attend church with some degree of regularity, and you
should provide opportunities for your employees to do
likewise (see ch. 5b, pt7, pp.140-143).

4. *Be a strong witness for Christ in both word and deed.*

> **"But you will receive power when the Holy
> Spirit comes upon you. And you will be my wit-
> nesses, telling people about me everywhere—in
> Jerusalem, throughout Judea, in Samaria, and to
> the ends of the earth" (Ac.1:8, NLT).**

> **"Behold, I send you out as sheep in the midst
> of wolves. Therefore be wise as serpents and
> harmless as doves" (Mt.10:16, NKJV).**

> **"Let your light shine before men in such a way
> that they may see your good works, and glori-
> fy your Father who is in heaven" (Mt.5:16, NASB
> '77).**

> **"Keep your conduct among the Gentiles [un-
> believers] honorable, so that when they speak
> against you as evildoers, they may see your good
> deeds and glorify God on the day of visitation"
> (1 Pe.2:12, ESV).**

Along with every other believer, you have been assigned
the greatest privilege in all the world, that of bearing witness for Christ throughout the world. Sharing about God's
love and the glorious salvation found in Him is the highest
privilege imaginable. But it is also a responsibility committed to you by our Lord Jesus Christ Himself. To accomplish
this task, He has equipped you with the power of the Holy
Spirit—*the very power* of God Himself. God's own Spirit

dwells within your heart and life so that you can carry out His great mission on earth.

a. **First, you are to witness to others by your word,** that is, verbally (Ac.1:8). Every day, as you go about your life, you are to tell others of God's saving love, forgiveness, and grace. Note that it is *you,* the believer, who is to witness. Imagine scientists knowing the cure for cancer but not sharing the news with anyone. It would be unforgivable! In the same way, you, as a Christian, know the cure, or the truth, for being saved from sin, death, condemnation, and hell. Why would you keep this wonderful news to yourself? Instead, be encouraged to bear strong witness and to make the glorious news of salvation known to everyone. At the same time, though, the Lord cautions you to be as wise as a serpent, and as harmless as a dove (Mt.10:16). He is sending you out as a witness into a world that is hostile to Him, and you will encounter individuals who do not want to hear about Jesus Christ. As a leader in your business, one who has authority over others, you risk being accused of harassment or of violating an individual's rights. Or, you may work for a company whose policies forbid you to speak about Christ or any religious topics on the job. Some of your clients may even discontinue doing business with you if they learn of your Christian faith or your stand for the truths of God's Word.

Nevertheless, you have a command from a higher authority, Jesus Christ, to witness as you go about your daily life. And Christ's first followers left you a principle to live by, an example to follow: when human authorities conflict with God's commands, you are to obey God (Ac.5:28-29). But, as Jesus instructed, you are to witness for Him wisely and harmlessly. Note what it means to be as wise as a serpent: in facing danger, the serpent...

- tries to escape

- takes shelter out of sight if possible

- is quiet
- does not expose itself needlessly
- seeks preservation first of all

Now, note what it means to be as harmless as a dove: the dove...

- is mild and meek
- bears no ill or hurt
- is innocent and inoffensive
- is a symbol of peace, not war

As you obey Christ's command to witness in an often-hostile world and business environment...

- you are to be wise in sensing threats and to respond calmly, respectfully, and kindly
- you are to provoke no one nor allow yourself to be provoked
- you are to wrong no one and to guard against being wronged
- you are to harm no one and to keep yourself from being harmed

The key to witnessing safely and effectively is walking in the power of the Holy Spirit. When you are consciously sensitive to the Spirit's leadership, He will guide you as to *when* to speak about Christ, *how* to do so, and *what* to say.

b. **Second, you are to bear witness to others in deed,** that is, by your life (Mt.5:16; 1 Pe.2:12). You are to live in such a way that unbelievers will be attracted to Christ by observing the way that you live. As you go about your daily business, you should always be conscious of this sobering fact: unbelievers are watching you. Your associates, employees, superiors, customers, clients, suppliers, the community in which you conduct business, and even unbelieving family members—they are all watching everything you do.

For this critical reason and others, God's Word instructs you to conduct yourself honorably, to always behave in the most excellent way possible (1 Pe.2:12). An *honorable* life is a good life, one that is pure, decent, upright, and noble. It speaks of a life that is without blame, that cannot be justly blamed of any wrongdoing or evil.

The world is watching to see if you really live what you profess. Therefore, as you lead your business from day to day, you should do so honorably, in a way that is consistent with your profession as a believer.

- You should operate with the highest ethical standards and utmost integrity.

- You should display a servant's spirit, one that seeks to help others and to provide what is best for them above what benefits you the most.

- You should live by the Golden Rule.

- You should show respect and kindness in the way you treat people, even the rudest customers and most belligerent employees.

- You should respond with self-control, patience, and kindness when someone provokes you.

- You should display unshakable faith in God, not panic or fear, even when a crisis strikes.

You are to live in such a way that, when people deal with you, they will have no doubt that they are dealing with a genuine follower of Jesus Christ. As you live honorably, you will experience the presence, strength, and peace of God—His care, guidance, and deliverance through the problems and crises of life. When unbelievers see your confidence in God and the peace you have when going through difficult times, they will be more likely to ask you about your faith when they face difficult, trying times. You may then have an open door to lead them to Christ (1 Pe.3:15).

On the other hand, if you do not display the character of Christ in your daily behavior, then everyone with whom you work and do business will see you as a hypocrite. Consequently, they will not be attracted to Christ. You should, therefore, be on guard at all times: make sure you are letting the light of Jesus Christ shine through your life and conduct. When unbelievers see His light—the good works you do, the patience and gracious attitude you have, the integrity with which you operate—they will sometimes be open to your witness and, again, you may have the privilege of leading them to faith in Jesus Christ.

5. *Give and be generous: Support the church and other ministries both locally and worldwide.*

> "Give, and it will be given to you; a good measure—pressed down, shaken together, and running over—will be poured into your lap. For with the measure you use, it will be measured back to you" (Lk.6:38, HCSB).

> "Now this *I say,* he who sows sparingly shall also reap sparingly; and he who sows bountifully shall also reap bountifully. Let each one *do* just as he has purposed in his heart; not grudgingly or under compulsion; for God loves a cheerful giver" (2 Co.9:6-7, NASB '77).

> "Honor the LORD from your wealth, And from the first of all your produce; So your barns will be filled with plenty, And your vats will overflow with new wine" (Pr.3:9-10, NASB '77).

God's Word teaches that He gives special gifts, abilities, or skills to His people (Ro.12:4-8; 1 Co.12:4-31). One of these is the gift of giving (Ro.12:8). Not surprisingly, God gives some believers an increased capacity to make money. He does this not for their own selfish purposes but to enable them to have plenty to help others and to spread the gospel throughout the world.

Now, God commands *every believer* to give tithes and offerings to Him. But, as stated, He gives some an increased capacity to make money so they can give more, more than most are able to give. Many of these gifted individuals become business owners, executives, or managers—some of large companies, others of small. And while many in leadership will not become wealthy, God also blesses many with the ability and opportunity to make far more money than they need. He does this so they can play an extraordinary part in providing the funds needed to fulfill the Great Commission of Christ (Mt.28:18-20).

As a business owner, executive, or manager, God may have chosen to bless you in this way. If He has, you have an important role to play in the mission of Christ. God's Word clearly declares that every God-given ability is equally important in the accomplishment of the Lord's mission. Your role is as critical as that of pastors who preach God's Word and of the evangelists and missionaries who take the gospel to the world (Ep.4:11). If God has blessed you with the ability to earn considerable wealth, He wants to use *you* to go beyond and to fund the Lord's servants and the ministries who take His Word to the world. The Lord has given you the ability to be shrewd in the world's system of making money so that the world's wealth can be used to help the needy and to carry the message of salvation and of eternal life to everyone (Lk.16:1-13).

What a privilege! What an honor! What a responsibility! Note what Scripture teaches about your giving.

a. **You should tithe**—financially support God's church—weekly (regularly) and generously.

> **"On the first day of every week, each one of you should set aside a sum of money in keeping with his income, saving it up, so that when I come no [special] collections will have to be made" (1 Co.16:2, NIV '84).**

> **"'Bring the whole tithe into the storehouse, so that there may be food in My house, and test**

Me now in this,' says the LORD of hosts, 'if I will not open for you the windows of heaven, and pour out for you a blessing until it overflows'" (Mal.3:10, NASB '77).

God is very specific about your support of His church and its mission. You are to give regularly, every Lord's day. This does not mean that you cannot tithe on a monthly or bimonthly basis, depending on when you get paid. But you are to be diligent about your tithing, giving the very week you receive your income.

In addition, you need to make sure that the amount you give is what it should be—an amount "in keeping with [your] income." Old Testament believers gave *at least* one tenth of their earnings, which is what is meant by the English word *tithe*, and New Testament believers continued this practice (He.7:8). The tithe is the starting point for you as a New Testament believer. But in light of all Christ has done for you, you may feel led to give substantially more.

b. **You should give** offerings in addition to your tithe to help others and to enable faithful ministries to take God's Word to the world (2 Co.9:6-7). In 2 Corinthians 9, Paul was clearly challenging the church to give a special offering in addition to their tithe to help meet the needs of fellow believers. In like manner, God calls you to give offerings in addition to your tithe in order to meet the world's desperate needs and to take the gospel to the ends of the earth. In addition, He calls groups of dedicated individuals to form ministries that take His Word to the world and that also train and equip ministers to better reach their communities for Christ.

These ministers and ministries must have funds to operate, and God's way of providing those funds is through His people. Note what Paul, the very first missionary, wrote to the church at Philippi:

"And you Philippians yourselves know that in the beginning of the gospel, when I left

> **Macedonia, no church entered into partnership with me in giving and receiving, except you only. Even in Thessalonica you sent me help for my needs once and again. Not that I seek the gift, but I seek the fruit that increases to your credit" (Ph.4:15-17, ESV).**

When you support those who are taking God's Word to the world, you enter into a partnership with them and the work they are doing (v.15). Indeed, the work they do is *your* work; you actually share in their labors, the accompanying joy and the eternal reward. Their results are *fruit* credited to *your* heavenly account (v.17).

Just think: when you partner with God's servants and ministries financially, you are as involved in God's work as those who are actually on the field. As you labor in your business or carry out the responsibilities of your position, you not only provide a beneficial service or product and employment for other people, but you also help fulfill the Great Commission of Christ Himself. This truth should give new meaning to your work. The tremendous burdens of the business world suddenly become lighter when you realize you are having a great impact for God, an eternal impact on others throughout the world. You have a purpose that transcends the stress, pressures, challenges, and exhausting hours of leading a business.

This purpose is why God has gifted you with the ability to make money and has given you the gift of giving. Naturally, He wants you to enjoy the fruits of your labors, but He does not want any of us living extravagantly or laying up treasures for ourselves here on earth. He wants us to invest our abundance in *His* work, to fulfill our vital roles in completing the Great Commission. He wants us supporting His servants and the ministries that take God's Word to the ends of the earth. He wants us to lay up eternal treasure in heaven (Mt.6:19-20).

c. **God makes a** motivating and assuring promise to you: when you prove faithful in giving to Him and His work, He will trust you with *more*. Scripture passages cited throughout this discussion repeatedly emphasize this promise. When you give obediently and sacrificially to the Lord, He promises not only to meet your needs, but also to trust you with even more to invest in His work. Note again what Paul wrote to the Corinthian church concerning giving an offering in addition to their tithe:

> **"The point is this: whoever sows sparingly will also reap sparingly, and whoever sows bountifully will also reap bountifully. Each one must give as he has decided in his heart, not reluctantly or under compulsion, for God loves a cheerful giver" (2 Co.9:6-7, ESV).**

When you give—sow your money into God's eternal work—He will *multiply your seed for sowing*. He will *enrich you in every way so that you can be even more generous in every way*.

God owns the earth and everything in it (Ps. 24:1;1 Co.10:26). So, He is the true owner of your business and all your personal assets, whatever money and possessions you have. God wants His wealth in circulation, being used to help the needy and to bring souls into His eternal kingdom. When you use what He has entrusted to you—your business, your abilities, your money—for His purposes, He will trust you with more. By committing yourself and your business to *His* purposes, you enter into a partnership with *Him*, a partnership that will yield *eternal* benefits.

Consider what God's Word teaches about giving, then ask these crucial questions: Can God trust *you* to use the ability and money He has given you to help the needy? Will you help carry the good news of His salvation to the world, whether directly or through the church or other ministries? Can you do more than you are currently doing? Pray for God's direction on this important matter and be open to His leading.

6. *Be a faithful steward (manager) of all the Lord has entrusted to you.*

" 'Again, it will be like a man going on a journey, who called his servants and entrusted his property to them. To one he gave five talents of money, to another two talents, and to another one talent, each according to his ability. Then he went on his journey. The man who had received the five talents went at once and put his money to work and gained five more. So also, the one with the two talents gained two more. But the man who had received the one talent went off, dug a hole in the ground and hid his master's money.

'After a long time the master of those servants returned and settled accounts with them. The man who had received the five talents brought the other five. "Master," he said, "you entrusted me with five talents. See, I have gained five more."

'His master replied, "Well done, good and faithful servant! You have been faithful with a few things; I will put you in charge of many things. Come and share your master's happiness!"

'The man with the two talents also came. "Master," he said, "you entrusted me with two talents; see, I have gained two more."

'His master replied, "Well done, good and faithful servant! You have been faithful with a few things; I will put you in charge of many things. Come and share your master's happiness!"

'Then the man who had received the one talent came. "Master," he said, "I knew that you are a hard man, harvesting where you have not sown and gathering where you have not scattered seed. So I was afraid and went out and hid your talent in the ground. See, here is what belongs to you."

'His master replied, "You wicked, lazy servant! So you knew that I harvest where I have not sown and gather where I have not scattered seed? Well then, you should have put my money on deposit with the bankers, so that when I returned I would have received it back with interest.

'"Take the talent from him and give it to the one who has the ten talents. For everyone who has will be given more, and he will have an abundance. Whoever does not have, even what he has will be taken from him. And throw that worthless servant outside, into the darkness, where there will be weeping and gnashing of teeth"'" (Mt.25:14–30, NIV '84).

"Moreover it is required in stewards that one be found faithful" (1 Co.4:2, NKJV).

The parable in the Matthew 25 passage is known as *The Parable of the Talents.* In it, the Lord teaches four vital principles concerning your business and your labor throughout life:

a. **First, you are** the Lord's servant (v.14). The Lord calls you His servant because He is your Creator. He created you and the universe and established the laws of nature that have brought everything forth. Consequently, everything in the universe belongs to God. You may be an executive or a manager within a business or the owner of a business and everything that goes along with it— the land, the buildings, the equipment, the inventory, and so on. But both you and all that you have belong to the Lord; He has simply entrusted it all to you.

b. **Second, the Lord has** given you a portion of His property or possessions to manage (v.15). He has given you your assignment to own or to lead a business or to handle a specific area of responsibility within a business.

Furthermore, God has uniquely equipped you to be successful in business and in carrying out your responsibilities:

- He created you, formed you genetically in your mother's womb with a natural propensity for what you are gifted to do. He gave you a mind and abilities to work and accomplish certain tasks in life.

- He brought into your life the things that you needed to prepare you for the responsibility you bear. It may have been the influence of good people, training, education, discipline, initiative, or all of the above.

- He gave you the opportunity to own or to lead part of a business, along with all the previous opportunities that led up to the vital position you now hold.

- He guided you, directing your steps and a host of other factors, many of which you cannot even fathom, to bring you to the place you are now.

All this simply says that God prepared you for *your* assignment in life and work. You should never think or boast that you are where you are or have achieved what you have strictly on your own, or solely because of your own efforts. Everything you are and everything you have is a gift from God, a trust committed to you. As Scripture says:

> **"For who makes you different from anyone else? What do you have that you did not receive? And if you did receive it, why do you boast as though you did not?" (1 Co.4:7, NIV '84).**

c. **Third, the Lord** expects you to be diligent in managing your area of responsibility (vv.16-18). Like the two hard-working servants in Jesus' parable, you are to be diligent in managing what the Lord has entrusted into your care (vv.16-17). Note what Jesus says about two of the servants:

- They were faithful and diligent. They used their abilities and energy, used what the Lord had given them.

- They were successful. Each servant gained and doubled what the Lord had given him. Although one man was given less to manage, both were *equally successful;* both *doubled* what the Lord had given them.

This is how you are to be. You are to work hard to be successful, using your abilities and energy and everything else the Lord has given you. You are also to be responsible, doing all you can to improve, expand, and grow the company that you own or for which you work.

Note that the third servant was irresponsible (v.18). He simply did not use the Lord's gift to the fullest of his ability. He hid it. His days, his time, and his energy were supposed to be used responsibly and productively, but he took his life and days into his own hands. What was he doing? We are not told, but his skills and efforts were not spent wisely. He served only himself. *He did not lose what had been entrusted to him, but he did not use it to produce more for the owner—the person (Lord) for whom he worked.* You are not to be like this servant, whom Scripture describes as *wicked* and *lazy* (v.26). You should not use what God has entrusted to you to benefit *only* yourself. You are to use what He has given you to the fullest of your ability.

d. **Fourth, you will** give an account to the Lord for your actions, your diligence and faithfulness in managing what He has entrusted to you (vv.19-30). The Lord is going to return, and you will stand before Him in judgment (v.19; Ro.14:12; 2 Co.5:10).

You will be judged for your diligence, for how faithfully you labored, not on your ability, nor on the size of the work you have been assigned. If you work faithfully, you will be able to face the Lord with confidence, just as the two hard-working servants in this parable did (vv.20–23). Like them, you will hear the Lord's glorious words, "Well done, good and faithful servant" (vv. 21, 23). And you will be greatly rewarded.

The lesson is clear: if you are faithful in using what God has committed to you, faithful to use it to the fullest of your ability, He will commit more to your trust. The Lord can do this in many ways. He may cause your business to grow, or He may bless you with additional businesses. He may promote you to a place of greater responsibility and influence. Or He may arrange circumstances to move you into something completely different, a new avenue of work and service where you can have an even greater impact throughout your community and society.

The important thing to remember is this: in all your work and labor, you serve the Lord God Himself. Everything you have is a trust from Him. If you are faithful, He will bless and use you in an even greater way, both in this life and in the coming kingdom of the new heavens and earth (2 Pe.3:10–13).

7. *Make sure your business and personal estates continue to carry on God's work when you are gone.*

> **"Besides, in my devotion to the temple of my God I now give my personal treasures of gold and silver for the temple of my God, over and above everything I have provided for this holy temple: three thousand talents of gold (gold of Ophir) and seven thousand talents of refined silver, for the overlaying of the walls of the buildings, for the gold work and the silver work, and for all the work to be done by the craftsmen. Now, who is willing to consecrate himself today to the LORD?" (1 Chr.29:3-5, NIV '84).**

> **"But God said to him, 'You fool! You will die this very night. Then who will get everything you worked for?'" (Luke 12:20, NLT)**

As David neared the end of his life, he made sure that a portion of his assets—the wealth God had entrusted to Him—would be used for the Lord after he was gone. He left a significant share of his own personal treasure to the work of God, the project to which he was most devoted, that of building a temple worthy of God (1 Chr.29:3-4).

In doing so, David, this man after God's own heart, left both an example and a challenge that extends to God's people today, over three thousand years later: "Who is willing to consecrate himself today to the Lord?" (1 Chr.29:5). David was essentially asking, "Who among you is so completely dedicated to God that you will follow my example and leave your personal wealth to His work?"

Though God owns the earth and everything in it, it is not all a part of His kingdom, not in this present world. Only what God's people dedicate to Him and use to accomplish His purposes is a part of His kingdom. Being a faithful steward of what God has committed to you—your assets, your business—calls for you to do everything you can to ensure that it continues to be a part of God's kingdom even after you are gone.

Consider this grim truth: after you are gone, your personal giving to God's kingdom will cease. The ministries you have regularly supported will lose the income God provided through you. By leaving a portion of your estate to them—perhaps through a trust or foundation that will produce annual interest or investment income—you can continue to support the ministries dear to your heart after you are in heaven. If you do this, your works will follow you; you will continue to bear fruit for the Lord on earth while you are serving Him in heaven, in His glorious presence and kingdom (Re.14:13).

If you own a business, consider its future. Right now, while you are alive and able to lead your business, it is part of God's kingdom, assuming you are using it as a means for doing or supporting His work. Either way, you are utilizing God's blessings to you to actively accomplish His purposes in the world.

This commitment of your business to God is your legacy as the owner. Do everything you can to assure that this legacy continues after you are gone. It is important that you set up a carefully and prayerfully established succession plan, both for your business's ownership and its leadership; and be sure that whomever you have appointed to carry out your wishes will do so faithfully.

Similarly, if at some point you decide to sell your business, you should, as a faithful steward of it, do all you can to ensure that it continues to serve God's kingdom and His purposes. Think for a moment: Do you want what you have invested your life in, what God has enabled you to build, to revert to the kingdom of this world?

If at all possible, you should patiently seek a buyer who is consecrated, or committed, to Christ, even as you have been. Pray that God will send a buyer who shares your values, your scriptural philosophy, your burden for the Lord's work, your dedication to accomplishing His purposes through your business. If you were to sell your business to someone who did not know the Lord, it would likely be lost from God's kingdom and become part of this world's kingdom forever.

Remember the sad example set by Solomon: he turned away from the Lord after achieving unparalleled success. As he faced death, he bitterly lamented that everything he had worked for would one day be left behind to others who might use it foolishly (Ec.2:18-21). He obviously failed to follow his father's (David's) excellent example.

As believers, we are called to be faithful stewards of everything God has entrusted to us. Faithful stewardship includes being wise in planning for what happens to our estates when we are gone. If we fail to make plans for our businesses and personal estates, regardless of size, we are almost guaranteeing that our life's work—all the Lord has blessed us with materially—will be lost.

Still, the most important legacy you can leave behind is a spiritual one. Solomon knew that his son would be his successor. Yet, he failed to impart to his son what would make him a wise king. Solomon was so busy building his kingdom that he neglected to invest in his son those things that would guarantee the future success of his kingdom. Solomon failed to walk with the Lord and, in doing so, he all but guaranteed that his son would not walk with the Lord either.

Wise investments, good decisions, hard work—all of these are important. Yet, without a spiritual foundation to sustain them, every person's kingdom—including yours—

will eventually crumble and fall. The most important thing you can do is to invest spiritually in your children and grandchildren, as well as in others who help you as you build and operate your business.

Like the rich man in Jesus' sobering parable, your appointment with death will come one day. The question God asked him is also His question to you:

> **"Then who will get everything you worked for?" (Lk.12:20).**

Wealth Creation Manifesto

Lausanne Movement
Connecting influencers and ideas for global mission

BUSINESS AS MISSION
BAM GL◉BAL

Background

The Lausanne Movement and BAM Global organized a Global Consultation on *The Role of Wealth Creation for Holistic Transformation*, in Chiang Mai, Thailand, in March 2017. About 30 people from 20 nations participated, primarily from the business world, and also from church, missions and academia. The findings will be published in several papers and a book, as well as an educational video. This Manifesto conveys the essentials of our deliberations before and during the Consultation.

Affirmations

1. Wealth creation is rooted in God the Creator, who created a world that flourishes with abundance and diversity.

2. We are created in God's image, to co-create with Him and for Him, to create products and services for the common good.

3. Wealth creation is a holy calling, and a God-given gift, which is commended in the Bible.

4. Wealth creators should be affirmed by the Church, and equipped and deployed to serve in the marketplace among all peoples and nations.

5. Wealth hoarding is wrong, and wealth sharing should be encouraged, but there is no wealth to be shared unless it has been created.

6. There is a universal call to generosity, and contentment is a virtue, but material simplicity is a personal choice, and involuntary poverty should be alleviated.

7. The purpose of wealth creation through business goes beyond giving generously, although that is to be commended; good business has intrinsic value as a means of material provision and can be an agent of positive transformation in society.

8. Business has a special capacity to create financial wealth, but also has the potential to create different kinds of wealth for many stakeholders, including social, intellectual, physical and spiritual wealth.

9. Wealth creation through business has proven power to lift people and nations out of poverty.

10. Wealth creation must always be pursued with justice and a concern for the poor, and should be sensitive to each unique cultural context.

11. Creation care is not optional. Stewardship of creation and business solutions to environmental challenges should be an integral part of wealth creation through business.

Appeal

We present these affirmations to the Church worldwide, and especially to leaders in business, church, government, and academia.

- We call the church to embrace wealth creation as central to our mission of holistic transformation of peoples and societies.
- We call for fresh, ongoing efforts to equip and launch wealth creators to that very end.
- We call wealth creators to perseverance, diligently using their God-given gifts to serve God and people.

Ad maiorem Dei gloriam - For the greater glory of God

Version 4.0: 23 April 2017

Subject Index

D

DAY OF WORSHIP (SEE **WORSHIP, DAY OF; REST**)

DEATH (SEE **LIFE, ETERNAL; SALVATION**)
Continuing to give, be fruitful for God after your **d.** 368-371
Defined. Separation. 344
Eternal **d.** Defined. 345
Inevitable for all. 213-214
Physical **d.** Defined. 344
Spiritual **d.** Defined. 345

DEATH, CHRIST'S
Accomplishes salvation. 346-347

DEBT (SEE **CREDIT; CREDITOR; FINANCES**)
Advised against, but not forbidden by Scripture. 90
Avoid as much as possible. 87-89
Collection of. 157, 168-174
Co-signing or guaranteeing another's **d.** 91-94
Pay when due. 89-91
When you cannot pay **d.** 157-167

DELEGATE 241-245, 284

DEPRESSED – DEPRESSION (SEE **ENCOURAGEMENT; FAITH; HOPE; PROMISES, GOD'S**) 22, 189, 211

DESIRE
For greatness. 7
For money and wealth. 315-316, 324, 327, 335-338
For power. 321
For success. 7, 36, 50, 64, 111, 257
Known by God. 32
Sexual **d.** 233, 236-240
To please God. 12, 32, 167

DESPAIR – DESPONDENT (SEE **DISCOURAGEMENT; ENCOURAGEMENT; FAITH; HOPE; PROMISES, GOD'S**)

DETERMINATION (SEE **PERSEVERANCE; PATIENCE**)

DEVOTIONS (SEE **WORSHIP; PRIVATE**)

DIFFICULTY (SEE **TROUBLES; TRIALS; ADVERSITY; PROBLEMS**)

DILIGENT – DILIGENCE
In daily work. 12-13, 111-118, 120, 127, 187, 210, 289-290
Over the responsibilities entrusted to you. 366-368

DIRECT – DIRECTION (SEE **DECISIONS; GUIDANCE; WISDOM**)

DISAPPOINTMENT (SEE **DISCOURAGEMENT**)

DISCERN – DISCERNMENT (SEE **WISDOM**)

DISCIPLINE (SEE **CORRECTION; EMPLOYEES**)

DISCOURAGE – DISCOURAGEMENT (SEE **COMFORT; ENCOURAGEMENT; FAITH; HOPE; STRENGTH**)
Causes. Unmet goals. 29.
Overcoming **d.**.
By being courageous. 182-185
By fighting, never giving up. 185-187
By focusing on the future. 187
By spiritual renewal. 186

DISCRIMINATION (SEE **JUSTICE; EQUALITY, HUMAN; PARTIALITY**)
Contrary to God's wisdom. 75-76
Guard against. 223-225, 231

DISHONEST – DISHONESTY (SEE **HONESTY; INTEGRITY; STEALING**)
Can result in profit or wealth. 11, 99
Dangers of. 11, 99
Detested by God. 95
D. sales tactics. 96-97
Examples of **d.** tactics. 216, 254
Guard against. 214-217
In communications. 262-265
Tolerating **d.** 169
Will be judged by God. 11, 97, 99, 137

On positive, excellent things.
  21-24
On service. 44-47
Right **f.** 22-24
Stay **f.** when facing problems. 37
Wrong **f.** 22

Forgive – Forgiveness
  Of debt. 167, 171
  Of delinquent customers.
    170-171
  Of enemies. 250-251

Forgiveness of Sins (See **Salvation**) 13, 65, 194, 318, 346, 348, 356

Frustration (See **Faith; Perseverance; Problems; Trials**)

Fulfillment (See **Contentment; Satisfaction**)
  Found in work. 8, 109, 297

Future
  Five attitudes. 213-214
  Focus on **f.**
    To overcome problems.
      197-198
    When discouraged. 187
  Preparing for. 85, 101-102
  Uncertainty of. 85

G

Generous – Generosity (See **Give - Giving**)

Gifts, Spiritual 363-364

Give – Giving
  Commanded and encouraged by
    God. 93, 323, 331, 359-363
  Gift of **g.** Explained. 363-364
  Is the essence of eternal life. 333
  Stirs God to bless you with
    more. 66, 362-363
  To help others. 66, 332
  To support ministries. 361-363
  To support the church. 360-361
  To take the gospel to the
    world. 36. 65-66, 295, 323,
    332, 361-363

Give up (See **Perseverance**)

Giving License (See **Indulging**)

Glorify God
  By having integrity. 12
  In every aspect of your business. 3-4
  Should be your first concern. 3

Goals (See **Vision**)
  Set **g.** for employees. 112
  Sufficient resources to accomplish **g.** 32-34
  Trust God in setting **g.** 29
  Unmet. Seven causes. 29-30

God's Word (See **Word, God's**)

Going to court (See **Lawsuits**)

"Golden rule" 41-42, 96, 98, 126

Gospel (See **Salvation**)
  Humanity's need for. 9, 52,
    184, 323
  Power of. 65
  Spreading, taking to the world.
    21, 36, 52, 65-66, 208, 295,
    332, 360, 361

Government (See **Citizenship**)
  Benefits of. 307-308
  Ordained by God. 302
  Respect for and submission to.
    301-306
    Exception. 304

Grace
  For trials and difficulties. 349
  Saving **g.** 356

Gracious - Graciousness
  In your treatment of others.
    17-18, 23, 173, 202, 229,
    265-267

Great – Greatness
  Comes from service. 8, 9

Great Commandment 41-44, 267

Great Commission 21, 65, 184,
  360, 362

Greed (See **Covetousness;
  Money, Love of**)
  A deadly enemy. 320-321

Scripture Quotations

Scripture Index

Bibliography

Albrecht, Karl. *Successful Management by Objectives: An Action Manual.* Englewood Cliffs, NJ: Prentice-Hall, Inc., 1978.

Anderson, Dave. *How to Run Your Business by the Book: A Biblical Blueprint to Bless Your Business.* Hoboken, NJ: John Wiley & Sons, Inc., 2011.

Barclay, William. *The Letters to the Philippians, Colossians, and Thessalonians.* Published as a volume in the "Daily Study Bible Series." Philadelphia, PA: Westminster John Knox Press, 1953.

_____. The Letters to Timothy, Titus, and Philemon. Published as a volume in the "Daily Study Bible Series." Philadelphia, PA: Westminster John Knox Press, 1953.

Blackaby, Henry and Richard. *God in the Marketplace: 45 Questions Fortune 500 Executives Ask about Faith, Life, and Business.* Nashville, TN: B&H Publishing Group, 2008.

Blanchard, Ken, and Phil Hodges. *Lead Like Jesus.* Nashville, TN: Thomas Nelson, 2005.

Blanchard, Kenneth, Ph.D., and Spencer Johnson, M.D. *The One Minute Manager.* New York, NY: Berkley Books, 1982.

Blue, Ron. *Splitting Heirs.* Chicago, IL: Northfield Publishing, 2004.

Boa, Kenneth, Sid Buzzell, and Bill Perkins. *Handbook to Leadership.* Atlanta, GA: Trinity House Publishers 2007.

Brooks, Phillips. *The Duty of the Christian Businessman.* New York, NY: Dodge Publishing Co., No date

Burkett, Larry. *Business by the Book: The Complete Guide of Biblical Principles for the Workplace.* Nashville, TN: Thomas Nelson, 1998.

_____. *Investing for the Future.* Wheaton, IL: Victor Books, 1992.

_____. *Surviving the 90's Economy.* Chicago, IL: Moody Press, 1992.

_____. *The Coming Economic Earthquake.* Chicago, IL: Moody Press, 1994.

Carnegie, Dale. *How to Win Friends and Influence People.* New York, NY: Simon & Schuster, 1981.

Cook, William H. *Success, Motivation, and the Scriptures.* Nashville, TN: Broadman Press, 1974.

Covey, Stephen R. *The 7 Habits of Highly Effective People.* Salt Lake City UT: Franklin Covey Co., 2015

Dale, Ernest, Ph.D. Management: *Theory and Practice.* New York, NY: McGraw-Hill Book Company, 1965.

Drucker, Peter F. *Managing for Results.* New York, NY: Harper and Row Publishers, 1964

_____. *The Practice of Management.* New York, NY: Harper and Row Publishers, 1954.

Engstrom, Ted W., and Edward R. Dayton. *The Art of Management for Christian Leaders.* Waco, TX: Word Books, 1976.

Ewing, David W. *The Practice of Planning.* New York, NY: Harper & Row, Publishers, 1968.

Floyd, Mike. *Supernatural Business.* Lake Mary, FL: Creation House, 2003.

Grudem, Wayne. *Business for the Glory of God: The Bible's Teaching on the Moral Goodness of Business.* Wheaton, IL: Crossway Books, 2003.

Guthrie, Donald. *The Pastoral Epistles.* Grand Rapids, MI: William B. Eerdmans Publishing Co., 1990

Henry, Matthew. *Commentary on the Whole Bible.* Old Tappan, NJ: Fleming H. Revell Co., Vol. 5.

Hampton, David R. *Modern Management: Issues and Ideas.* Belmont, CA: Dickenson Publishing, 1969.

Heyel, Carl, Editor. *The Encyclopedia of Management, Vols. I & II.* New York, NY: Reinhold Publishing Corporation, 1963.

Hill, Alexander. *Just Business: Christian Ethics for the Marketplace.* Downers Grove, IL: InterVarsity Press, 1997.

Johnson, C. Neal. *Business As Mission: A Comprehensive Guide to Theory and Practice.* Downers Grove, IL: InterVarsity Press, 2009.

Jones, Laurie Beth. *Jesus the CEO: Using Ancient Wisdom for Visionary Leadership.* New York, NY: Hyperion, 1995.

Longman, Tremper, III. *Reading the Bible with Heart & Mind.* Colorado Springs CO: NavPress, 1997.

Miller, Theodore J., Editor. *Invest Your Way to Wealth.* Washington, DC: Kiplinger Books, 1998.

Moore, Donald. *What if Jesus Carried a Briefcase?* Greenville, SC: Ambassador International, 2015.

Moore, Gary D. *The Thoughtful Christian's Guide to Investing.* Grand Rapids, MI: Zondervan Books, 1990.

Nash, Laura L. *Believers in Business.* Nashville, TN: Thomas Nelson, 1994.

Pink, Michael Q. *The Bible Incorporated in Your Life, Job and Business.* Mt. Juliet, TN: Hidden Manna, Inc., 1988.

Pryor, Austin. *Sound Mind Investing.* Chicago, IL: Moody Press, 1993.

Reddin, W.J. *Effective Management by Objectives.* New York, NY: McGraw-Hill Book Co., 1971.

Robertson, A. T. *Word Pictures in the Old Testament.* Vol. 4. Nashville, TN: Broadman Press, 1930.

Rodin, R. Scott, Editor. *Christ-Centered Generosity.* Colbert, WA: The Global Generosity Network and Kingdom Life Publishing, 2015.

Silvoso, Ed. *Anointed for Business: How to Use Your Influence in the Marketplace to Change the World.* Bloomington, MN: Chosen Books, 2002.

Stanley, Charles. *Success God's Way.* Nashville, TN: Thomas Nelson, 2000.

Steward, David L. with Robert L. Shook. *Doing Business by the Book.* New York, NY: Hyperion Books, 2004.

The Bible Promise Book, NIV. Uhrichsville, OH: Barbour Publishing, Inc., 2004.

The Businessman's Bible, NKJV. Nashville, TN: Thomas Nelson, Inc., 1989.

The Businessman's Topical Bible. Tulsa, OK: Honor Books, 1984.

Van Duzer, Jeff. *Why Business Matters to God (And What Still Needs to Be Fixed).* Downers Grove, IL: Inter-Varsity Press: 2010.

Van Fleet, James K. *The 22 Biggest Mistakes Managers Make and How to Correct Them.* West Nyack, NY: Parker Publishing Co., 1973.

What an Executive Should Know About... Series. Chicago, IL: Dartnell Press, 1963-1964.

Wong, Kenman L., and Scott B. Rae. *Business for the Common Good: A Christian Vision for the Marketplace.* Downers Grove, IL: InterVarsity Press, 2011.

LMW (Leadership Ministries Worldwide) publishes the world's leading outline commentary Bible series, *The Preacher's Outline & Sermon Bible®*. Our mission is to provide pastors in the global church with this and other gospel-centered resources:

The Preacher's Outline & Sermon Bible® - a 44-volume series in KJV and NIV
What the Bible Says to the Believer – The Believer's Personal Handbook
What the Bible says to the Minister – The Minister's Personal Handbook
What the Bible Says to the Business Leader – The Business Leader's Personal Handbook
What the Bible Says about the Tabernacle
What the Bible Says about the Ten Commandments
The Teacher's Outline & Study Bible™ - various New Testament books
Practical Illustrations
Practical Word Studies in the New Testament
Old Testament Prophets Supplement
Study Booklets:
Faith
Prayer
The Passion of Jesus
Wisdom

All books are available at **lmw.org**, on **amazon.com**, and at your local bookstore. *The Preacher's Outline & Sermon Bible®* is also available for sale digitally from Wordsearch, Logos, Olive Tree, Accordance and others.

Proceeds from sales, along with donations from donor partners, go to underwrite our translation and distribution projects. These projects equip pastors and leaders in the global church who have limited access to the books, resources, and training they need to prepare them to preach the Word of God clearly, plainly, and confidently.

Visit LMW's website at **lmw.org** to learn more about our mission and how you can partner with us:

PRAY: Please pray for the spread of the gospel and our role in it. Go to **lmw.org/stories** to join our prayer network.

CONNECT: LMW partners with other like-minded ministries around the world. Do you know someone who might like to connect with us? Let us know at: **info@lmw.org**

GIVE: The work of LMW is sustained by faithful giving. Impact the world with God's Word at **lmw.org/give.**

LMW is a 501(c)(3) ministry founded in 1992 to share God's Word, clearly explained, with pastors, Bible students and Christian leaders worldwide.

lmw.org   1928 Central Ave.   1-(800) 987-8790
info@lmw.org   Chattanooga, TN 37408   (423) 855-2181

www.ingramcontent.com/pod-product-compliance
Lightning Source LLC
Chambersburg PA
CBHW070015100426
42740CB00013B/2508